# Becoming an Expert Witness for the Family Court

I0130618

Written from the perspective of a clinician, this book builds on readers' existing professional skills to guide them through the maze of specialist knowledge needed to act as an expert witness in the family courts. Offering a single comprehensive reference for practitioners spanning across disciplines, this book focuses on the specific orientation, knowledge base and nuances involved in ensuring fairness, justice and the protection of family life when working within the courts.

Firmly grounded in practical case examples, this book explores the rationale, procedures, processes and priorities of the court and highlights legal imperatives and their impact on families. Readers will benefit from learning how to translate their existing skills to providing expert witness testimony. Topics explored include, but are not limited to:

- Children's welfare and the law, including child abuse and exploitation
- The family procedure rules that experts must follow
- Guidance on providing an assessment and evidence in court
- Cultural and language barriers to justice
- Vulnerable families and contentious issues, such as domestic violence and ruptured parent-child relationships
- Data security, costs, invoicing and developments in technology.

*Becoming an Expert Witness for the Family Court* is an essential read for any mental health or medical practitioner interested in, or new to, working within the family courts. It will be of particular interest to psychologists, psychiatrists, counsellors, therapists, paediatricians and practitioners in other related medical specialisms.

**Joyce Scaife** is a clinical psychologist with over 25 years of experience as an expert witness carrying out assessments for the family court. She is the former Director of Clinical Practice, Clinical Psychology Unit at the University of Sheffield.

# Becoming an Expert Witness for the Family Court

## A Comprehensive Guide for Mental Health and Medical Practitioners

Joyce Scaife

Routledge
Taylor & Francis Group

LONDON AND NEW YORK

Designed cover image: Getty Images

First published 2026
by Routledge
4 Park Square, Milton Park, Abingdon, Oxon OX14 4RN

and by Routledge
605 Third Avenue, New York, NY 10158

Routledge is an imprint of the Taylor & Francis Group, an informa business

© 2026 Joyce Scaife

The right of Joyce Scaife to be identified as author of this work
has been asserted in accordance with sections 77 and 78 of the
Copyright, Designs and Patents Act 1988.

For Product Safety Concerns and Information please contact our
EU representative GPSR@taylorandfrancis.com. Taylor & Francis
Verlag GmbH, Kaufingerstraße 24, 80331 München, Germany.

Trademark notice: Product or corporate names may be trademarks
or registered trademarks, and are used only for identification and
explanation without intent to infringe.

British Library Cataloguing-in-Publication Data
A catalogue record for this book is available from the British Library

ISBN: 978-1-032-59184-1 (hbk)
ISBN: 978-1-032-59186-5 (pbk)
ISBN: 978-1-003-45339-0 (ebk)

DOI: 10.4324/9781003453390

Typeset in Times New Roman
by codeMantra

# Contents

# Figures

# Tables

# Preface

When I first began working as an expert witness, I searched in vain for a reference text that would assist me with the task. Over 25 years later I have attempted to write the book that I wanted then. The aim of this book is to provide a single comprehensive reference resource for beginning experts in the family court. It is intended to be an introductory text and companion volume to *Deciding Children's Futures*, which describes an approach to assessment of children and families characterised by a compassionate and critically reflective stance. This volume is addressed to the procedural and technical rather than relational aspects of the expert's role: *what* you need to know, rather than *how* to conduct assessments.

Expert witnesses appointed by the family court include practitioners within the disciplines of psychology, psychiatry, paediatrics, other medical specialisms and social work. Typically, these specialists have gained their expertise within their discipline, through working in health and social care professions. Although the task of an expert witness benefits from knowledge and skills associated with clinical roles, it requires a different orientation and additional knowledge which is not readily available to novice experts and may conflict with habitual orientations to the work. In court work, there appear to be more imperatives – 'musts' and 'shoulds' – than is typical of clinical work. The reasoning behind this is to ensure fairness and justice for those families who find themselves in the family court system.

Most families who find themselves in family court proceedings are in some way vulnerable through unfamiliarity with court processes and procedures, social conditions of poverty or isolation, challenges to their health and well-being, unstable relationships, experiences of trauma and/or discrimination. What is at stake is their right to family life as they wish to live it. The state can be a very powerful entity in deciding whether or not they are able to exercise this right. It thus behoves expert witnesses to conduct themselves with integrity, commitment to children's welfare, understanding extended to all parties and an overriding sense of fairness and justice. In my opinion, this cannot reliably be accomplished without extensive knowledge of court processes and the role played within these by experts.

I have attempted to illustrate and make accessible a mass of information that is pertinent to the role through examples of case reports, personal reflections of participants in the process and my own experiences of working as an expert witness.

The latter are composite accounts based on 'real' narratives but with details and identifiers altered in order to ensure confidentiality. Although this text may give an impression of certainty and unassailable universal 'truths', these are nevertheless told through my personal lens, reflecting my values and what I take to be important. I am very likely to have given more air-room to topics that engage me, and the reader may detect particular slants on the content of which I may or may not be aware.

My experience lies within the family court in England. Since the inception of devolved governments, some relevant legislation has diverged. Where it is within my knowledge, this is referenced in the text, but there may be some undocumented instances where policies and procedures in Scotland, Wales and Northern Ireland differ from those in England. One overarching difference between England and Scotland is that the Children Act 1989 extant in England has been replaced in Scotland with the Children (Scotland) Act 1995, covering similar areas of child law.

To my knowledge, the information contained in this volume has been obtained from reliable and verifiable sources listed in the reference section. In a constantly evolving social and political landscape bombarded by social media and content generated with the assistance of AI, I have attempted to be assiduous in checking original sources. Although I have adopted terminology following that used in legal texts and government documents, this does not always reflect contemporary values and beliefs. Biological parents tend to be referred to as 'mother' and 'father', whilst non-cisgender identities may use other terms. 'He' appears in some legislation to represent 'he', 'she' and 'they'. I acknowledge that some families are not represented by normative labels. I have tried to reflect the increasingly pluralistic and diverse cultural histories and individual identities of the people whom I encounter in this work, and to use language that shows respect for our differences.

Sometimes this work can be very challenging, particularly when being cross-examined by a barrister with an incisive and contesting style. It is their job to do the best for their client by testing the evidence to the full. But an expert's evidence can be crucial in ensuring justice and enabling people who are 'stuck' in dysfunctional ways of interacting to move on. Such was the case in Re W[1] when Dr Kate Hellin provided an assessment that was credited by the judge as helping to repair a deeply polarised relationship between care workers and the parents of a child with serious disabilities for whom a care order application had been made.

The child used a wheelchair, suffered from epilepsy, a swallowing disorder, breath-held until he lost consciousness and self-harmed such that he required one-to-one care at all times. The care agency complained that the parents had insisted on overseeing the training of carers and had refused to call an ambulance when the child suffered a hypoxic episode in which his blood oxygen levels fell to a dangerous level. This went against the guidance in the care package being followed by staff. Dr Hellin's instruction was aimed at achieving a better understanding of what was happening in interactions between the parents and professionals. The judge said that he had not expected the report 'so comprehensively' to capture the dynamic between them.

The report noted that a previous traumatic experience in which the child suffered a brain haemorrhage and bowel intussusception had left the mother with a heightened level of resting anxiety which was a rational response to the abnormal circumstances. It required recognition that these were 'ordinary' parents dealing with extraordinary life-threatening circumstances. They cared for their son with a passion and with a depth of experience of his complex individual needs. It was difficult for them to have confidence in substitute carers and to manage their anxiety when he was in the care of others. This explanation of the parents' seemingly difficult behaviour led to the resolution of differences between the parties, averting the need for a contested hearing. For me, the opportunity to make a difference is the most powerful motivator for doing this work.

## Note

1  Re *W (A Child)* [2021] EWHC 2844 (Fam).

# Acknowledgements

During the time that I have spent as an expert witness, I have been privileged to work with clients across a spectrum of society whom I would like to thank for sharing the intimacies of their lives and for the learning opportunities that our encounters have provided. I would also like to thank the many professionals I have met along the way – legal representatives and practitioners in a range of disciplines whose knowledge and experience have been invaluable to my practice.

My heartfelt thanks are due to readers who shared ideas and critical and encouraging feedback on earlier drafts of the manuscript. Family members Jon and Hannah Scaife always give generous amounts of time to read everything I ask them to critique and invariably provide thoughtful and insightful comments and suggestions with love and support. Anthony Theakston of Hogan's solicitors, one of the most considered and thorough advocates whom I have had the good fortune to connect with during my court work, provided invaluable feedback on the first three chapters. Lisa Crowther of Carter Brown Associates updated me on recent developments as well as providing incisive and expert critique from her extensive and up-to-date knowledge of the field. Maria Downs shared her wide experience of working with refugees, asylum seekers and interpreters as well as offering encouragement and helpful feedback on the text.

Acknowledgement is also due to Napper Architects for permission to reproduce their illustration of a courtroom layout in Figure 6.1, published on their website at https://www.napperarchitects.co.uk/sheffield-law-courts/.

I am grateful as always to the staff at Routledge including Grace McDonnell who supported commissioning of the text, Lauren Redhead, Stacey Carter and staff at codemantra who have steered this book through all its various stages with efficiency and good humour.

# Chapter 1

# Introduction

I became an expert witness by accident. Working in a CAMHS service for many years, I was asked to provide information about the work that I had carried out with a client whose child became subject to care proceedings. This role was that of fact witness (also known as 'witness of fact' or 'professional witness'), providing a description of intervention and outcome. It was on the back of this that I was asked to consider whether I would like to provide expert testimony in future family proceedings.

I found it hard to decide whether I qualified as an expert witness. What level of education, skills and experience constituted adequate expertise? Many well-qualified professionals, including psychologists, can experience a condition in which they feel fraudulent – known as 'imposter syndrome', something that I had felt myself on many occasions, and I often encountered it in students studying to be clinical psychologists. The term was coined by Clance and Imes (1978) when studying professionally accomplished women who constantly felt they were underachieving and just fooling others about their competence. Professionals tend not to talk about it as the experience includes fear of being found out. Much subsequent research has confirmed the feelings to be widespread, not just amongst women. In a systematic review (Bravata et al., 2020) prevalence rates varied from 56 to 82% amongst graduate students, college students, nurses, medical students and other professions. It is thought to be more prevalent amongst minority groups, arising within discriminatory systems and structures (Tulshyan and Burey, 2021).

I have found it helpful to assure myself that I do know how to do some things such as talk and listen to people with compassion and my full attention, think whilst listening so that I maintain some control over an interview, evaluate relevant research literature and write coherently and accessibly about technical matters. There are many other activities in which I am not skilled and it is important that I recognise and accept this rather than feeling that I have to know everything.

DOI: 10.4324/9781003453390-1

The British Psychological Society (BPS) offers the following definition of an expert:

> An expert is a person who, through specialist training, study, or experience, is able to provide a court, tribunal, or hearing with relevant scientific, technical, or professional information or opinion, based on skills, expertise, or knowledge that is likely to be beyond the experience and knowledge of the representing lawyers, judge, jury or panel.
>
> (British Psychological Society, 2021: no page numbers)

The BPS (2023) also lists what the courts may expect regarding the typical training and expertise of different categories of practitioner psychologists who describe themselves with protected titles such as 'clinical psychologist', 'forensic psychologist' or 'counselling psychologist'. In my experience, courts prefer experts who are reflective, cautious and considered about their opinions and will be 'on guard against the over-dogmatic expert, the expert whose reputation or amour proper [sic] is at stake, or the expert who has developed a scientific prejudice' (Davis, 2021).

During the years that I have worked as an expert witness I have encountered many pitfalls, most of which I have somehow managed to escape, and when stumbling into one, from which my learning has accelerated. This book is intended to address *what* you need to know in order to safeguard yourself and your clients in the context of the family court. *How* to carry out the role is addressed in a companion volume.

## Aims and Remit of the Family Court

The remit of the family court is to make decisions in the best interests and for the welfare of children. This is its chief purpose and is known as the paramountcy principle. It does this by making court orders that specify the arrangements for care of the child. It is also argued that 'the court's role should be focused on protecting the vulnerable from abuse, victimisation and exploitation and should avoid intervening in family life except where there is clear benefit to children or vulnerable adults in doing so' (Ministry of Justice et al., 2011: 182). Orders made by the family court must also be proportionate to the risks, if any, identified by the court.

The sorts of families who find themselves in the family court are those who have been found to be providing inadequate or harmful care to their children (public law cases) and separating parents who are unable to resolve through other means the disputes between them over the care of the children (private law applications). Not all separating parents make recourse to the courts to help them settle their disputes but the number is significant with 51,473 new private law applications started in 2024 (Ministry of Justice (MoJ), 2025a) in England and Wales, and 15,980 new public law applications. The Children and Family Court Advisory and Support Service (CAFCASS) (2025a) figures are consistent with these, with 16,055 new public law cases being referred between April 2023 and March 2024, and 39,661 new private law cases in the same period. Of the private law cases, the MoJ reported that in 19% of cases both parents were represented and in 39% of cases neither were. Approximately one-third of private law cases proceeded to a final hearing. Many cases are resolved without the assistance of an expert witness.

Whilst in this book I discuss what might largely be called technical issues, I want at the outset to say that these issues are by no means only technical for the people involved – not only parents and children but the professionals of all persuasions who come into contact with them. In both public and private law proceedings, parents are under a great deal of stress as they contest their right to share their lives with the beings who are almost invariably of the utmost importance to them. Emotions run high and it behoves us in completing expert assessments to take the greatest possible care in what we do, and to show sensitivity, kindness and compassion.

During the Covid-19 pandemic, courts rapidly had to adapt to remote hearings, which resulted in members of the legal profession reflecting on the family court process as it took place within the physical space of the court. In a survey by the National Family Justice Observatory (Ryan et al., 2020: 19) a strong theme, as with an earlier survey, 'is that family justice is not simply administrative adjudication but is dealing with personal and often painful matters, which require an empathetic and humane approach'.

> Some of our decision-makers commented on the pressures they felt themselves. One spoke about the difficulty of 'seeing a mother on her own in her flat, of watching her hear me say I'm making a placement order or removing the child to local authority care' when there was no one there to provide the mother with support.
>
> (McLean and George, 2021: 5)

Another judge said:

> You cannot tell how people are engaging or reacting. A respondent to a family law act injunction application was in her kitchen during the hearing and threatening to kill herself..... The cues, body language, subtle indications that we have always used during hearings to ensure that people are as engaged as possible with the hearing are lost. Similarly, all the pointers that would be there to be seen to warn us that a party was becoming angry, and thus allow us to step in at an early stage, have gone. It's appalling. We are making decisions even at case management about children's lives on the basis of a telephone call.
>
> (Ryan et al., 2020: 21)

Whether the decision is made with everyone present in court or not, the parent will later have to return to the new reality of their life and deal with the outcome. Experts are not immune to the intensity of feeling of those involved in this work. Whilst ensuring that the families are treated with compassion and respect, I need to be aware that lawyers, barristers and judges are similarly connected to their clients' anguish. I need to be sensitive to their feelings and to have systems in place to look after my own.

## The Welfare Checklist

Returning to the paramountcy principle, in order to determine what the child's best interests are, the court considers the issues in the Welfare Checklist which can be found in Section 1 Paragraph 3 of the Children Act 1989 (National Archives, 2023). The court has to show that these have been considered before making any legal order that affects the care of the child.

## The Welfare Checklist Criteria

1   The ascertainable wishes and feelings of the child concerned (considered in the light of his age and understanding)

Local authorities are obliged under the Children Act 1989 to take children's wishes and feelings into account in most actions that will concern them. This is also underlined in statutory guidance, such as the 'Framework for the Assessment of Children in Need' and the 'Working Together to Safeguard Children 2023' guidance. The latter states that:

> Anyone working with children should see and speak to the child, listen to what they say, observe their behaviour, take their views seriously, and work with them and their families and the people who know them well when deciding how to support their needs. Practitioners should also be aware that children may find it difficult to always speak about what they need, what is happening to them or what has happened to them. Legal duties under the Equality Act 2016 must be complied with, including putting special provision in place to support dialogue with children who may not be able to convey their wishes and feelings as they may want to. This might include, for example, those who have communication difficulties, unaccompanied children, refugees, those children who are victims of modern slavery and/or trafficking and those who do not speak English or for whom English is not their first language.
>
> (HM Government, 2023: 12)

No age or stage limit applies to children's right to have their views and feelings heard. Even pre-school children are able to contribute a perspective but a great deal of skill is required to evaluate a child's expressed wishes and feelings which may be subject to the influence of multiple factors. It can be particularly challenging to distinguish between expressed and ascertainable wishes and feelings. In private law proceedings, it is not infrequently alleged that the child is being unduly influenced by the parent with whom they live, even to the extent of being deliberately coached to take a negative position and make false allegations against the other parent. The complexities of ascertaining a child's wishes and feelings with a degree of confidence will be explored in more depth in later chapters.

In order genuinely to include a child's perspective, my preference is to make an audio-recording of my meetings with children and to obtain their views through the use of a range of media and activities that are described in a companion volume (Scaife, 2024). This can be through the use of posting boxes, drawings, toys, puppets, tests and questionnaires. I include quotations from the child in my report which can provide readers with a sense of genuineness and insights not necessarily apparent from a third-party account.

2  His physical, emotional and educational needs
The court has to consider the child's needs, both immediate and longer-term, in each developmental domain. These will often be framed as a question in the letter of instruction to an expert. Whilst there are needs common to all children, some have special needs as a result of their genetic or congenital history, environmental conditions and experience of care-giving. As children's needs develop over time, the court has to consider whether the proposed living arrangements will be adaptive to the child's changing developmental status.

3  The likely effect on him of any change in his circumstances
The court is concerned with the stability of the arrangements for the care of the child. In care proceedings a child may have been removed from a parent unable to meet their needs, then subjected to multiple damaging changes of placement whilst looked after by the local authority. In private law, parental applications that involve changes of school, long travelling distances and/or separation from extended family and friends may be looked upon unfavourably. Courts seek to make decisions that will cause the least disruption to a child's life.

4  His age, sex, background and any characteristics of his which the court considers relevant
It is not always obvious how such factors might impact decisions regarding the care of the child. With increasing age, it becomes more difficult to make arrangements counter to the expressed wishes of children since they will likely 'vote with their feet' and move themselves from an imposed to a preferred arrangement, which may put them in considerable danger.

John Burnham (2013) developed the acronym 'social graces' (GGRRAAAC-CEEESSS) to represent aspects of visible and invisible difference in beliefs, power and lifestyle, both voiced and unvoiced. The acronym currently references gender, geography, 'race', religion, age, ability, appearance, class, culture, ethnicity, education, employment, sexuality, sexual orientation and spirituality. Courts may be faced with decisions that need to weigh cultural norms, economic well-being, educational opportunities and family structure. In the matter of M children heard by Sir James Mumby and Lord Justice Singh in the High Court on 20 December 2017 the court was required to balance choice of gender identity with the child's membership of a particular religious or spiritual community. An appeal was made against a decision to reject an application for contact between children belonging to a Charedi Jewish community and their father who identified as transgender. The original judgment had reached the conclusion that the likelihood of the children and their mother being marginalised or excluded by the ultra-Orthodox community is so real, and the consequences so great, that this one factor, despite its many disadvantages, must prevail over the many advantages of contact.[1]

(Child Rights International Network, 2018)

The family court has to weigh such factors in making decisions in a child's best interests. In my experience, a particularly challenging decision can be whether to separate children of different ages who have grown up together so that one of them stands a greater chance of permanence.

5    Any harm which he has suffered or is at risk of suffering
The court will explore harm that the child has suffered and harm that the child is at risk of suffering in the future. Harm is defined as 'ill treatment or the impairment of health or development' and can be in any developmental domain. It includes, for example, 'impairment suffered from seeing or hearing the ill-treatment of another' (Adoption and Children Act, 2002, Section 120). Frequently included in the letter of instruction to an expert witness is the question of whether a child has suffered or is at risk of suffering harm which can be physical, emotional, sexual, vicarious as in domestic abuse, medical as in Fabricated or Induced Illness (FII) or any other form.

6    How capable each of his parents, and any other person in relation to whom the court considers the question to be relevant, is of meeting his needs
The court will want to ensure that parents are putting the child first and are able to meet the child's needs. No assumptions are made about whether fathers or mothers are best placed to do this. Where parents are considered to be failing in this regard, the local authority is required first to explore whether extended family members or close friends are able to meet the child's needs through kinship care.

7    The range of powers available to the court under this Act in the proceedings in question
This is a key principle of family law which is set out in Section 1 of the Children Act 1989. The court is instructed to make no order unless there is evidence to suggest that an order would be in the child's best interests. Even if no application has been made for a particular order, the court will consider every option and can make a wide range of orders. For example, in private law proceedings, should it emerge that the parent with whom the child lives intends to relocate permanently without seeking the consent of the other parent who holds Parental Responsibility (PR) for the child, the court may grant a prohibited steps order preventing movement away from the jurisdiction.

## Structure and Processes of the Family Court

The processes of the family court are set in train by an application which may be made by a parent in private law proceedings or by the local authority in public law. This is summarised in Figure 1.1.

**The Processes of the Family Court in Regard to Children**
The Family Court hears issues concerning the care of children
An application is made for a legal order to the Family Court

**Private Law**
Application made by parents/carers
in disputes over care of children

**Public Law**
Application made by local authority

Before making an application, attempts should be made to reach agreement which can be formalised by a Consent Order (England and Wales) or a Minute of Agreement (Scotland). Parents are required to attend a MIAM (mediation information and assessment meeting).

Where there are concerns about a child's welfare and proceedings are brought by the local authority.

CAFCASS officer appointed to represent interests of the child/children
Legal representation of child automatic in public law, may be appointed in private law.
(In public law proceedings and where the child is legally represented in private law proceedings the CAFCASS officer is referred to as the 'children's guardian' or in N. Ireland 'guardian ad litem'.)

**First Hearing and Dispute Resolution Appointment (FHDRA)**
Parties may appoint and fund own legal representative or act 'in person' i.e. represent themselves. If there is evidence of domestic abuse, the victim may claim LAA funding.

All parties entitled to legal representation with funding from Legal Aid Agency (LAA)

First hearing is the **Case Management Hearing (CMH)** which identifies major issues and sets a timetable ideally to complete within 26 weeks. In cases such as alleged non-accidental injury, a fact-finding hearing may take place first, providing a baseline.

Possible **Fact Finding Hearing** at which the judge decides on the facts. **These cannot be challenged by an expert.**

*Expert may be appointed to assist with 'just resolution' of issues*

**Dispute Resolution Appointment**

**Issues Resolution Hearing**

**Final Hearing**
Possible orders the court may make:
- Child Arrangements Order including 'lives with' and 'spends time with'
- Specific Issue Order e.g. school attended
- Prohibited Steps Order e.g. child cannot be taken out of the UK without other parent's permission.

**Final Hearing**
Possible orders the court may make:
- Care Order
- Supervision Order
- Special Guardianship Order (in favour of connected persons or kinship carer who has been caring for the child)
- Child Arrangements Order (in favour of a parent or connected person)
- Emergency Protection Order (at the start)
- Secure Accommodation Order
- Placement Order (finalised by an Adoption Order for which the adoptive parents apply.)

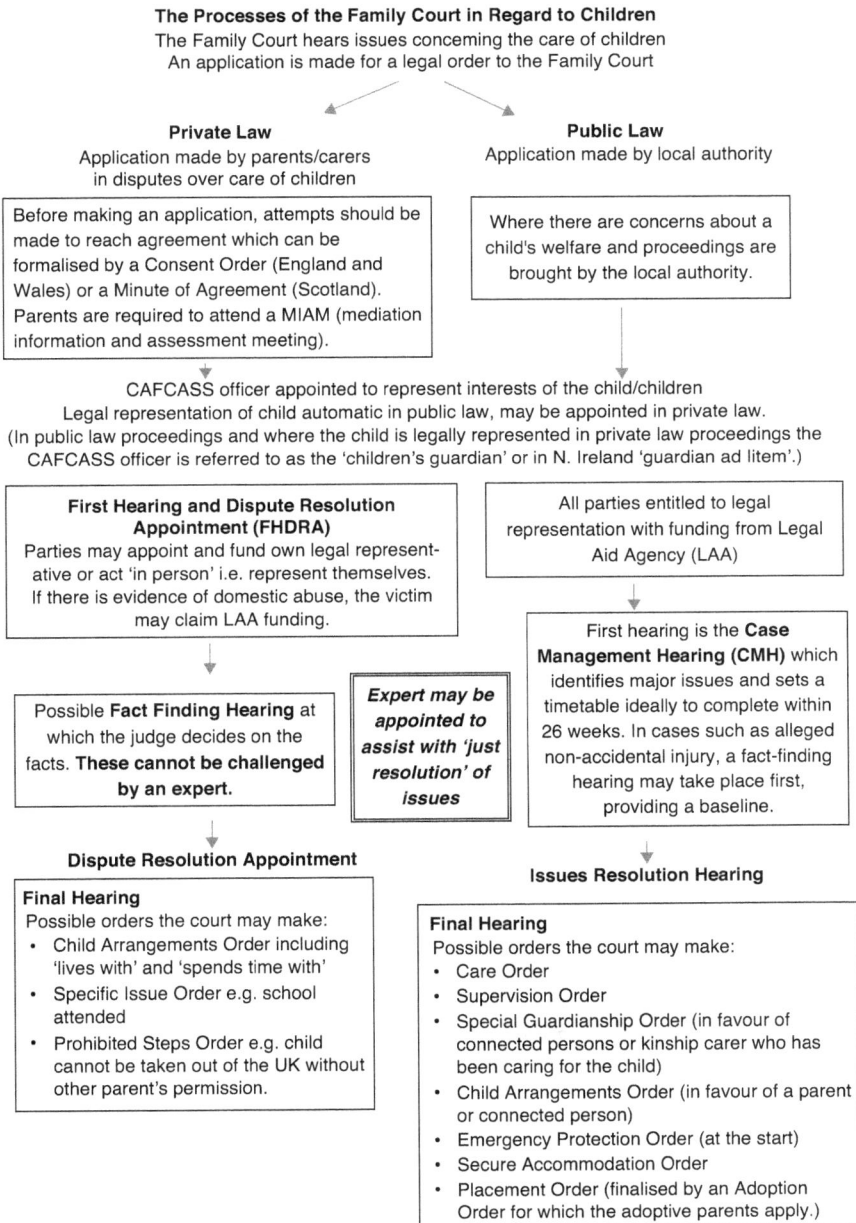

*Figure 1.1* The Processes of the Family Court in Regard to Children.

The decision maker/s in hearings within the family court occupy a specific hierarchy. Magistrates (lay people who generally sit in a panel of two or three supported by a legal advisor) hear relatively straightforward cases, district judges are drawn from barristers and solicitors of at least five years' standing (and since 2010, legal executives may also be appointed). Circuit judges (known as recorders if they work part-time) must satisfy the judicial-appointment eligibility condition on a seven-year basis, and judges in the High Court (Family Division) need extensive legal expertise and must successfully navigate a competitive application process involving written tests, interviews, and assessments. The level of the court is determined by the complexity of the issues.

Often also present at hearings in the family court is an officer employed by CAFCASS or CAFCASS Cymru in Wales, and each party to the proceedings who will either represent themselves or be represented by a member/members of the legal profession. This means that there can be a lawyer and barrister for each party. In public law a mother is automatically a party, as is a father if he holds parental responsibility, in default of which he must make an application to be made a party by the court. This also applies to same-sex parents who are married or in a civil partnership.

### Role of CAFCASS

The role of CAFCASS is to advise the court on the best interests of the children. At the outset they are responsible for carrying out routine safeguarding checks on the parents through police and local authority records. They also ask parents at this stage about safeguarding issues such as domestic abuse, drug or alcohol dependency. The CAFCASS officer will provide this information to the court and typically participates in the first hearing whether in person or remotely. In public law the officer acts as a guardian for the children (formerly 'guardian ad litem' to distinguish the role from 'legal guardian') and represents the best interests of the children, carries out assessments and provides reports. They are professionally qualified social workers with considerable experience of working with children and families but act independently of the local authority. It is often on the advice of the guardian that an expert report is recommended.

In public law there is always a CAFCASS officer to represent the child (or children), whereas in private law the guardian only becomes involved after the initial hearing if directed by the court. In cases regarded as complex, the judge can make a direction under Rule 16.4 of the Family Procedure Rules 2010 to make the child party to the proceedings. When this happens, a guardian is appointed for the children to give the court an independent view of their perspectives. Sometimes in private law, the child's guardian is employed by the National Youth Advocacy Service (NYAS). The guardian will also instruct a solicitor to represent the child. The solicitor is responsible for presenting the child's case in court, including calling witnesses for the child. The guardian is responsible for advising the solicitor about appropriate plans for the child's well-being and what information should be put before the court.

## Court Rationale

The family court is currently based on an adversarial approach which aims to resolve disputes by the people involved presenting their respective positions before an impartial decision-maker. Private law typically involves disputes between parents, public law between parents and a local authority (the parties). A parent or local authority applies to the court for an order (the applicant), and whoever disagrees with the request responds (the respondent). In this approach, the court relies upon the parties' discretion to select the evidence that they wish to put before the court, limited only by a duty to tell the truth. This means that they can present or leave out whatever they so choose. However, judges are expected to be proactive in considering which aspects of the evidence are required to enable the court to determine the relevant or key issues in dispute.

Public authorities such as the police and social work organisations are in addition under a duty to make honest disclosure of the facts known to them. This includes compliance with orders from the court to disclose all material arising from investigations that they have carried out. In a case heard by Mr Justice Peter Jackson[2] the police failed to supply a covert recording that had been made of the mother following the death of a child. This became apparent in criminal proceedings against the father. It was deemed that this should have been made available to the family court which meant that further consideration had to be given to the matter, causing anxiety for the mother and significant expense for the public purse although in this case it made no difference to the outcome.

A consequence of Article 6 of the Human Rights Act, the right to a fair trial, is that each party has the right to see and comment upon documents relied upon by the other party (European Court of Human Rights, 2022). For the expert witness, this means that any documents provided to them by any of the parties and upon which they rely for their opinion, must be shared with all of the parties. This can be accomplished by submitting them to the lead solicitor. The process being adversarial may be reflected in the parties' reactions to the professional's report whereby they will each be seeking to emphasise the opinions with which they agree and counter the opinions with which they disagree.

Interviews with clients have much in common with those conducted in clinical settings, but a major difference lies in the absence of confidentiality. Whatever clients say and whatever information they provide in the way of documents, emails, text messages, photographs or other media has to be shared with all of the parties. I find that clients not infrequently want to discuss something 'off the record', in response to which I stop them in their tracks and remind them that there is no such thing as confidentiality in this interview. When a parent feels the need to maintain secrecy over an issue, perhaps for fear of giving a negative impression, it can present a barrier to gaining insight into family functioning. This may pertain, for example, when a new romantic partnership has been established. A child in such a household may also be under pressure to keep this 'secret'.

The adversarial approach in the family court has been the subject of controversy, particularly since the introduction of restrictions to the provision of legal aid which may leave litigants in person (those who are not legally represented and present their own case) at a significant disadvantage. The process is not seen as providing a level playing field. The approach has also been criticised as harmful with respect to families when allegations of domestic abuse and other serious offences are involved, to the extent that a review (known as the Harm Panel report) was commissioned by the Ministry of Justice (Hunter et al., 2020). This highlighted how vulnerable individuals can feel threatened, experience re-traumatisation when giving evidence and may face the prospect of being questioned by or having to question a former partner whom they experienced as abusive. Repeated applications for court orders in themselves may serve to continue a process which is experienced as an attempt to maintain control even after separation. Since publication of the Harm Panel report, changes to legislation and court procedure have been made including plans published in October 2025 (Ministry of Justice, 2025c) to repeal the presumption of parental involvement (Children Act, 1989) where safety concerns pertain.

Contrasting with the adversarial approach is an inquisitorial process which shifts management of the process of investigation from family members to the judge. In this approach it is the judiciary who act as enquirers, determining what evidence is to be presented, its relevance, and how it is to be evaluated and tested. It is similar to an official enquiry (Hardcastle, 2005). The family justice system in England and Wales is reported to reflect characteristics of both approaches.

> Our system, and for good reason, is essentially adversarial, even in the Family Court. But it is a system very different from the adversarial system of yore. Then the judge functioned as little more than an umpire, adjudicating on whatever claim the litigant chose to bring, the only limitations being the need for some recognised cause of action and the requirement that the evidence had to be both relevant and admissible. Those days have long since gone. Modern case management imposes on the judge the responsibility of deciding what issues will be argued and what evidence will be permitted. The process before the judge may still be adversarial, but it is a dispute fought in accordance with an agenda set by the judge, not by the parties. But that, of course, assumes that the parties are represented. Where they are not, then the judge must take a more active role. The hearing is more likely to produce the right and just result if the judge adopts a more inquisitorial approach.
>
> (Munby, 2014: 12)

Judges in the family court are mandated to act in children's best interests. This may mean reaching conclusions or making an order that none of the parties has proposed. Nevertheless, the basis of the process continues to be adversarial which is considered potentially bruising for professionals, stressful for parents, and difficult for children who may wish to participate, for example by requesting to meet with the judge (Welbourne, 2016).

The Family Solutions Group has argued that the language of the court serves to reinforce its adversarial nature. At webinars hosted in 2023 they invited legal professionals to explore the use of solutions-focused rather than combative or battle terminology. Sir Andrew McFarlane, President of the Family Division, said, 'It's blindingly obvious that the language we have been using is not appropriate and only goes to stoke the minds of those in a combative mindset, rather than direct them in a different way' (Family Solutions Group, 2022). They made some very specific recommendations to replace words such as 'versus' with 'and', 'dispute' with 'issue to be resolved' and 'contact' with 'parent time' or 'family time'. They argued the case for the language used in court to be collaborative rather than combative, constructive rather than destructive and focussed on the future rather than recriminations about the past.

## The Expert Witness Role in the Family Court

Experts are appointed by and owe their duty to the family court. They are governed by Part 25 of the Family Procedure Rules (Justice, 2022) and are required to comply with the Standards for Expert Witnesses in Children Proceedings in the Family Court which are set out in the Annex to Practice Direction 25B (Justice, 2017). The Directions define issues such as the expert's duty to the court, the content of the report, their qualifications and experience, impartiality, and compliance with codes of conduct.

The role requires the expert to provide an opinion on questions documented in a letter of instruction (LOI). I find it helpful to keep in mind that I am being asked for an opinion, not an objective assertion of 'the correct opinion'. Lee Ross (2018) described what he termed the '*truly* fundamental attribution error': the illusion of superior personal objectivity. He cited Mark Twain: 'In all matters of opinion our adversaries are insane'. So long as I can have confidence in my opinions and the processes by which I reached them, I can allow that someone else's opinion is different and may be just as valid. The court may also give feedback that my opinion was not helpful. This was the case when I was asked to give an opinion regarding the attachment of a four-year-old (who had spent her early years in the care of her mother who was thought to have suffocated her younger brother) to her father. I could not say with certainty whether her behaviour reflected a pattern of insecure attachment arising from inconsistent early care, and/or that she was struggling with the sudden loss of her brother and mother, and/or that there were aspects of her father's care to which she was averse.

A significant proscription in work for the courts is to avoid expressing an opinion outside one's own area of expertise. There are times, for example, when it is apparent that a medical condition may be impacting a parent's behaviour and I will remark upon this whilst noting that the issue is outside my area of expertise.

Instructions to experts, which contain the questions on which an opinion is sought, are generated by the parties. Approaches to experts are made by solicitors representing the parties with a request for an up-to-date CV, hourly rates, hours needed to complete the assessment, and timescales for providing a report. The child's solicitor is usually designated as the lead solicitor who will provide the expert with a letter of instruction documenting the issues in the case and the questions which the expert is requested to address. The lead solicitor will also provide the 'bundle' of documents already submitted to the court, any other relevant documents and communications, and is the advocate with whom the expert will usually communicate about any issues arising.

The court is keen that the appointment of an expert witness does not cause delay to the proceedings as this is seen as counter to the best interests of children. The court attempts to keep care proceedings to a 26-week timetable, a directive that was introduced in the 2014 Children and Families Act. It is imperative that experts adhere to the filing date for their report in order to ensure adherence to the timetable. If they fail to do so, even for valid reasons, the expert may be found in violation of their duties as a witness and fees may be revoked.[3]

Although experts may quote higher hourly fee rates, the base rates for completing an assessment are defined by the Legal Aid Agency (LAA) (2025) and may not be exceeded without prior authority (before work on the report commences) from the LAA which is applied for by the instructing solicitor. The Legal Aid Agency (2025) stated that the requirements for prior authority are that the complexity of the material is such that an expert with a high level of seniority is required, or the material is of such a specialised and unusual nature that only very few experts are available to provide the necessary evidence. The LAA also provides benchmarks for the number of hours that it is expected the expert will need for the work. Prior authority needs to be sought if it is anticipated that these hours will be exceeded. The application needs to justify the proposed additional expense, typically in cases which involve a great deal of reading material such as very extensive medical records, where additional time arises from the need for an interpreter, or for interviews with additional family members or professionals.

In the family court, a single joint expert is usually appointed whose report is shared between the parties, although a second expert may be allowed if, for example, 'certain medical evidence is pivotal and difficult to challenge without a second opinion' (Davis, 2021: no page numbers). In private law,

> the rules require the parties to apply for the court's permission to obtain expert evidence as soon as it becomes apparent that it is necessary to make it and no later than the First Hearing Dispute Resolution Appointment (FPR, r 25.6).
>
> (Gordon, 2023: no page numbers)

In public law the application needs to be made and report submitted prior to the Issues Resolution Hearing. Ideally, and in line with the statutory timescale set for the completion of public law procseedings, the application for permission to instruct an expert should be made prior to the initial Case Management Hearing.

The expert chooses how to address the questions in the letter of instruction through interviews, observations, test administration, and reading documents provided by the parties and other professionals. It may be necessary to request documents that do not appear in the bundle. Within the report experts describe their approach, highlighting relevant factors and generating possible explanatory accounts for their findings. The report needs to discuss any competing explanatory accounts and describe the reasons for choosing one over another. This will probably reference relevant research literature. If appropriate, the report may take a 'balance sheet' approach to the evidence for and against an opinion. Improving accessibility of the report by limiting and/or explaining technical terms is desirable, as is an attempt to express opinions in as concise a way as possible in order to constrain the length of the report. Practice Direction 27A paragraph 5.2A.1 suggests a 40-page limit for expert's reports with an executive summary of no more than four pages.

I find it helpful to include all of the evidence on which my opinion is reached within the report so that readers can follow my reasoning process. Experts do not make decisions or assert 'the facts' as this is the prerogative of the judge. 'The expert advises but the judge decides' (Davis, 2021: no page numbers). For this reason, I do not include a section entitled 'Conclusions' but instead prefer to entitle it 'Summary', meaning the summary of my opinion in relation to the questions posed.

Experts can be asked to clarify their report by additional questions submitted within ten days of its receipt. They may also be asked to attend an experts' meeting in which areas of agreement and disagreement are clarified. This is a relatively infrequent occurrence since there is usually a single joint expert in the family court, but I have been asked to meet with and/or consider the reports of practitioners from other disciplines such as psychiatrists and paediatricians. The purposes of such a meeting are to explore the reasons for disagreement on any expert question and to decide what, if any, action needs to be taken to resolve any outstanding disagreement and to provide an explanation of existing evidence or additional evidence in order to assist the court to determine the issues. One of the aims of specifying the issues for discussion is to limit, wherever possible, the need for the experts to attend court to give oral evidence (Practice Direction 25E). Jointly instructed experts are advised not to attend any meeting or conference unless it is a joint one, or all the parties have agreed in writing, or the court has directed that such a meeting may be held, and it is agreed or directed who is to pay the expert's fees for the meeting or conference.

In public law Children Act proceedings, experts may also be asked to attend a court-directed professionals' meeting. This takes place between the local authority, other parties/their representatives and any relevant named experts for the purpose of providing assistance to the local authority in the formulation of plans and proposals for the child (Practice Direction 25E 5.1). It is arranged, chaired and minutes taken in accordance with the directions given by the court, typically by the lead solicitor.

If it is determined that the expert is required to give oral evidence, they will be invited to the final hearing on a specific date. Attendance may be in person or remote. Their evidence is usually given on day one or two of the hearing. Going to court often involves much waiting time and additional documents may be provided for the witness to read and consider during this time outside the courtroom.

The process begins with taking an oath or affirming that the witness will tell the truth and is repeated after the clerk of the court. The witness gives their 'evidence in chief' through statements and questions posed by the lead solicitor, and is then questioned (cross-examined) by the other parties or their lawyers or barristers who attempt to further their client's case through these questions. The judge may also ask questions. The process is described fully in Chapter 6.

Whilst the process typically takes between an hour and three hours, I have spent a whole day in the witness box and returned at a later date to continue giving evidence. This was very unusual and occurred because there were a large number of children of different ages and several parents involved. Each party had an advocate and a barrister. The court takes breaks, for lunch and to provide time for the parties to explore issues outside the hearing or obtain relevant documents that were not available in advance. Whilst under oath (which continues during breaks) the witness cannot discuss anything related to the case with the parties. I have been strongly discouraged from responding to a parent's greeting during such breaks. I tend to make myself scarce in order to be clear that I am not being influenced in my opinion by any discussions with parties on the day.

In contrast, additional evidence may be put before the expert at the hearing, following which they may be asked to reconsider their opinion. The court views it as important for experts to be open to changing or modifying their opinions if new evidence so warrants rather than rigidly adhering to an initial position. It is good practice for the expert to let the parties know of any resulting change of opinion. Modifying an opinion may help to clarify the significant issues in the case. The judge will respect the thoughtful, reflective expert who is open to revision of their opinion.

The family court differs from the criminal court in regard to the standard of proof required. It makes decisions based on the civil standard of proof: 'the balance of probabilities' and not the criminal standard of proof: 'beyond reasonable doubt'. The family court can make a finding that someone has harmed a child but they can be found not guilty in the criminal court.

This was the case in respect of 13-month-old Poppi Worthington. After a post-mortem found suspicious injuries in her anus, the coroner concluded that Poppi had died from asphyxiation after her father brought her into his bed and abused her. Mr Justice Peter Jackson, a High Court family judge sitting at Liverpool Crown Court, found that on the 'balance of probabilities', Poppi's father had perpetrated a penetrative anal assault on her, either using his penis or some other unidentified object. Poppi died shortly afterwards from a cause which the judge was unable to ascertain. The Crown Prosecution Service (CPS) reviewed the evidence against her father in 2016 and found that there was 'no realistic prospect' of a conviction in the criminal court as police had failed to collect vital evidence (Dolan, 2018).

---

## Key Points from this Chapter

- Involvement with the family court can be stressful and harrowing for both parents and professionals.
- First and foremost, the family court prioritises the welfare of children, which is known as the 'paramountcy principle'.
- The court determines what is in the child's best interests by reference to the Welfare Checklist.
- The basis of the family court is an adversarial approach in which a primary caregiver or local authority (the parties) seeks the making of an order concerning arrangements for the care of children. Other parties contest this and each puts forward the evidence that they choose to support their case. However, judges are expected to be proactive in considering which aspects of the evidence are required to enable the court to determine the relevant or key issues in dispute.
- The judge in the family court may also take an inquisitorial approach which shifts management of the process of investigation from the parties towards the judge.
- Court hearings take place in a particular order and to set dates. The need for an expert witness is determined early in the process and they must adhere to the court timetable in order to avoid delay to the proceedings which can be harmful to children. Expert witnesses may only be appointed if determined to be necessary for justice to be achieved.
- Experts are appointed by and owe their duty to the family court. They are governed by Part 25 of the Family Procedure Rules (Justice, 2022) and are required to comply with the Standards for Expert Witnesses in Children Proceedings in the Family Court which are set out in the Annex to Practice Direction 25B (Justice, 2017).
- In the family court a single joint expert is usually appointed and shared between the parties, rather than each appointing their own expert.
- The expert provides a report, answering questions posed by the parties in a letter of instruction. If the expert's opinion is contested by a party/the parties they may, in the interests of justice, be required to give evidence in a final hearing.

---

## Notes

1  J v B [2017] EWFC 4 (20 January 2017).
2  Cumbria County Council v M and Others [2016] EWFC 27.
3  X and Y (Delay: Professional Conduct of Expert) [2019] EWFC B9.

Chapter 2

# Children's Welfare and the Law

## The Children Act 1989

The Children Act 1989, with subsequent amendments, is the primary legislation that governs child protection in England. Parallel legislation was introduced in Northern Ireland and Scotland in 1995 when the Children (Northern Ireland) Order and the Children (Scotland) Act were passed by Parliament. The Act applies in Wales except for Part III which has been replaced by the Social Services and Well-being (Wales) Act 2014. The 1989 Act has 12 parts, within which there are 108 sections.

It is parts 1 to 5 that are of greatest relevance to expert witnesses. These govern:

1  The welfare of the child, parental responsibility (PR), appointment of guardians and welfare reports.
2  Orders with respect to children in family proceedings. These relate to private law proceedings and include Child Arrangements Orders, Specific Issues Orders and Prohibited Steps Orders. Special Guardianship and Family Assistance Orders are also covered in this part of the Act. An amendment passed in the Children and Families Act 2014 emphasised that without evidence to the contrary, the involvement of parents in the child's life will be taken as beneficial to the welfare of the child (Holt, 2019).
3  Arrangements for the support of children and families provided by local authorities in England.
4  Care and Supervision Orders that may be granted to a local authority (LA) by the court when children's welfare is compromised or is likely to be compromised if action is not taken.
5  Child Assessment Orders and Emergency Protection Orders.

The original legislation integrated public and private law provisions and was a result of consensus following public inquiries into the deaths of children at the hands of their carers. Safeguarding agencies (a wide range of agencies working together to protect vulnerable individuals including health, local authorities and police) were regarded as having failed to work together to protect children, particularly when parents were hard to engage. Statutory guidance published in 'Working

DOI: 10.4324/9781003453390-2

Together to Safeguard Children 2023', provides detailed information about the core legal requirements. The guidance aims to ensure multi-agency cooperation to help, protect and promote the welfare of children.

The Children Act 1989 enshrines several key principles, including:

- The concept of PR and what kinds of rights and responsibilities this entails.
- That anyone who has legal PR for a child can generally act alone in making a decision about the child's welfare. Where there is a major decision to be made about the child's life, all those with PR need to be consulted. If one parent wants to make a change such as to the child's name or to move abroad with the child, all those with PR must agree.
- That a child's welfare is the main consideration (is paramount) when the court is exploring a question about a child's upbringing.
- That delay is likely to prejudice the welfare of the child.
- That children are best looked after by their families unless intervention in family life is essential.
- That the court should not make an order unless to do so would be better for the child – the 'no order' principle.

## Part 1: Introductory

Part 1 of the Act introduces these key principles of the legislation and defines the concept of PR. A mother automatically has PR for her child from birth. A father usually has PR if he is married to the child's mother or is listed on the birth certificate (after 1 December 2003, depending upon in which part of the UK the child was born). If a child's father is not married to their mother and does not appear on the birth certificate, PR can be sought through a voluntary arrangement or by court order. Same-sex partners will both have PR if they were civil partners at the time of the treatment (donor insemination or fertility treatment).

For same-sex partners who are not civil partners, the 2nd parent may obtain PR by either applying for PR if a parental agreement was made or becoming a civil partner of the other parent and making a PR agreement or jointly registering the birth (Gov.uk, undated a). Legal rights in surrogacy arrangements may be found at Gov.uk (undated b). PR may also be sought by others who are connected to the child such as a step-parent or additional parent. Grandparents can obtain it through a child arrangements order or special guardianship. More than two people may hold PR for the same child.

For births registered in Scotland a father has PR if married to the mother when the child is conceived or marries her at any point later. From 4 May 2006 he has PR if named on the child's birth certificate. For births registered in Northern Ireland a father has PR if married to the mother at the time of the birth or if he marries the mother later and resides in Northern Ireland at the time. From 15 April 2002 an unmarried father has PR if he is named or becomes named on the child's birth certificate.

Whilst this may seem relatively straightforward, there can be complexity, particularly around the status of a parent from the child's perspective. When a child is conceived, the mother may either be unaware of the identity of the father, unwilling to inform the father of the pregnancy or completely disengaged from the relationship with the father. If she develops another relationship whilst pregnant, the second man may be named as the father on the child's birth certificate. If the mother separates from this man soon after and forms a third enduring relationship, the third father is the man who is providing the fathering and the only father the child has known. Such children may be entirely unaware of this history, and an expert witness may be asked to offer advice on how to, when to, and who should tell the child about it. PR can only be removed under exceptional circumstances and this would have to be regarded as in the best interests of the child.

PR is important because anyone who has it can act alone in making day-to-day decisions about the child's welfare, although major decisions require consultation with other holders of PR. In the event that holders cannot agree, an application may need to be made to the court.

When there are disputes regarding arrangements for the care of a child, Practice Direction 12B of the Family Court Procedure Rules regarding the Child Arrangements Programme (CAP) comes into effect. It includes mandatory police and LA checks of applicants and respondents in any application for a Child Arrangements Order, and checks may be directed by the court to be undertaken in any other private law case (Justice, 2023a).

Part 1 of the Act also provides for requests to be made by the court to the Child and Family Court Advisory and Support Service (CAFCASS) or an LA for an assessment of the welfare of the child, which is known as a Section 7 report. It is usually requested when parents are unable to resolve their dispute about the arrangements for care of the children and is intended to assist the court in reaching a decision. The content of the report is specified, central to which is consideration of the welfare checklist (see Chapter 1) in relation to this child. The child or children are usually seen individually, their wishes and feelings noted, and an opinion offered as to whether these have been formed spontaneously or under pressure. Separate meetings will usually be held with each carer for whom the issues are in dispute. As part of the process, the author of the report may speak to the parents, wider family members and engage with a variety of professionals such as the child's GP, health professionals and the child's school. The assessment includes safeguarding information obtained through requests to the police and other authorities.

### Part 2: Orders with Respect to Children in Family Proceedings

Part 2 of the Act applies to private law proceedings and outlines the range of orders which the court can issue regarding with whom a child will live and spend time. These used to be termed Residence and Contact Orders. They have been replaced by Child Arrangements Orders which can include 'lives with' and 'spend time with' elements. These can be quite detailed, defining exactly what periods a child will spend with carers, including specific times and dates. How the child will spend holiday periods when schools are closed may also be tightly specified.

Prohibited Steps Orders prevent a carer from exercising some elements of their PR. They are typically made to block a child being removed from a particular school, changes being made to their family name, or being taken out of the UK. They can last for several months or several years, depending upon the court's opinion about what best serves the child's interests. If it does not end sooner, the order comes to an end when children reach their 16th birthday, or in exceptional circumstances on their 18th birthday when they legally become an adult. They can be sought under Section 8 of the Children Act 1989.

Specific Issues Orders are made to determine questions and conflicts about a child's upbringing including medical treatment such as immunisation or surgery, religious affiliations or arrangements for the child's education. Such orders may also arise from disputes about a child's name or geographical location and whether a particular individual is allowed to have contact with them. Unless there are exceptional circumstances, a Specific Issues Order will not be made once a child is aged 16 years and if extended, ends at the age of 18 years. Such orders cannot be made if a child is in the care of a local authority.

Disputes between separated parents over arrangements for the care of the children can reflect and often amplify already overwhelming feelings of distress, rage, fear, disgust, jealousy and hurt. One parent may feel seriously wronged by the other and allegations can fly back and forth about domestic abuse, betrayal, substance misuse, deliberate alienation or coaching of a child against the other parent. What appear to be watertight Child Arrangements Orders can be fiercely contested with allegations by both parties that they are failing to comply. They are viewed from the perspectives of people in conflict; interpretations differ:

Father:

After we separated, at first we had an informal arrangement for me to see Bella and it worked okay but then Fiona started to say that I couldn't come after work and it was difficult to fit it in between school and work. When I was supposed to have her, her mother would invite a friend to stay over so Bella wouldn't want to come. I hated not seeing her and it all felt at the whim of Bella's mum so I made an application to court and the judge made a final order. I was collecting Bella from school on a Friday and taking her back there on Monday mornings but after a couple of weeks her mum collected her early and told school that I had threatened to run away with her so when I went to pick her up she wasn't there. I hadn't had the written order by then so I had nothing to show the school. I went to get her from her mother's but she wouldn't let me in and she wouldn't answer her phone and I didn't know what she was saying to Bella. Fiona and her lawyer devised a plan to build a case against me. She started to say that I'd been abusive when we lived together and that I'd interfered with Bella. She applied for a non-molestation order. I was arrested and interviewed by the police, and it was so shameful and degrading when they came to my workplace. They took no further action; it was all a conspiracy to prevent me from seeing my daughter.

Mother:

> I used to let Mark see Bella whenever he wanted but he started to come later and later after she was in bed. It was all about what fitted for him and not what was best for Bella. I'd been for counselling because I was depressed after we separated, and my counsellor helped me to see how controlling he had been. My self-esteem was rock bottom. He was always calling me fat and telling me what a bad mother I was. She helped me to see that I could be someone and I started to make friends and got a part-time job. When I wouldn't let him in to see Bella after her bedtime, he started to get pushy and aggressive, demanding that I open the door and let him see her whenever he wanted. On one occasion I called the police because he was really scary. And I didn't want Bella overhearing us arguing every time he collected her. So I applied for a non-molestation order and the judge granted it. Bella started to come home from contact upset about him shouting at her and she didn't have a bed of her own so she was sleeping in his and it worried me. I discussed it with her teachers and they thought it wasn't right either. When she said he had told her that he was going to take her out of the country to see his family she was scared she wouldn't come home and I felt I had to protect her. I rang social services and they told me to stop contact. When we were together he never showed much interest in her – he was always working. He just wants to carry on controlling me like he used to.

In family conflicts such as this, an expert witness may be asked by the court to explore the family dynamics and account for the difficulties, but it is not the prerogative of the expert to reach conclusions about the facts. That is the job of the judge, and the expert needs to be very careful not to stray into the domain of deciding on the facts, lest their report be dismissed in entirety.

## Special Guardianship (Section 14 of the Children Act 1989)

The Adoption and Children Act (2002) introduced special guardianship and Special Guardianship Orders. Special guardians usually have a close relationship with a child, often as a member of the wider family, former foster carer or family friend. The order places a child with the guardian permanently and they are awarded PR. Existing holders of PR retain it but their ability to exercise PR is severely restricted by the special guardian's authority to make day-to-day decisions regarding the child without the need to consult others. The order usually lasts until the child is aged 18 years. The term 'guardian' is not to be confused with the children's guardian working for the courts within CAFCASS.

## Family Assistance Orders

This order may be made under Section 16 of the Children Act either in private or public law applications. The emphasis is upon short-term involvement and giving assistance to families. The order will usually have a very specific remit to achieve its goals within a maximum of 12 months. It is typically made where general support requirements are considered to be insufficient. The emphasis is on help and assistance, rather than serving the function of a safety measure. Either the LA or CAFCASS staff may be nominated to effect it. Consent must be obtained from the adults named in the order. The Family Assistance Order 'may direct the officer concerned to give advice and assistance as regards establishing, improving and maintaining contact to such of the persons named in the order as may be specified in the order' (National Archive, 2024a: no page numbers). The assistance may involve helping with practical arrangements for contact, facilitating communication between parents, and/or providing emotional support for family members whilst they adjust to the new arrangements. If an expert considers that it would be appropriate to suggest the making of a Family Assistance Order, this is probably best accomplished after discussion with relevant professionals and carers, since agreement to the proposal is usually necessary. However, the court may make a Family Assistance Order without agreement of the local authority, providing that they have had an opportunity to make representations about whether an order should be made.

## Part 3: LA Support for Children and Families

### Children in Need

A child in need is defined under Section 17 of the Children Act 1989 as one who is unlikely to experience a reasonable standard of health or development without assistance from the local authority, or their health or development is likely to be significantly impaired without assistance, or they have a disability. The definition is wide-ranging to cover physical and mental health; emotional, social, intellectual, physical and behavioural development. A Child in Need Plan outlines the support that the child and family need and how it will be provided in order for the child to experience adequate health and development. Such assessments also seek evidence as to whether a child is suffering, or is likely to suffer, 'significant harm' due to parental actions or omissions. The Act specifies the requirement to take account of the child's wishes and feelings regarding the provision of support services. The LA has a duty to provide or facilitate others to provide services for children in need.

Traditionally, assessments of children in need have been carried out only by qualified social workers, but the revised 'Working Together to Safeguard Children' legislation has broadened the definition to 'lead practitioner' who may be a family support worker, drug and alcohol practitioner, domestic abuse or youth worker (Samuel, 2024).

### Accommodation and Looked After Children

A child who is in the care of an LA or provided with accommodation for more than 24 hours is referred to as a 'looked after child'. This is often abbreviated to 'LAC' which children and young people have reported can result in them feeling depersonalised and as if they 'lack' something (NSPCC, 2023). Children under a Section 20 (voluntary) arrangement are 'looked after' but not 'in care'.

Under Section 20 of the Act local authorities are required to provide accommodation for any child in need when no one with PR is able to care for them. Section 20 can be used in circumstances when a child has nowhere to live; no one to look after them due to parental illness or difficulties such as serving a short prison sentence; when the carer is attempting to leave an abusive partner; or when the parent feels that the child is beyond their control and therefore at risk. Under this section of the Act, consent is required from the person/s with PR, and it is often referred to as 'voluntary care' or 'voluntary accommodation'. Sometimes an LA will ask parents to sign a 'Section 20 agreement' which means that the parent is consenting for the child to live elsewhere, often in foster care. The child is being looked after without the need for the LA to obtain an order of the court. There is a risk of this allowing the child to languish in alternative care without a formal planning process and can be seen as a 'back door' way for a Care Order to be obtained (Child Protection Resource, 2021).

Consideration needs to be given to children's views when deciding where to accommodate them. Sibling groups are usually best placed together and accommodated near their home if possible. In my experience, if a parent who has consented to the provision of alternative care, often because they are finding that they cannot meet the needs of the child, revokes their consent, but the LA considers that the risk to the child returning to their care would be too great, a court order may be sought. In this circumstance, furious parents have raged about the deceit of the LA, whom they said had told them that the child could return home as soon as their parental consent was withdrawn. This mother was struggling with her physical and mental health to the point where she was unable to provide the care that her daughter needed:

> My health was getting worse and worse and I was in pain all the time. The hospital didn't know what was wrong with me and it made me short-tempered and upset. Charlie was doing dangerous things, climbing out of the window and walking on the window ledge, smearing faeces all over her bedroom walls and stealing from her brother. I didn't have the energy to cope. I'd been asking social services for help for months but all they gave me was respite one weekend a month. I was at my wit's end and I was frightened I might hurt her. I didn't want to, but I knew if I told the social worker that, she'd have to do something. I agreed to her being in voluntary care and the social worker told me I could have her back home any time. So when she was moved to a place that she didn't like and begged me to come home I went to pick her up. That's when things turned

nasty and they took me to court and got an order. I felt massively let down. I felt cheated. I needed someone to come and work with me and Charlie, not a police van turning up to take her away to a children's home miles away.

Devolved governments have slightly different definitions of a looked-after child and follow their own legislation, policy and guidance. Scotland includes within its definition children under a supervision order to the LA who are still living in their birth family. A looked-after child is usually living with foster carers, or sometimes in a residential children's home or specialist residential setting such as a school or secure unit.

In England, if a child is to be placed in secure accommodation, Section 25 of the Act sets out the 'welfare' criteria, either of which must be met before a looked-after child can be placed in a secure setting. The criteria are:

1  The child has a history of absconding and is likely to abscond from any other description of accommodation; and if the child absconds, he is likely to suffer significant harm or
2  If the child is kept in any other description of accommodation he is likely to injure himself or other persons.

(Section 25, Children Act 1989)

The welfare principle (established in Section 1 of the Act), although still relevant, is not of paramount consideration under Section 25. In exceptional circumstances, if a child is not 'looked after' or the placement of the child is thought to constitute a deprivation of the child's liberty (even though it is not its primary purpose), an application would need to be made to the High Court to exercise its inherent juris-diction. Prior to admission to a secure facility, a written agreement concerning the placement should be made between the LA and the parents to include the purpose of admission, expected duration and arrangements for bringing the placement to an end. Further details regarding deprivation of children's liberty is available for each of the devolved governments from legislation.gov.uk.

## Part 4: Care and Supervision

### Care and Supervision Orders

Under Section 31 of the Act, Care and Supervision Orders may be sought either by an LA or (in England, Northern Ireland and Wales) by the NSPCC which also has statutory powers to protect children. In Scotland, children may be subject to a Child Protection Order (when a child is at immediate and serious risk) or a Compulsory Supervision Order made by a Children's Hearing or sheriff. The latter requires a child to comply with specified conditions (such as where they live) and the LA to support and provide assistance to the child and family. In England, Wales and Northern Ireland no Care Order or Supervision Order may be made with respect to a child who has reached the age of 17 (or 16, in the case of a child who is married). Applications for these orders are regulated by the Public Law Outline (PLO) which is addressed in a later chapter.

Care orders set out a long-term plan for a child but when an LA believes that a child has suffered, or is likely to suffer, significant harm whilst remaining in their birth family, an interim order may be sought. An Interim Care or Supervision Order is typically in place whilst assessments and interventions are continued and is effective until the conclusion of the proceedings or a final order is made. Whilst in place, interim orders carry the same weight as full orders.

A court may only make a Care Order or Supervision Order if it is satisfied that 'the child concerned is suffering, or is likely to suffer, significant harm; and that the harm, or likelihood of harm, is attributable to the care given to the child, or likely to be given to him if the order were not made, not being what it would be reasonable to expect a parent to give to him; or the child's being beyond parental control'. These are known as the 'threshold criteria'. When applying for an order under this section of the Act, an initial statement by the LA will typically set out the issues demonstrating that the threshold has been reached. A separate, condensed threshold document will also be produced. A response statement by the carer will set out which of these are agreed and which are contested. The evidential burden of proof that needs to be met by the local authority's statement is the civil standard of 'balance of probabilities' which allows for considerable discretion. A link has to be established between the facts relied upon in the threshold document and the conclusion that a child has suffered, or is at risk of suffering significant harm. And there is a requirement to tolerate inevitable diverse and unequal standards of parenting, 'including the eccentric, the barely adequate and the inconsistent'[1] (Re: L). The requirement to evidence the threshold criteria rests on the applicant for a Care Order as applied in the decision Re B (2008)[2] and as documented in the landmark case of Re A.[3]

The court may grant a Care Order in place of a Supervision Order if it is believed to be more appropriate or vice versa. Both orders require that the threshold be met, but a Care Order confers PR on the LA in addition to the parties by whom it is already held. A Supervision Order places a responsibility on the LA to 'advise, assist and befriend' the child and by extension, the people with whom the child lives. There is no requirement for a care plan to be made but the LA will usually agree a 'supervision contract' or 'supervision order support plan' with carers. A Supervision Order is designed to enable oversight of the child through a plan submitted to the court during proceedings. This is designed to be specific and purposeful in its aim of reducing risks and building on strengths within the family. Under a Supervision Order a 'responsible person' is designated as any person who has PR for the child and/or any other person with whom the child is living. With their consent the order may oblige them to take all reasonable steps to ensure that the child complies with the responsible person's directions. They may be directed to attend with the child, including medical or psychiatric appointments.

The LA supports the responsible person in ensuring that the supervised child complies with specific directions (National Archives, 2024a):

- To live in the place or places specified for stated periods of time
- To attend a particular place or places on a day or days specified
- To participate in activities specified
- Under certain circumstances to submit to medical or psychiatric assessment or treatment. (Where children have sufficient understanding to make an informed decision, they are required to consent to the inclusion of this requirement.)

'It shall be for the supervisor to decide whether, and to what extent, he exercises his power to give directions and to decide the form of any directions which he gives' (National Archives, 2024a: no page numbers). Supervision orders can be in effect for one year and may be extended to a total of three years.

A Care Order sets out the long-term plan for the upbringing of the child concerned. This may specify that they live with a parent, member of the wider family or friend of the child's family (kinship care), be placed for adoption (a Placement Order followed by an Adoption Order would be required) or in any other form of long-term care. The plan needs to set out the impact on the child concerned of any harm suffered or that was likely to be suffered; the current and future needs of the child (including needs arising out of that impact); and the way in which the long-term plan for the upbringing of the child would meet those current and future needs. Questions based on these requirements are often included in the letter of instruction to an expert.

During the time that children are in care, parents and carers are expected to be given reasonable amounts of contact (known as 'family time') with the child unless otherwise directed by the court. However, in urgent situations to protect the child the LA may refuse contact for up to seven days. Should the LA seek to refuse contact for longer than seven days, it must apply to the court to prevent contact in order to safeguard or promote the child's welfare.

Children's experiences of being in care vary greatly but for many, the alternative arrangements are never quite 'home', no matter the quality of care being provided or the amount of harm suffered. This child could not put aside her love for her father and sense of belonging to her birth family:

> We've had the social for three years now, three years in February. And all our social workers have said that it's all fine and everything. But then with the social worker we've got now, she just didn't care at all to think about what we need. As soon as we had her she ordered us to go to court to get a Care Order on us 'cos she thought that we, I don't know… In my foster family there's this, this little, how shall I put this, whinge-bag baby and I've had enough of it. He won't shut up and I get angry and punch my pillow, and sometimes the wall. I've got a teddy there and so I always put my dad's shorts on it so I can cuddle them in the

> night with the teddy. I just, when I'm in bed I feel like I belong with him because I've got his shorts but I don't belong at the foster carer's, I belong with my dad, and all the lot of us as a family. I've just got a picture of him in my head. I want to see him in real life and live with him so I see him all the time.

Sometimes during assessments, children make impassioned pleas to be reunited with a family member by whom they truly feel loved and wanted:

> I've had a really bad time in care and do *not* get on with this foster carer. She couldn't care less what happens to me. I'm always being accused of stuff I haven't done and apparently I'm a bad influence on the other foster child. I'm begging you to get me out of here and put me with my nana who cares a lot about me and makes sure I have everything I need. I won't run away if you put me with my nana but I would run away if I was placed with another foster carer. I just want to be happy right now but I'm not. I hate it here a lot. I'd be real happy at my nana's. I'd have my bike again. I'd still have that freedom that other kids have to go to the park and kick a football around. I'd have my noodles again 'cos I haven't had them for ages.'

### Children's Guardians and CAFCASS

Children's guardians ('guardian ad litem' in Northern Ireland) are appointed by the court to safeguard and represent children's interests. They have social work expertise but function independently of the local authority. Whilst they are typically appointed in public law proceedings, they have become increasingly involved in private law disputes when the child is joined into the proceedings under Practice Direction 16A of the Family Procedure Rules 2010, Section 16.4. They are sometimes referred to as a '16.4 guardian'. This occurs when the child has a standpoint or interest which is inconsistent with or incapable of being represented by any of the adult parties; the views and wishes of the child cannot adequately be met by a report to the court; there are complex medical or mental health issues or other unusually intricate issues to be determined; or there are complex international issues aside from child abduction which may require inquiries to be undertaken abroad. The appointment of a children's guardian gives children legal representation and a voice so that their own views can be heard by the court. In many cases the appointment follows from a CAFCASS recommendation or an application by one of the adult parties but it is also possible for a child to apply to court to be joined to the proceedings.

The guardian explores the issues with the parents, professionals and others with relevant knowledge. Guardians are invariably represented by a solicitor and if older children disagree with the views of the guardian they can instruct their own solicitor to act on their behalf. Experts may be asked to assess whether a child has capacity directly to instruct their own solicitor. This was the case in Re C[4] when an expert concluded that the influence over a child by his father was extreme and damaging to the extent that the child had absorbed his father's belief system.

## Part 5: Protection of Children

This section of the Act is about caring for children who cannot safely be looked after within their birth families. LA staff at all levels are urged to look after these children in the same way that they would care for their own under the banner of 'corporate parenting'. Seven corporate parenting principles are defined. They are

> not about applying a formulaic approach to how services are delivered in relation to looked-after children and care leavers. Rather they describe the behaviours and attitudes expected of councils when they are acting as any good parent would do by supporting, encouraging and guiding their children to lead healthy, rounded and fulfilled lives.
>
> (Department for Education, 2018)

These principles are:

- to act in the best interests, and promote the physical and mental health and well-being, of those children and young people
- to encourage those children and young people to express their views, wishes and feelings
- to take into account the views, wishes and feelings of those children and young people
- to help those children and young people gain access to, and make the best use of, services provided by the local authority and its relevant partners
- to promote high aspirations, and seek to secure the best outcomes, for those children and young people
- for those children and young people to be safe, and for stability in their home lives, relationships and education or work; and
- to prepare those children and young people for adulthood and independent living.

> (Department for Education, 2018: 8)

Under Section 47 of the Children Act 1989 an LA must make enquiries to decide whether it should act to safeguard or promote a child's welfare where it has reasonable cause to suspect that a child who lives, or is found, in its area is suffering, or is likely to suffer, significant harm; or is informed that a child in its area is the subject of an Emergency Protection Order or is in police protection. Each LA provides guidance about how to conduct Section 47 enquiries with a view to minimising distress to the child and family, systematically obtaining as much information as possible to illuminate the issues, and making sure that each of the children and carers is fully involved. This includes assessing the child's understanding, their wishes and feelings. On occasion, criminal proceedings (in addition to the civil proceedings) may be brought against a carer for which the child's evidence may be sought. In this case, meetings with the child need to avoid the use of leading questions and follow the relevant guidance (Ministry of Justice, 2023). Before meeting with children for the purposes of an expert witness assessment, the expert needs to be familiar with the stage of proceedings and whether a concurrent criminal case is planned in order to avoid questioning the child in a way that could compromise the prosecution. The standard of proof in the criminal court is 'beyond reasonable doubt' which means that different conclusions may be reached from those in the civil court 'on a balance of probabilities'.

Under part V of the Act a number of different orders may be sought:

### Child Assessment Orders

This order requires a child to be made available for assessment. Children's services may apply for this when they suspect the child is at risk, but the parents are refusing to allow the child to be assessed. The court can only make an order if it agrees there is reason to suspect the child is suffering or likely to suffer significant harm and that the assessment will not happen unless the order is made. A Child Assessment Order lasts for seven days and cannot be extended (Family Rights Group, undated). If the parents refuse to comply with such an order the LA may then apply for an order that enables them to protect the child.

### Emergency Protection Orders (EPOs)

This order can be sought if it is believed that a child is likely to suffer significant harm if they are not taken to, or remain in, a place of safety. The order gives the LA PR for the child though this should only be exercised when necessary to safeguard or promote the child's welfare. The court can direct the conditions in which contact between the child and parents takes place, and order medical examinations of the child. An Emergency Protection Order lasts up to eight days and may be extended only once for a period up to seven days. During this period the LA may apply for a Care Order.

If it is believed that a particular person constitutes a significant risk to the child, an Emergency Protection Order may include an exclusion requirement which can stipulate that a person must leave or not enter the home of the child or must stay away from the area in which the child lives. The carer who continues to look after the child at their home must agree to this requirement. If a child's whereabouts cannot be established, although someone is believed to know where they are, the court can order them to provide the information they hold. The court can also authorise entry into a property to search for a child, if necessary with a police warrant.

### Police Powers of Protection (PPP)

Under Section 46 of the Act, where a police officer has reasonable cause to believe that a child would otherwise be likely to suffer significant harm, the child may be kept in or moved to suitable accommodation for protection, for example, a relative's home, a hospital, a police station, a foster home, children's home or other suitable place. No child may be kept in police protection for more than 72 hours. These powers are only used in exceptional circumstances as a last resort, where there is insufficient time to seek an EPO, or for reasons relating to the immediate safety of the child. As no court order is required, they may be made out of working hours. Parents and children removed from their families through such orders have described to me their feelings of intense fear and distress in a process that can be highly charged and traumatic, to be used only as a last resort.

> I was at my aunt's house and I looked at my phone. There were loads of missed calls, messages and emails. They said we were going to be taken away. Mum had no money to get home because we was planning on staying at my aunt's house. What's even going on?' Our aunt gave us some money for a taxi and when we got home, there was loads of papers about how it was all going to happen. Next day my mum was making breakfast when the police arrived and I cried and cried, then I packed and carried on crying. We all spent the day crying. I didn't know what was going to happen and I was terrified. I thought, 'What if I don't ever see my mum again? What if I never get to live with her again? What if I never see my brothers again? What if I never get to live in this house again? I went and gave my bed a hug. Bye bye bed.

This parent was struggling with mental health issues:

> I just wouldn't let them take Killean. I kept him with me as long as I could. I took him out and didn't come home till midnight. They'd been looking for me. I wouldn't let anybody in. I wasn't thinking straight. I threatened to dangle Killean out of the window so they would all disappear and go away but they didn't. I thought I could stop them from taking him. I was screaming and all the neighbours were out on the street. I didn't intend to harm him. I was frightened. I was crying and shaky. I felt sick. Killean was as well. Eventually they kicked the door down to get him. I just handed him over when they came in and they took him and locked me up. I wouldn't have let them come up and drag him. If I'd done that they would have dragged him and he was frightened enough as it was. You can't really explain to a two-year-old can you? He wasn't crying or owt like that. The situation got completely out of hand.

## Adoption and Children Act 2002 (Amended 2014)

This Act aligned adoption law with the relevant provisions of the Children Act 1989 in privileging children's welfare as the paramount consideration in all decisions relating to adoption. It placed a duty on local authorities to maintain an adoption service, it set out new regulatory structures, made provision for the process of adoption and stated the conditions for making Adoption Orders. Adoption support services were identified as having a role in assisting adopted adults to obtain information about their adoption and their birth relatives. It introduced restrictions on arranging adoptions and advertising children for adoption other than through adoption agencies, and provided additional limitations on the adoption of children from overseas (The National Archives: undated b). It extended adoption orders to single people, married couples and unmarried couples.

The government's intention was to encourage the wider use of adoption, particularly of children looked after by local authorities, and to improve the performance of adoption services. The revised system aimed to provide greater certainty and stability for children by dealing as far as possible with consent to placement for adoption before they were placed; to minimise uncertainty for prospective adopters, who possibly faced a contested court hearing at the Adoption Order stage; and to reduce the extent to which birth families were faced with a 'fait accompli' at the final adoption hearing.

The Act also introduced the new legal option of Special Guardianship Orders (see above) in which the child's legal relationship with the birth parents is not severed.

More recently there have been legal developments towards open adoption, acknowledging the necessity, particularly for older children, of sustaining links with some members of their birth families. The report published by the Public Law Working Group (PLWG) (Courts and Tribunals Judiciary, 2024a) recommended significant changes to enable adopted children to maintain relationships with their birth families when safe, to improve access to records and provide clearer guidance for international adoption. Research on open adoption and adoption outcomes for children is explored extensively in Scaife (2024). Whilst maintaining links with birth families can assist a child's developing identity, sense of continuity and understanding of their origins and history, it may generate conflicts of loyalty and be emotionally challenging. Substantial resources are needed to educate prospective adoptive parents and to facilitate and monitor ongoing direct contact. The PLWG recommended a tailor-made approach providing for individualised arrangements, ongoing support for birth families and the use of digital platforms to facilitate enduring relationships between adopted children and birth family members.

## Children Act 2004

This development brought in amendments and clarifications to the original Act. (Foster, 2023). These included creation of the post of Children's Commissioner for England to promote and protect the rights of children, and to improve the oversight and regulation of childcare facilities. It introduced a duty for other local safeguarding agencies and services to partner with the LA to improve the well-being of all children in their area. This was achieved by the development of Local Safeguarding Children Boards (LSCBs). The government published 'Every Child Matters' (HM Government, 2003) which outlined five key rights of children to be healthy, stay safe, enjoy and achieve, make a positive contribution and to achieve economic well-being.

## Children and Families Act 2014

This Act enshrined in legislation the need for proceedings to be concluded as swiftly as possible, making specific mention of a 26-week time limit on length of cases in the family court. The PLO, first introduced in 2008 had suggested a 26-week template for proceedings. The Act introduced a 'timetable for the child' drawn up at the beginning of the proceedings, having regard to the impact on the welfare of the child and on the way that proceedings are conducted. An extension is allowed 'in order to resolve the proceedings justly'. In fact, proceedings often take longer than this and became extended in part as a result of the impact of Covid-19. The average time for a care and supervision case to reach first disposal throughout 2024 was 40 weeks, down 2 weeks from 2023 (Ministry of Justice, 2025a). The Act altered Section 25.1 of the Family Procedure Rules to restrict expert evidence to that which is necessary to assist the court to resolve the proceedings justly.

The Act altered the allowable duration of interim orders according to the specifics of the case, now made at the beginning of proceedings and envisaged to last until the final hearing date. It made changes to the way that care plans should be scrutinised by courts; clarified the local authority's duty to promote an ongoing relationship between children in care and their parents; introduced a fostering for adoption arrangement; removed the requirement to consider ethnicity when selecting a long-term placement for a child; and made changes to post-adoption contact, allowing the court to make an order requiring adopters to allow the child to visit, stay with or otherwise have contact with the person named in the order, or to prevent such contact (Cox, 2020).

## Children and Social Work Act 2017

The Children and Social Work Act 2017 amended the Children Act 2004, replacing LSCBs with new local arrangements for safeguarding and promoting the welfare of children. Three safeguarding partners – the local authority, NHS Integrated Care Boards (ICBs) and police forces were made responsible for determining how safeguarding arrangements should work in their area for them and all bodies and groups within the area that play a crucial role in coordinating the safeguarding and welfare of children.

## Government Reform Proposals 2023

In February 2023, following the review of children's social care by Josh MacAlister (2022), the Government published an implementation strategy and consultation on reforming children's social care in England entitled 'Stable homes, built on love'. This resulted in a plan to lay the foundations for reform of the whole system beginning with a pathfinder programme in 12 pilot areas. The changes proposed included a new Family Help service removing the distinction between early help and children in need services, greater investment in kinship care and foster carer recruitment and retention, establishment of an early career framework for social workers, and movement towards child protection functions being led by a multi-agency group of staff (Foster and Danechi, 2023). There is evidence for the subsequent implementation of some of these proposals (Samuel, 2025).

## Human Rights Act

The Human Rights Act 1998, which came into force in the UK in October 2000, sets out the fundamental rights and freedoms to which everyone in the UK is entitled. It incorporates the rights set out in the European Convention on Human Rights (ECHR) into domestic British law. Those human rights covered by the Act are listed by the Equality and Human Rights Commission (2018). In the family court, Article 8 which states that: 'everyone has the right to respect for his private and family life, his home and his correspondence' can be particularly relevant.

In one example, the High Court refused an application for reporting restrictions in relation to a family in which two parents were accused of murdering one of their twins. The case was heard in the family court whilst the parents were prosecuted in the criminal court. The LA argued under Article 8 that it would be contrary to the surviving child's interests to be identified in the community as having parents subject to murder charges, and that prospective adopters may be deterred from coming forward. The press submitted that the case was not exceptional and that all children would benefit from the public being made aware of the seriousness with which the deaths of children are treated (B, R and G, 2022).[5] The press cited Article 10 relating to freedom of expression to support their case. In such clashes between different Articles of the Act, Kitan Ososami (2021: no page numbers) argued that 'Rigorous scrutiny must be applied when deciding whether interference with a child's rights under Article 8 is proportionate and necessary'.

I have encountered the use of Article 8 in relation to parents contesting the right to remain in the UK. Children born in the UK to migrant or refugee parents without legal status can apply for indefinite leave to remain (ILR) if they have lived in the UK for at least seven years previously. This is known as the 'private life' route. Once a child has successfully obtained the right to remain, and provided that the parent meets specific criteria, separated parents can apply for a UK Parent Visa (Reiss Edwards, 2024). The parent needs to show that they have joint or sole PR and will take an active role in the child's upbringing. A parent who has limited involvement with the child (particularly if they believe that the other parent is preventing contact) may seek evidence from the family court in the form of a Child Arrangements Order, that they are playing a role in the child's upbringing. An expert witness may be asked to make an assessment of the quality of the relationship of the child with the parent, and to disentangle the effects of hostilities between separated parents upon the arrangements for the care of the child. The expert needs to be aware that the issue of right to remain may be a factor in a parent's application to the court regarding the arrangements for the care of the child, and needs to include in their assessment enquiries about migrant parents' status in the UK.

## Criminal Justice Bill

There is currently no general statutory obligation for individuals in England to report child abuse. The statutory guidance on safeguarding states 'anyone who has concerns about a child's welfare should consider whether a referral needs to be made to local authority children's social care and should do so immediately if there is a concern that the child is suffering significant harm or is likely to do so' (Foster, 2024). There is an expectation that those working with children will comply with the guidance unless there are exceptional circumstances.

> In addition, some individuals are required to report child safeguarding concerns under standards or codes of conduct set by their professional regulatory body. A failure to adhere to such standards may result in misconduct or fitness to practise proceedings against them.
>
> (Foster, 2024: no page numbers)

Within the Criminal Justice Bill (2025) the government introduced mandatory reporting of sexual abuse, thereby strengthening this requirement.

Court-appointed experts are no exception to this expectation. Expert witnesses have a duty of care to both their clients and the public. The British Psychological Society (BPS, 2023: no page numbers) states, 'Any allegations of abuse, either ongoing or historic, must be taken seriously and consideration must be given about breaking confidentiality especially in cases where other vulnerable people may be at risk.' When working in the family court, no undertaking of confidentiality can be given to clients.

## Legislation Relating to Gender Questioning in Young People

Commissioned by NHS England, in April 2024 Hilary Cass published her report into gender identity services for children and young people. Concerns had emerged in 2018 about services being provided by the Gender Identity Development Service (GIDS) at the Tavistock clinic (Barnes, 2024). In 2020, Keira Bell, a leading claimant in proceedings against the Tavistock Trust, reported that she had been given puberty-blocking drugs after just three or four appointments, had been prescribed testosterone and later via adult services had undergone a double mastectomy, all of which, by the age of 22 years, she regretted. She said that no alternatives had been proposed. From 2014, children as young as nine years could be referred to GIDS for puberty blocking drugs. In 2022 GIDS was closed down and replaced by new regional services.

In England, Wales and Scotland, the Equality Act 2010 prohibits discrimination relating to gender reassignment. The Department for Education (DfE) guidance on the Equality Act states that protections apply to those who are undergoing, have undergone, or are proposing to undergo, a process (or part of a process) of reassigning their sex by changing physiological or other attributes. In 2023 the DfE (2023a) published non-statutory guidance on gender-questioning for schools and colleges, and in April 2024 the House of Commons library (Long, 2024) published a research briefing regarding provisions to support gender-questioning children in schools.

Subsequent to the Cass report, the Department of Health and Social Care (2024a) introduced a temporary ban on the prescription of puberty blocking drugs for under-18s who were not already taking them. The ban applied to the sale or supply of these drugs for gender incongruence or dysphoria and also prevented the supply from prescribers registered in the EEA or Switzerland for any purpose to those under the age of 18 years. With some exceptions, it has become a criminal offence for a pharmacist, doctor or other person to dispense puberty-suppressing drugs to patients under the age of 18 years. The introduction of the legislation has been controversial.

I include this legislation here as children referred to the family court may question their assigned gender during the course of the assessment, and experts may be asked to suggest relevant services:

> I hate it, I hate these (pointing to her breasts). I feel uncomfortable with them. I want a binder but I don't know where to get one. I want the operation to get rid of them. I daren't look down at myself, I daren't put a swimming costume on. I don't like getting photos. I hate periods and everything about being a girl. I'm getting my hair shaved the same as my brother's. I wear boys' clothes. I've been finding out about hormone blockers. My brain tells me I'm a boy.

New arrangements for the referral of children to what is now called 'NHS Children and Young People's Gender Services' came into effect in September 2024 and were updated in March 2025. Arden and Greater East Midlands Commissioning Support Unit (Arden and GEM) manages all referrals which must be made by NHS community and hospital paediatric services or NHS Children and Young People's Mental Health (CYPMH) services. These children can be particularly vulnerable and it is advised that plans are drawn up by the referrer and local professional network to ensure that their needs are being met in the interim.

Until 2025 the NHS issued new NHS numbers and changed 'gender' markers to individuals who transitioned. This was terminated following the Sullivan Review (Department for Science, Innovation and Technology, 2025) which made a clear distinction between the characteristics of sex assigned at birth and gender identity. 'Legal sex' is a shorthand for people who have transitioned and includes holders of a Gender Recognition Certificate.

---

### Key Points from this Chapter

- The primary legislation that governs the family court in England is the Children Act 1989. There is parallel legislation in the devolved governments.

- A Section 47 enquiry, also known as a Child Protection enquiry or S47, is a statutory investigation into whether a child is at risk of significant harm. The purpose of the enquiry is to determine what action is needed to protect the child.
- PR is an important construct in that it allows anyone who holds it to make day-to-day decisions about a child without the need for consultation with others.
- Without evidence to the contrary, it is taken by the family court that involvement of both parents is beneficial for children.
- It is considered that delay is likely to prejudice the welfare of children. Experts need to ensure that they are able to meet the deadlines to which they have agreed for reporting purposes. Delay is inimitable to the courts' aim of managing public law cases to completion within a 26-week timetable.
- The court follows the 'no order principle' unless an order is deemed necessary for the welfare of the child.
- To assist with private law decisions, the court may order a Section 7 report from a children's guardian.
- In private law proceedings the court may make Child Arrangements Orders, Prohibited Steps or Specific Issues Orders.
- Courts refer to 'threshold' criteria which are the facts that the LA must prove if they are requesting the court to make a Care or Supervision Order.
- In a particularly difficult or complicated private law family case, the judge may decide to make the child a 'party' to the case under rule 16.4 of the Family Procedure Rules. A guardian is appointed to represent the child and is sometimes called a '16.4 guardian'.
- Different sections of the Human Rights Act can be brought to bear within children's proceedings and these may be in conflict with each other.
- In the UK, although there is currently no general mandatory requirement for professionals to report concerns about a child's welfare, statutory guidance behoves anyone working with children to report concerns if they believe a child is suffering significant harm. Some practitioners must report child safeguarding concerns under standards or codes of conduct set by their professional regulatory body.
- Within the Criminal Justice Bill (2025) the government introduced mandatory reporting of sexual abuse, thereby strengthening this requirement.

## Notes

1  Re L (Care: Threshold Criteria [2007].
2  Re B (Children) [2008] EWCA Civ 282.
3  Re A (A Child) [2015] EWFC 11.
4  Re C (Child: ability to instruct solicitor) [2023] EWCA Civ 889.
5  B, R and G (a Child) [2022] EWHC 320 (Fam).

## Chapter 3

# Family Procedure Rules

### The Court's Approach to Expert Evidence

The court's approach to expert evidence reflects the role of the expert in relation to the court. It is the expert who advises and the judge who decides the issues. This was put succinctly in the McFadyen lecture (2024) by the Right Honourable Dame Siobhan Keegan:

> The correct position remains that expert reports serve as an interpretive aid to the court. They distil complex data or information with which the court is naturally unfamiliar and present the information to the court in clear and accessible terms. From there, where necessary, the expert will be entitled to offer their opinion on what this evidence tells us. But that does not mean their conclusion is determinative of the whole case. The reality is that their conclusion will often be but one piece of a larger puzzle.
>
> Put simply, the conclusions of the expert may hold significant weight in the outcome of a case; but equally they may not. The final decision rests with the judge, who is under their own obligation to provide a closely reasoned judgment that sets out how they weigh each piece of evidence, and how it has informed how they have concluded. To do otherwise may amount to an abuse of process.
>
> (Judiciary NI, 2024)

I have always experienced respect for my opinion, even if cross-examination can put it to a hard test. Judges often ask questions themselves, with a view to clarification of the issues which may be specific to the family in question or more general. In this they may be exercising an inquisitorial role, beyond the adversarial nature of the court process. One issue about which I have been questioned by judges is that of attachment, where misunderstandings may have arisen because terms from ordinary language have been ascribed technical meanings. Because misconceptions are common, I digress here for a brief exploration of attachment theory as originally conceived. More detail may be found in Society for Emotion and Attachment Studies (SEAS) (2021).

DOI: 10.4324/9781003453390-3

Reports in the bundle sometimes reference 'strength' of attachment of a child to a caregiver. The attachment literature emphasises not strength but *security* of attachment because strength of attachment does not reflect the quality of the relationship or its benefit to the developing child. Hostages may become strongly attached to their captors as in 'Stockholm syndrome' when they develop a reciprocated emotional bond with their captors. 'Trauma-bonding' is used to describe one-way empathic responses from an abused person to their abuser. Whilst these terms all describe attachment which may be strong, and can be adaptive in the short term, it is unlikely that sustaining these relationships would be considered to be in a child's best interests.

In order for a child to learn positive self-esteem and develop the capacity to self-soothe when distressed, an argument instead is made for the concept of secure/insecure attachment. In response to sensitive care-giving a child is believed to develop a sense of self-worth – their needs appear to be important to the carer – and to develop trust towards the carer who is reliable and sensitive in meeting their needs. Children learn that they are valuable and that others can be trusted and relied upon. It is thought that this learning becomes relevant as they develop other relationships in the wider community.

Some children learn that the best way to obtain sensitive care is by making very few demands on a carer who finds the child's fussing and crying aversive. The child learns to avoid making demands and develops what is known as an avoidant insecure pattern of attachment. Nevertheless, the child is able to make sense of and respond to what the carer offers and may develop particular skills in self-reliance. On the other hand, a child may learn that making a big fuss is the only way to obtain a carer's attention and proceeds to do so whenever their needs remain unmet. This would be known as an anxious insecure pattern, but again the carer's behaviour is relatively predictable.

The most challenging care-giving is that which is unpredictable: warm and affectionate at times, hostile and rejecting at others, frightening at yet others. In this context it is thought that children struggle to know how to behave in order to have their needs met and may develop extreme behaviours as they attempt to make sense of the carer's response to them. This is known as a disorganised pattern, which makes it very difficult for a child to develop a sense of themselves as a worthwhile individual and to develop trust in adults.

This is just one example where the expert may assist the court by explaining discipline-specific concepts in as simple a way as possible. I have known judges to ask for such explanations in order to help parents who are present in the court to understand the long-term harm that may result from their actions or omissions and the court's decision to remove a child from their care.

## The Expert's Role

The expert's role is to provide specialised knowledge and express opinions that clarify complex issues. They bridge the gap between the legal and psychological aspects of a case. Judges do not have to accept an expert's evidence or opinions, but if they disagree they are required to explain why the evidence or opinion is being rejected. In Re B (1996)[1] the judgment included the following:

> The expert advises but the Judge decides. The Judge decides on the evidence. If there is nothing before the court, no facts or no circumstances shown to the court which throw doubt on the expert evidence, then, if that is all with which the court is left, the court must accept it. There is, however, no rule that the Judge suspends judicial belief simply because the evidence is given by an expert.

The expert's opinion is thus an important contributor to the decision-making process. In order to fulfil their role, experts are bound by and need to be familiar with the relevant Family Procedure Rules (FPR, 2010) which provide a structure to guide professional practice. They came into effect in 2011 and govern the procedures of the family court in England and Wales. They are made and regularly updated by a committee (the Family Procedure Rule Committee) whose membership includes the President of the Family Division, various judges, barristers, solicitors and staff from CAFCASS/CAFCASS Cymru and a lay member. There are 36 parts within the rules, Part 25 pertaining specifically to expert witnesses who need to be conversant with the rules and state their compliance with them in their reports. Amendments and updates are located at Justice (2025).

### Family Procedure Rules Part 1

Part 1 of the rules defines the overriding objective of enabling the court to deal with cases justly, having regard to any welfare issues involved. The court must ensure that the issues are managed expeditiously and fairly, and are proportionate to the nature, importance and complexity of the issues; ensure that the parties are on equal footing; save expense and allot to the case an appropriate share of the court's resources (Justice, 2020).

Whilst I am sure that the court strives towards these objectives, I have my doubts about the extent to which clients are on equal footing. A study conducted in 2021 (Hood et al., 2021) reported a strong social gradient in children's social care. When comparing 32,000 small neighbourhoods in England, rates of referral increased from 100 per 10,000 children for the least deprived neighbourhoods to 1,370 per 10,000 children for the most deprived neighbourhoods. This 'social gradient' increased at each subsequent level of intervention by children's social care. 'Researchers found that a 10% increase in an area's deprivation was associated with a 62% increase in a child's chances of being referred to children's services, a 64% increase in the rate of child in need plans, a 69% rise in child protection investigation rates and an 80% increase in the rates of child protection plans' (Preston, 2021: no page numbers). Measures of deprivation include income, employment, education, health, crime, barriers to housing and the quality of the living environment (Ministry of Housing, Communities and Local

Government, 2019). My experience suggests that parents who are experiencing significant deprivation are much less well equipped to understand and respond to or avoid interventions by the state than would be their neighbours from wealthy suburbs, even though their representation is funded by the state. The legal terminology and procedures involved in care proceedings can be experienced as confusing and overwhelming.

This inequality is not only applicable to public law. In private law, one of the parties is often much better resourced than the other, either by virtue of economic disparity between ex-partners or through the public funding rules which can exclude inadequately resourced parents from legal aid. The Legal Aid, Sentencing and Punishment of Offenders Act (LASPO) of 2012 removed funding from most private family cases after April 2013 which has led to an increase in the number of litigants in person; those parents who are representing themselves. In a study by Trinder et al. (2014), the major reason for self-representation was the inability to afford a lawyer. These parents invariably felt that they were disadvantaged by their lack of representation. Only a small proportion of litigants in person were able to represent themselves competently in all aspects of the proceedings, even if they were well-educated professionals. Around half of the parents studied were experiencing one or more vulnerabilities which often compounded their difficulties with self-representation. These included impairments or ill-health, learning difficulties, problems with emotional control, extreme nerves and anxiety and limited English language skills:

> I have not slept since Friday night. I was up all night Saturday and I was up all night last night getting this paperwork to come in today. I am too tired to give a monkey's and my son has been poorly so…Every other time I have been physically sick with stress and worry and meeting deadlines and the first time was horrendous, it was just really bad. I did not sleep for three or four nights before, erm… I had panic attacks, I had chest pains, it was horrible. The times in between have been as bad.
>
> (Trinder et al., 2014: 34)

Whilst I have observed judges do their best to assist litigants in person, their inexperience in cross-examining expert witnesses (and presumably other witnesses) is glaringly apparent – and is just the 'tip of the iceberg' in terms of complexity and the challenge posed by the family court process.

### Family Court Procedure Rules for Experts: Part 25

Wherever possible, expert evidence should be obtained from a single joint expert (SJE) instructed by both/all of the parties. To that end, a party wishing to instruct an expert should as soon as possible give the other party or parties a list of the names of one or more experts in the relevant speciality whom they consider suitable to be instructed. If the parties cannot agree on the specific expert, permission can be sought for the instruction of separate experts, but in my experience this has been very rare. With the aim of adhering to the PLO timetable, there is an imperative for advocates to identify a preferred expert at an advocates' meeting preceding the Case Management Hearing (Courts and Tribunals Judiciary, 2024a).

A Part 25 Application is made to the court to seek permission for an expert or professional to prepare a report or assessment within the domain of their expertise in order to assist resolution of the proceedings. Experts are required to comply with the duties outlined within Practice Direction (PD) 25B. They are instructed to provide an accurate assessment to the court without being influenced by the person who is paying for it. In public proceedings, carers and children are automatically entitled to be legally represented and funding is provided from the public purse. The local authority and the other parties usually pay equal shares which need to be invoiced once the report is distributed and lodged with the court. In private law proceedings, one or more of the parties may be self-funding and may not agree with the decision to seek a report which can nevertheless be ordered by the court. This can present issues with reimbursement, which some experts manage by requesting payment from self-funding individuals in advance. The process of assessing costs and invoicing is addressed in Chapter 6.

Expert evidence can only be put before the court with the court's permission and has to be restricted to that which is necessary to assist resolution of the proceedings. The court's permission is required not only to instruct an expert but also for a child to be examined or assessed. This permission should be stated in the relevant court order and it is appropriate, if in any doubt, to check with the lead solicitor before seeing a child. Sometimes experts' reports are commissioned prior to the commencement of proceedings (known as pre-proceedings), which can assist with meeting the 26-week timescale for public law proceedings to be concluded. If a pre-proceedings report is commissioned, the expert is still bound by the duties set out in PD 25B, and the court nevertheless needs to give permission for their evidence to be put forward, or it is otherwise inadmissible.

Enquiries are made of potential experts by the advocates in advance of requesting the court's permission to instruct. Potential experts need to confirm that acceptance of the instructions will not involve them in any conflict of interest, that the work required is within their domain of expertise, and that they can complete the work within a specified timescale. They will need to provide information about availability to attend court, and of the cost and likely hours needed to carry out the assessment, to attend any experts' meetings and to give evidence.

Having provided this information, the expert then waits to find out whether the court has granted permission for the assessment, and whether they or someone else is to be instructed. It is not necessarily the case that the enquiring solicitor will come back to the expert with this information. In order to manage workload, I find it useful to specify for how long I will maintain the availability (typically for two weeks), lest I find that I have no work or a deluge. If I have received no further communication after this period expires, I assume that I am not being instructed. Sometimes the solicitor will come back after two weeks to enquire as to whether the availability is still extant. A system is necessary in order for experts to manage their workload.

## Information that Should Be Provided to the Expert

At the initial point of enquiry, experts should be provided with adequate information about the nature of the proceedings and the issues requiring determination by the court for which the expert's opinion is sought. This is often sketchy, but it is important nevertheless to try and assess whether the proposed work falls within your area of expertise. It is at this stage that I will often refuse the invitation or seek further information to ensure that I am an appropriate expert. In the subsequent letter of instruction (LOI), the expert can expect to be provided with the questions on which opinion is sought (including any ethnic, cultural, religious or linguistic contexts), whether permission is to be requested to instruct an additional expert in the same or a related field, the volume of anticipated reading, whether or not permission has been given for seeing a child, whether and with whom the expert is expected to conduct interviews, the likely time-table, a report filing date, anticipated court hearing dates, the option to make representations to the court about being named in any judgment, information about funding and to whom invoices are appropriately directed.

In agreement with the other parties, one of the advocates (usually the lead solicitor who acts for the child) takes responsibility for providing the LOI setting out the questions approved by the court, which the PD observes should be clear, focused and direct, and reflect what the court is requesting. Annex A of PD 25C provides suggested questions for an LOI to experts belonging to different professions. A paginated bundle of documents is provided which outlines the issues under consideration. It contains previous and current court orders, statements and responses by the various parties. It may contain police, medical and other reports. The expert may be advised that they have a right to talk to relevant people concerned with the proceedings provided that an accurate contemporaneous record is made of the discussions. I typically do discuss relevant issues with a range of professionals and carers, making a record, and particularly where there may be liability issues, sending this to them in order to check for accuracy. Experts may be asked to explain their choice of people with whom they have decided to confer.

Although this is what is meant to happen in theory, the practice may fail to live up to these standards. Whilst the rules advise that the expert is to be fully and properly instructed, the busy schedules of solicitors can interfere with the process. Everyone involved is supposed to have looked carefully at the proposed LOI before it is forwarded to the expert, but in many cases, when I ask the people I am interviewing about whether they know its contents, they look at me blankly. Sometimes, I have agreed to provide a report to a relatively short deadline and the LOI is still circulating among the parties. It may arrive in time for my meetings or, on occasion, still be outstanding. I have on occasion arranged appointments in anticipation of the LOI, but an expert may be subject to a complaint if acting without agreed instructions as it is not possible otherwise to ensure compliance with PD 25. If the delay to the LOI means that the report cannot be completed by the filing date, advice needs to be sought from the lead solicitor and the expert needs to be very clear about the impact of the delay. On acceptance of instructions it is wise to conduct a thorough study of the bundle in order to identify any additional documents that will be needed in order to keep to the timescale.

Sometimes circumstances change after the letter is agreed. Further updating information may then need to be provided. Often I am promised medical records which fail to materialise, and I end up chasing them myself. If they fail to arrive in time, I need to state a caveat in my report that my opinion may change in light of information contained therein, or, if I consider them essential to forming an opinion, to state this in my report by indicating that without sight of them I am not able to give an opinion in relation to specific questions. For some disciplines, medical records will be essential reading and often parties prefer all matters to be covered in one report to prevent further burden on the public purse. When in doubt, it is advisable to seek advice from the lead solicitor.

The bundle of court documents can be overwhelming, but needs to be read in detail in order to give a full picture of the evidence concerning the issues. Sometimes, there have been previous proceedings but the bundle may contain nothing of them, possibly for good reason. It is important not to offer an opinion based on only a proportion of the available evidence. If something is missing, it needs to be requested with a deadline after which it would be too late fully to consider and incorporate into any opinions reached. If it cannot be provided, the impact of the unknown on the expert's opinion needs to be acknowledged with relevant caveats in the report. Updating documents that are provided to the court between receipt of the LOI and the hearing need to be made available to the expert so that their opinion may be updated accordingly.

Falling foul of these procedure rules can be very damaging to the families being assessed. The decisions made by the court are of enormous import to them and to children's lives, as in the case of C [2018].[2] The expert was found to have reached conclusions based on 'an appropriate but perhaps novel psychometric measure' which she therefore needed to explain and give her qualifications for using it. She was found to have based her assessment of the father on suppositions rather than proven facts. She had not read updating documents and had given evidence poorly as a result of feeling unwell on the day. Expert reputations may be harmed; this judgment was published and at Paragraph 46 stated:

> … 3 days of court time has been wasted… This case has now had to be adjourned to July of next year… The orders sought are of the utmost seriousness and are sought against a background where X has suffered no outwardly discernible harm and the concerns of the local authority and guardian are primarily about the historical performance of mother in her previous partnership with the violent father of her older children or on her own and the risk of future harm. For me to

make such orders I must be satisfied that nothing else will do. The evidence…
falls well below that threshold.

BAILII (2018)

### Directions to Expert Witnesses

Experts are required to comply with the PD. They are instructed to provide advice that conforms to the best practice of their profession and to answer the questions about which their opinion is being sought. Their opinion must be independent of the parties instructing the expert and confined to matters material to the issues in the case. The expert must stay within their areas of expertise, and where a question falls outside the scope of their experience, state this at the earliest opportunity, and if appropriate, suggest another expert who may be instructed for their opinion on this specific issue.

When trawling through evidence and in compiling my report, there are times when an issue arises that is outside my domain of expertise, and yet I think it may be material to the matter at hand. Excluding its consideration has the potential adversely to affect outcomes. For example, one mother I saw described to me her diagnosis of a rare medical condition, some symptoms of which were shared in common with a state of inebriation – slurred speech and unsteadiness on the feet which had been cited as evidence that her capability to provide adequate parenting was compromised. In another, a child had been diagnosed with a medical condition that I was concerned may have resulted from her carers' false reports of symptoms and inappropriate interpretation of and responses to the child's behaviour. In such circumstances, whilst raising the issues in my report, I state clearly that these are outside my area of expertise. In the latter, I immediately contacted the lead solicitor, recommended an urgent consideration of the child's safety and a medical review of the evidence.

Perhaps the best-known example of an expert being accused of going beyond their realm of expertise is the case of paediatrician Sir Roy Meadow, who told the jury in criminal proceedings against Sally Clarke that the chance of two children dying naturally in these circumstances was one in 73 million. He had not calculated the statistic himself but took it from a government-funded multi-disciplinary enquiry entitled the Confidential Enquiry into Stillbirths and Deaths in Infancy (CESDI), reported by Fleming et al. (2000), to which he was writing a preface. But he did not consider other studies of sudden infant death syndrome or quote the figure for the probability of two children being murdered by their mother, an even rarer eventuality. This is an example of the importance of exploring a range of relevant studies, considering the issue from a range of perspectives, consulting with colleagues and being circumspect in reporting.

In expressing an opinion, the expert is required to take into account all of the material facts including any relevant factors arising from issues of diversity, of which many are possible (Burnham, 2013). As cultural mores change it can be challenging but essential to give careful consideration to the range of variability of cultural experiences of the families that we assess. I find it particularly taxing to form and express opinions to my satisfaction in the context of differences of culture, ethnicity and associated values. The UK is traditionally regarded as an individualistic culture in which children are taught to question authority and be curious, where parents are encouraged to play with children, where personal choice and freedoms are encouraged, and physical chastisement is not endorsed. Collectivist cultures are more likely to be characterised by obedience to authority, greater emphasis on social responsibilities rather than play, and physical chastisement as a more acceptable disciplinary style (Edwards, 2021). I have encountered some anxiety expressed by a Malaysian parent about her return there after a period of education in a UK university, since her children had been encouraged to question their teachers, a practice that they were likely to find unacceptable in their Malaysian school. In families in which each parent hails from a different cultural context, I have encountered confusion in the children about how to conform to their different expectations. One parent expects obedience and exacts strict punishment for failure to comply, whilst the other encourages the child to challenge and question authority. How to bring up children was highly contentious at times in my own experience of parenting, when my partner and I were ostensibly from similar cultural contexts. How much more difficult it must be with greater diversity of background. When assessing other families, it is incumbent upon us to hold in mind awareness of the impact of our personal and cultural histories on our own values, prejudices and biases.

Whilst this example is one of differences of ethnicity, challenges are also posed when assessing the impact and role of diversity of educational attainments, employment, gender, sexual orientation, spirituality and religion (and the wider range of 'social graces' described by Burham, 2013). One child whom I assessed got into fights at school when he told classmates that he had two mummies and no daddy (adopted by a same-sex couple) and they responded with disbelief and laughter. It can be particularly difficult to conduct a fair assessment of parents with learning disabilities. For a more extensive discussion of these issues see a companion volume (Scaife, 2024).

'Taking into account all of the material facts' may seem uncontroversial but claims made in the process of reaching an opinion can be categorised as: unproblematic or self-evident' (almost everyone within the community of practice would be expected to agree with the claim), 'personal' ('*I* think' or 'on the basis of my experience'), and 'other' which, for purposes of credibility, need to be substantiated with evidence. In the last case, support may come from the strength of argument that can be made from the practitioner's data, test scores, or from academic books or papers that have been peer reviewed prior to publication (Scaife, 2024). Experts are expected to distinguish between those facts they know to be true and those facts which they assume (Judiciary, 2014). It is the judge who determines disputed facts. Experts are advised against carrying out fact-finding exercises of their own.

I confess to being unclear in this context about what constitutes a fact-finding exercise. I often interview people who have been involved with the family, such as teachers, probation officers, foster carers and supervisors of family time. This has never been queried, but if in doubt about whether to interview someone, it is advisable to check with the lead solicitor. I have also made up 'tests' and activities designed to explore contested issues. On one occasion, a child had written a letter to their teacher describing harmful actions by a parent. Whether the child was capable of correctly spelling the words used was in dispute. Months after the letter was sent, I created and reported the results of a spelling test given to the child which included the disputed words. This was not queried by the court.

The status of the facts on which the expert relies benefits from being made clear in the report. Practitioners may not agree on what constitutes a fact, and if there is controversy it is important to lay out the conflicting opinions and provide an argument as to why one interpretation is preferred over another. Courts sometimes order a fact-finding hearing in which a judge is the final arbiter in determining the facts. These are then incontrovertible and if the expert disagrees with them, their report is almost certain to be discarded in its entirety.

### Expert Evidence in Fact-Finding Hearings

Fact-finding hearings are essentially like a 'mini-trial' in which the judge decides, on the basis of the evidence put by the parties (usually the parents and/or local authority) the facts of the case. They usually take place when allegations are made by the parents against each other or by the local authority against the parents when, should they be correct, the welfare of a child is compromised. These allegations may be about direct abuse or harm of the child, or involve domestic abuse witnessed by a child. The court orders witness statements from the contesting parties and might also require them to produce a Scott Schedule which, in tabular form, clearly sets out the allegations in dispute with dates, the applicant's response, and the findings (Table 3.1).

The court also may order witness statements from other people, videos, recordings, police reports, medical records, and statements from professionals such as teachers who may be able to provide further evidence.

The allegations are put before the court and the judge decides, on the basis of the evidence provided and on the balance of probabilities, what did and did not happen. The judge then makes a finding of fact. This is unassailable. The law operates a binary system – the fact either happened or it did not. It is not possible for the judge to find that it might have happened. The burden of proof always remains with the party that brought the allegation. In cases where the local authority is making the allegation, they must be able to provide evidence that a reasonable explanation offered by the parents is false.

Fact-finding hearings in care proceedings often relate to allegations of physical, sexual or emotional abuse within the family. Whatever the allegations, the key

Table 3.1 Hypothetical Respondent's Scott Schedule

| Date | Respondent's allegation | Bundle reference | Applicant's response | Applicant's bundle reference | Judge's finding |
|---|---|---|---|---|---|
| 15.07.2022 | The applicant raped the respondent | Respondent's narrative statement dated 17.10.24 (C7)<br>Police report dated 16.07.22 (E22) | Denied. The sex was consensual. | Applicant's response statement dated 15.11.24 (C12)<br>Police interview dated 16.07.22 (E24)<br>Confirmation of no further action CPS dated 30.07.22 (E28) | |
| 20.09.2022 | The applicant punched the respondent on the back when she refused his sexual advances | Respondent's narrative statement dated 17.10.24 (C8)<br>Police report dated 21.09.22 (E24)<br>Hospital records dated 21.09.22 (E156) | Denied | Applicant's response statement 15.11.24 (C13)<br>Police interview 21.09.22 (E28) | |
| 17.12.2022 | Verbal abuse in front of the children – called the respondent 'fucking whore' | Respondent's narrative statement 17.10.24 (C10) | Denied. Applicant refused to hand over the children and called him a 'fucking paedo nonce' | Applicant's response statement 15.11.24 (C18) | |

questions for the court are usually: (a) how was the injury caused? and (b) if it was inflicted, by whom?

In some cases, there is no explanation as to how an injury occurred, and no memorable or witnessed event which suggests an accidental explanation either. Some children are clumsy and often present with multiple bruises in places where they are unexpected if caused accidentally. One such is my six-year-old grandson who has scars on his head from three memorable accidental injuries resulting in trips to Accident and Emergency and often several other bruises and scratches of indeterminate cause. The inability of a parent to explain an event is inadequate for finding an event proven. The burden of disproving a reasonable explanation put forward by the parents falls on the local authority.

## Resolutions Model

Sometimes a judge may conclude that an injury was non-accidental but a specific per-petrator cannot be identified from a pool of two or more, as when a child was in the family home with both of their parents when the injury occurred, or if more people were present and nobody admits to being responsible. If an individual parent or someone from the pool is determined to have caused the injury but everyone continues to deny wrongdoing, the likelihood is that the court would conclude that it would be too risky for the child to return home. The Resolutions Model recognises that there are some situations where a child could be returned home, even if a parent with findings made against them, either personally or as a pool finding, continues to deny responsibility.

Five factors are considered when deciding whether safeguards can be put in place to protect the child in their home environment:

- Do the parents acknowledge that professionals have legitimate concerns given the medical evidence and any finding of the court?
- Are they prepared to work in partnership with professionals in an open and hon-est manner?
- Are they willing to examine the way they care for their child and be willing to make changes to care routines in order to help ensure their child's safety?
- Are they willing to accept a high level of professional support and monitoring of their child's welfare?
- Is there a credible support network composed of safe extended family mem-bers or friends who are willing and able to be involved in helping to ensure the child's future safety?

This approach requires a great deal of commitment not only from the parent but also from their family and wider support network over a long period of time. It is very demanding of social workers and the children's guardian in managing the process and solving any problems that arise along the way. This is evident in Re J.[3]

Fact-finding hearings are not always constructive. They can be counter-productive, and particularly in private law, worsen an already fraught parental relationship. They may also be considered potentially harmful to the relationship between a parent and child, as in the following example where different accounts were given by an eight-year-old and her father. The child's teacher noticed that as the end of a school day approached, she began to behave in an atypically agitated manner which led the teacher to enquire if there was something wrong. The child burst into tears and was taken aside. The teacher enquired what was the matter. Sobbing and trembling, the child said:

> I don't want to go home. Please please please don't make me go home. My dad got really angry last night because I wanted to carry on playing on my Nintendo and he asked me to put it down to stop my little brother from banging into the cupboards on his scooter. He shouted and screamed at me and took off his belt and hit me on my legs and it really really hurt. When he dropped me off at school this morning he said that he hated me and he'd kill me when I got home. Please don't make me go.

The veracity of this account was brought into question because the child had a history of making a previous allegation against a member of staff at the school, which the evidence had not supported. There was no sign of any injury that would have been consistent with her account. But on this occasion, the extreme emotional presentation of the child and the fact that she had not raised the issue until the teacher asked what was wrong provided some evidence to support her claim.

The father's account was that when asked to put down her Nintendo the child had responded by shouting and swearing at him. He was under stress at work and from trying to look after his three children whilst keeping the house in order and making the evening meal. In anger he had shouted back at the child and flicked a tea towel that he was holding against her legs. When he dropped her off at school, she had opened the door and undone her seatbelt before the car came to a halt. He had grabbed her by the arm to prevent her from exiting into the path of an oncoming vehicle and shouted at her out of fear.

A fact-finding hearing might have been ordered, but may also have been rejected on the grounds that the case could be determined without recourse to the same. Were one of the accounts found to be factual, this would have meant that either the father or the child had lied, a matter which they would then need to negotiate with each other after the child returned home, as was being proposed, a course of action with which the child was by then in agreement. An expert may be asked for an opinion about what the child should be told about the judge's decision. I would typically advocate telling her the facts of the matter – for example that the judge had decided it was not necessary to know exactly what had happened in order to decide where her best interests lay.

Scott schedules are regarded as inadequate for documenting more insidious and subtle chronic abuse in the form of coercive and controlling behaviour. The Domestic Abuse Act, 2021 was intended to raise awareness and understanding about the devastating impact of domestic abuse on victims and their families, further improve the effectiveness of the justice system in providing protection for victims of domestic abuse and bringing perpetrators to justice, and strengthen the support for victims of abuse by statutory agencies (Home Office, 2024). This is now enshrined in definitions of domestic abuse:

> any incident or pattern of incidents of controlling, coercive, threatening behaviour, violence or abuse between those aged 16 or over who are, or have been, intimate partners or family members regardless of gender or sexuality. The abuse can encompass, but is not limited to psychological, physical, sexual, financial, emotional. Domestic abuse can take different forms, including: physical abuse, sexual abuse, financial abuse, coercive and controlling behaviour, and gaslighting/emotional abuse, digital/online abuse, so-called 'honour-based' violence, forced marriage, female genital mutilation (FGM).
>
> (Victim support, 2022: no page numbers)

It is now acknowledged that applications for child arrangements orders may in themselves be part of a pattern of coercive or controlling behaviour which could be as abusive as any particular factual incident that might be included in a Scott Schedule. Coercive and controlling behaviour involves a range of acts designed to render an individual subordinate and to corrode their sense of personal autonomy. This is through a pattern or series of acts perpetrated cumulatively. The court's current guidance, arising from Re H-N and Others[4] states that in every case where domestic abuse is alleged, the parties should be asked to describe orally and in a statement, the overall experience of being in a relationship with each other.

The case of K v K [2022][5] provided guidance on when to have a fact-finding hearing. This set down that the allegations needed to have a direct impact on the child's welfare. The judge needs to decide on the allegations only to the extent that they are relevant and necessary to determining issues relating to a child's future welfare: the paramount concern of the court:

> A fact-finding hearing is not free-standing litigation. It always takes place within proceedings to protect a child from abuse or regarding the child's future welfare. It is not to be allowed to become an opportunity for the parties to air their grievances. Nor is it a chance for parents to seek the court's validation of what went wrong in their relationship. If fact-finding is to be justified in the first place or continued thereafter, the court must be able to identify how any alleged abusive behaviour is, or may be, relevant to the determinations of the issues between the parties as to the future arrangements for the children.
>
> BAILII (2022, no page numbers)

The advisability of holding a fact-finding hearing was also considered in Re P and E.[6] The judge confirmed that the court should consider the principles as set out by

Justice McFarlane (as he then was) in the 'Oxfordshire' case, as it is known[7], and summarised in Re H-D-H at Paragraph 22:[8]

i    When considering *the welfare of the child*, the significance to the individual child of knowing the truth can be considered, as can the effect on the child's welfare of an allegation being investigated or not.

ii   *The likely cost to public funds* can extend to the expenditure of court resources and their diversion from other cases.

iii  *The time that the investigation will take* allows the court to take account of the nature of the evidence. For example, an incident that has been recorded electronically may be swifter to prove than one that relies on contested witness evidence or circumstantial argument.

iv   *The evidential result* may relate not only to the case before the court but also to other existing or likely future cases in which a finding one way or the other is likely to be of importance. The public interest in the identification of perpetrators of child abuse can also be considered.

v    *The relevance of the potential result of the investigation to the future care plans for the child* should be seen in the light of the s. 31(3B) obligation on the court to consider the impact of harm on the child and the way in which his or her resulting needs are to be met.

vi   *The impact of any fact-finding process upon the other parties* can also take account of the opportunity costs for the local authority, even if it is the party seeking the investigation, in terms of resources and professional time that might be devoted to other children.

vii  *The prospects of a fair trial* may also encompass the advantages of a trial now over a trial at a possibly distant and unpredictable future date.

viii *The justice of the case* gives the court the opportunity to stand back and ensure that all matters relevant to the overriding objective have been taken into account. One such matter is whether the contested allegation may be investigated within criminal proceedings. Another is the extent of any gulf between the factual basis for the court's decision with or without a fact-finding hearing. The level of seriousness of the disputed allegation may inform this assessment. As I have said, the court must ask itself whether its process will do justice to the reality of the case.

If the expert's opinion changes, they are required to inform those providing the instructions as soon as possible, giving the reason for the change. This most typically occurs when further compelling evidence is provided. Courts advise not being afraid to change or modify an opinion in the light of new information or facts. Judges will appreciate the capacity to reflect, keep an open mind and prioritise assisting the court rather than taking a dogmatic position.

### Content of the Expert's Report as Defined in PD 25B

The report is the culmination of the expert's investigations. Errors within it are likely to undermine confidence in the opinions expressed. I also see it as a testimony of what the expert believes to have led to the current circumstances, to which the parties may return not only in the context of the current proceedings, but in the future. In my view the report needs to reflect a genuine attempt to understand how even the most appalling behaviour might be explained, whilst not excused. It is not an account of evil people doing evil things, but a 'story' that reflects compassion for each of the protagonists and a best attempt to explain how things got this way. Studies of the prevalence of adverse childhood experiences (ACEs) amongst prison populations are a testament to the complexity of victim-perpetrator distinctions (Johnson, 2023). Whilst the report may document parental weaknesses, it may also highlight strengths on which people may draw to improve matters. If a child become adult were to read the report, would it help them to understand their childhood predicaments and those of their struggling caregivers? But no matter how persuasive, some of the participants will cling nevertheless to intransigent firmly-held beliefs about the abject faults of the child's other parent or agencies of the state. PD 25B makes clear the rules about the content, the *what,* of the expert's report, but not *how* it is to be expressed.

The report must give details of the expert's qualifications and experience, include a statement listing the documents provided and on which the opinion is based, and an explanation of any opinions or conclusions, summarising the facts and instructions that are material to the opinions expressed. The report needs to state who carried out any tests or examinations, their qualifications, and whether the work was carried out under the expert's supervision. The report needs to address the questions about which an opinion is sought, and in expressing an opinion to the court:

a   take into consideration all of the material facts including any relevant factors arising from ethnic, cultural, religious or linguistic contexts at the time the opinion is expressed, identifying the facts, literature and any other material, including research material, that the expert has relied upon in forming an opinion;
b   describe the expert's own professional risk assessment process and process of differential diagnosis, highlighting factual assumptions, deductions from the factual assumptions, and any unusual, contradictory or inconsistent features of the case;
c   indicate whether any proposition in the report is an hypothesis (in particular a controversial hypothesis), or an opinion deduced in accordance with peer-reviewed and tested technique, research and experience accepted as a consensus in the scientific community;
d   indicate whether the opinion is provisional (or qualified, as the case may be), stating the qualification and the reason for it, and identifying what further information is required to give an opinion without qualification;

Where there is a range of opinion on any question to be answered by the expert, the report should

a   summarise the range of opinion;
b   identify and explain, within the range of opinions, any 'unknown cause', whether arising from the facts of the case (for example, because there is too

little information to form a scientific opinion) or from limited experience or lack of research, peer review or support in the relevant field of expertise;

c  give reasons for any opinion expressed: the use of a balance sheet approach to the factors that support or undermine an opinion can be of great assistance to the court;

The report should contain a summary of the expert's conclusions and opinions. It also should contain a statement that the expert:

a  has no conflict of interest of any kind, other than any conflict disclosed in his or her report;
b  does not consider that any interest disclosed affects his or her suitability as an expert witness on any issue on which he or she has given evidence;
c  will advise the instructing party if, between the date of the expert's report and the final hearing, there is any change in circumstances which affects the expert's answers to (a) or (b) above;
d  understands their duty to the court and has complied with that duty; and
e  is aware of the requirements of FPR Part 25 and this practice direction;
f  in children proceedings, has complied with the Standards for Expert Witnesses in Children Proceedings in the Family Court which are set out in the Annex to this Practice Direction;
g  be verified by a statement of truth in the following form –

> 'I confirm that I have made clear which facts and matters referred to in this report are within my own knowledge and which are not. Those that are within my own knowledge I confirm to be true. The opinions I have expressed represent my true and complete professional opinions on the matters to which they refer.'
>
> Where the report relates to children proceedings the form of statement of truth must include -
>
> 'I also confirm that I have complied with the Standards for Expert Witnesses in Children Proceedings in the Family Court which are set out in the Annex to Practice Direction 25B-The Duties of an Expert, the Expert's Report and Arrangements for an Expert to Attend Court'
>
> (Justice, 2017: no page numbers)

The issue of conflicts of interest may be relatively non-controversial, but worthy of consideration. Conflicts of interest can be a 'financial interest, a personal connection or an obligation, for example, as a member or officer of some other body' (Shek, 2015). Where there is any personal connection between the expert and anyone else involved in the case, either the parties or their representatives, it is essential for these to be declared or for the expert to decline the work. Even the perception of a conflict of interest may alone be sufficient to distress some participants in proceedings. I have known parents to complain that their own advocate is too cosy with the other legal representatives in court in a conspiracy against them. They observe professionals consulting with each other to their own exclusion. Under the pressure of care proceedings it is easy to let the imagination run wild.

Conflicts of interest sometimes arise when the level of concern about a child points towards precipitate action. A general practitioner, with whom a mother and her children were all registered, had become concerned that the mother may have fabricated or induced illness (FII) in her children, one of whom had been diagnosed with autism and epilepsy, and both of whom had been referred for investigations of suspected cardiac issues (E and H, 2023).[9] The mother also worked in the GP's surgery. She had told other staff and the children's teachers, falsely, that she was suffering from breast cancer. She had claimed at work, also falsely, that her son was seriously ill in hospital. Additionally, she was found to have been accessing her own and her children's medical records, a matter designated as gross misconduct. A strategy meeting was called involving three consultant paediatricians, social workers, the police, the headteacher of the children's school and others. Reference to the Working Together guidelines suggested in such cases the importance of referral to a consultant paediatrician who assumes lead responsibility for the child's health, but this was not undertaken. The lead was taken by the family GP who held multiple role-relationships with the mother. A subsequent strategy meeting resulted in the granting of an Emergency Protection Order and removal of the children from their home in the middle of the night by police banging on the door which was described by the judge as having a lasting and adverse impact upon the whole family.

A judgment by HHJ Vincent concluded that the general practitioner, the safeguarding lead for the surgery, who was regarded as having driven the decision-making about the family, was not the appropriate person to undertake this role as a result of conflicts of interest. She was too personally involved as the mother's employer and general practitioner (BAILII, 2023). A more measured response was needed from a paediatrician whose specific role was to take a lead for the children's health.

In another example, if a practitioner offers not only an expert witness service but also provides or has links with therapeutic intervention services to which assessed clients could be referred, it could be argued that there is motivation to recommend referral to these particular services.

Recommendations for interventions deliverable only by the instructed expert or their associates are inconsistent with [transparency]. It increases the risk of bias, can limit appropriate oversight of interventions and risks delay as it may create barriers to families accessing appropriate, timely support local to them. The court should be extremely cautious when asked to consider assessment and treatment packages offered by the same or linked providers.

Family Justice Council (2022, no page numbers)

## Arrangements for Giving Evidence

It is expected that experts will be given adequate notice of dates and times for attending court if required. They should be given an indication as to the length of time that they will be needed and the option to participate by telephone conference or video link in order to minimise disruption to their professional schedules and minimise costs. The parties' advocates should have identified the issues that the expert is required to address and arranged a logical sequence to the giving of evidence.

## Standards for Expert Witnesses in Children Proceedings in the Family Court

Experts must comply with standards 1–11 in the Annex of PD 25B (Justice, 2017), which I would advise to read in full, whilst I have summarised key points as follows:

1   The expert's area of competence is appropriate to the issue(s) identified by the court and is evidenced in their CV.
2   The expert must evidence sufficient relevant experience and recent activity related to the issues in the case, and be familiar with the breadth of current practice or opinion.
3   The expert needs to have working knowledge of relevant social, developmental and cultural norms, and accepted legal principles applicable to the case, and have cultural competence[10] to deal with the circumstances of the case.
4   The expert is up-to-date with Continuing Professional Development appropriate to their discipline, and engaged in supervisory mechanisms relevant to their practice.
5   If the expert's current professional practice is regulated by a UK statutory body, they are in possession of a current licence to practise or equivalent.
6   If a member of a regulated profession, the expert must hold a current licence to practise or otherwise show evidence of appropriate professional accountability.
7   The expert should be compliant with any necessary safeguarding requirements and information security regulations, and carry professional indemnity insurance.
8   If the expert's current professional practice is outside the UK they need to demonstrate that they are compliant with the FJC 'Guidelines for the instruction of medical experts from overseas in family cases'.
9   The expert should have undertaken appropriate training, updating or quality assurance activity – including actively seeking feedback about cases for which they have provided evidence in the family courts in England and Wales within the last year.
10   The expert needs to have working knowledge of, and comply with, the requirements of PD 25B. This includes compliance with the requirement to identify where their opinion on the instant case lies in relation to other accepted mainstream views and the overall spectrum of opinion in the UK.

11  The expert should state their hourly rate in advance of agreeing to accept instruction and give an estimate of the number of hours the report is likely to take.

In spring 2025 (Gov.uk) the government launched a consultation on the standards required for expert witnesses. The aim of the proposed changes was to improve consistency of standards and ensure that only experts with the relevant qualifications, experience and oversight were instructed in the family court.

Whilst not referenced in the standards for expert witnesses, any practitioner who is involved professionally in work with children or vulnerable adults needs to have completed an enhanced Disclosure and Barring Service (DBS) check. Enhanced DBS checks are the most detailed level of examining someone's background and they cannot be applied for by the individual concerned. They can only be requested in connection with a specific job by an employer. This poses a problem for experts who are not employed in any other capacity or by a company for whom they work as an associate expert witness. There are umbrella companies that, for a fee, will undertake this task on behalf of self-employed experts. They can be found at: https://www.gov.uk/find-dbs-umbrella-body. It is advised that it may be necessary to visit the company in person in order to verify identity.

## Meetings between Experts

Because the court normally instructs an SJE, meetings between experts are rarely required in the family court. I have only once been asked to meet with a member of a related profession, on this occasion when we were both giving evidence, in order to clarify areas of agreement and disagreement. PD 25E makes it clear that jointly instructed experts should not participate in any meeting or conference which is not a joint one, unless all of the parties have agreed in writing, or the court has directed that such a meeting may be held.

More often, in public law proceedings, I have been asked to attend a professionals' meeting which has involved the guardian, social worker and the parties' advocates. The court may give a direction that a meeting shall take place between the local authority and any relevant named experts for the purpose of providing assistance in the local authority's formulation of plans and proposals for the child. Minutes of such meetings are usually taken by the lead solicitor and circulated for corrections to be made by the attendees.

There have been occasions following such meetings when I have subsequently been contacted for further advice or discussion, but this is not permitted unless authorised by the court, even if it is thought most likely to be of benefit to the child. The appropriate action is to contact the lead solicitor for advice.

## Family Procedure (Amendment No 2) Rules 2023

In April 2024 specific amendments to the Family Procedure Rules which apply to private proceedings came into effect. It has been my experience that when separated parents take the arrangements for caring for children to court, the process tends to escalate whatever conflict between them was already extant. This amendment was designed to keep such disputes out of court and resolve differences at an early stage. Disputing parents had already been required to attend a Mediation Information and Assessment (MIAM) meeting as a first stage in the process. The new rules expanded the definition of non-court dispute resolution to include, but not limited to, 'mediation, arbitration, evaluation by a neutral third party (such as a private FDR process) and collaborative law'. A new form (FM5) required parents to explain the reasons for seeking a court order despite having attempted to resolve the issues by a non-court means. Parents became obliged to state a legitimate reason for being exempt from attending a MIAM (such as being subject to domestic abuse). The aim was to make attending the MIAM more than just a tick box exercise and to discourage a 'win-lose' attitude towards the resolution process.

## Family Procedure Rules and the Expert Witness

The family court is obliged to follow the Family Procedure Rules which are designed to specify 'what' to do in the family court, supplemented by PDs which specify 'how' to proceed. Expert witnesses need to ensure that they stay within these rules and keep abreast of changes and amendments. The overriding objective of the rules is to enable the court to deal with cases justly, with children's welfare at the forefront. In my opinion, they protect experts from unwarranted hubris, encouraging the expression of highly considered opinions, open-mindedness and consultation with others when in doubt.

---

### Key Points from this Chapter

- The expert advises and the judge decides but expert evidence can only be discounted if doubt is thrown upon it.
- Experts are bound by Part 25 of the Family Procedure Rules with which they need to be conversant. They testify to this at the end of their reports.
- Children should not be seen unless permission has been granted by the court for them to be examined or assessed. This should be stated within the relevant court order in the bundle.
- Referrals should only be accepted when the issues lie within the expert's domain of expertise. If in doubt it is advisable to check and err on the side of caution.
- Accurate contemporaneous records need to be kept of any conversations with family members, professionals or others. Where appropriate the respondent may be asked to check for accuracy.
- It is important not to give an opinion unless it can be supported with adequate data. If information or data is missing, such as medical records,

request it. If it is not forthcoming, the opinion either needs to be qualified or the opinion not expressed in its absence. It is acceptable to say that a question in the LOI cannot be answered in the absence of this data.

- Experts are expected to anticipate pending documents and request them if not supplied.
- Bundles may seem overwhelming but need to be read in detail to give a full picture of the evidence.
- It is judges who determine contested facts, whilst experts are expected to rely on the facts accepted within their community of practitioners. Where these are contentious, experts are expected to lay out the conflicting arguments and explain why one interpretation is preferred over another.
- Findings of fact made by the court are unassailable. If the expert expresses a counter view, their report is likely to be dismissed in its entirety.
- PD 25B lays out the rules about the content of reports but *how* the opinion is expressed is best done with understanding and compassion.
- It is perfectly acceptable to change an opinion in light of new evidence. This is preferred to taking a dogmatic position.
- Experts need to comply with standards 1–11 published in the appendix to PD 25B.
- Experts need to be cautious about contacts made other than by the lead solicitor, either whilst a case is open or after it is closed. It is wise to check with the lead solicitor whether and how to respond.
- Throughout, experts need to be aware of their own cultural histories; the impact that these are having on their own values, prejudices, biases and the lenses through which they are viewing the people and the data that they are examining.

## Notes

1  Re B (Care: Expert Witnesses) [1996] 1 FLR 667.
2  C (interim judgment on expert evidence) [2018] EWFC B9.
3  J (A Child)(Resolutions Model) (Rev 1) [2021] EWFC 58.
4  Re: H-N and Others (Children) (Domestic abuse: finding of fact hearings [2021] EWCA Civ 448.
5  K, Re [2022] EWCA Civ 468.
6  Re P and E *(Care Proceedings: Whether to Hold Fact Finding Hearing) [2024] EWCA Civ 403.*
7  *A Local Authority v DP, RS and BS [2005] EWHC 1593 (Fam).*
8  *Re H-D-H (Children) [2021] EWHC Civ 1192.*
9  E and H (Care Proceedings - Alleged FII - Costs) [2023] EWFC 69.
10  NB It has been argued that claiming we can achieve competence in any culture is untrue, dangerous and based on content-oriented training. Instead, an ongoing process of learning through taking a position of 'cultural humility' is advised (Lekas et al., 2020).

Chapter 4

# Data Generation, Organisation and Report Writing

At the outset of an assessment for the family court, the expert is provided with a letter of instruction (LOI) and a bundle of documents. These enable the construction of a plan for conducting the assessment and inform the format of the report. Although not always possible, I find it preferable at this stage to read the entire bundle and begin to construct the report. Bundles are typically divided into sections that contain preliminary documents such as case summaries and statements documenting how the threshold for local authority intervention has been met (in the case of public law), position statements from CAFCASS, court applications and orders, statements from parents and professionals, care plans where relevant, expert reports and miscellaneous documents. There may also be separate sections for medical and police records, previous proceedings and records of supervised contact between parents and children. In my experience, bundles vary greatly in their degree of organisation, completeness and length. There may be hundreds or even thousands of pages, sometimes even in one section such as medical records. When reading is extensive, the expert can request that the parties arrive at an essential reading list. The contents of the bundle are usually agreed by all parties, and in the event of any disagreement, the judge may intervene. Practice Direction 27A deals with the bundle in family proceedings.

Unless operating outside the Legal Aid Agency (LAA) guidance regarding fees and hours, experts need to restrict the amount of time that they spend on the assessment process. Consequently, although I find it desirable to read the entire bundle, at this stage some sections may have to be skimmed. But, when it comes to giving an opinion, this must be based on all of the available information that the expert asserts that they have relied upon in reaching their position and this will include the entire bundle.

Arising from a review of the bundle, key issues and positions can be identified from which the assessment plan is developed. This will usually involve interviews with parents and/or children, discussions with third parties such as a child's teacher or foster carer, and decisions regarding the administration of tests and formal assessment measures. It may also be helpful to observe interactions between parents and children during contact or family time. As experts may be questioned on their choices, it is important to have a rationale for them. Justification may need

DOI: 10.4324/9781003453390-4

to be made for interviewing particular individuals who are caring for or have cared for a child, whilst omitting others.

It is important to decide as early as possible what kinds of data will be needed to address the questions in the LOI, and if data is missing this should be requested as early as possible. Some data may not be available for the filing date of the report, in which case caveats need to be included as to how the expert's opinion may change in light of evidence that emerges at a later stage. Sometimes experts may be asked to provide an 'either-or' opinion, dependent upon what will later be judged to be the facts.

## The Assessment Plan

Letters of instruction typically begin with questions about the parents, requesting a psychological profile including assessment of any mental health difficulties and aspects of functioning that might negatively impact parenting or cooperation between parents. In order to address these questions I find it necessary to arrange meetings with individual carers. I much prefer face-to-face meetings since they incorporate body language, nuances of communication and variations in pace and phrasing. Remote interviews can make eye contact more challenging, be impacted by the vagaries of technology with unreliable connectivity, or by the presence of off-screen third parties exercising a degree of control over the interviewee.

My initial contact with the parent will usually be by email or text message, requesting a time when a phone call would be viable for them. The message explains that I have been asked to meet with them, that there is a choice of venue for such a meeting, that I will be asking questions about their opinions and that I will be asking them to complete some questionnaire measures. I suggest that the meeting may take about four hours, with the aim of dispelling expectations of fitting a brief meeting into their busy schedule. My subsequent phone call to the parent then offers opportunities to explore the content of the message and to make arrangements that take into account other parental commitments.

I find that most parents face an interview by a psychologist with a degree of trepidation and anxiety. Sometimes they tell me so. This behoves me to make the context and approach as relaxed and parent-friendly as possible. Particularly in public proceedings, parents have already been found wanting and their involuntary relationships with professionals have often been transacted through mistrust, fear and hostility. My aim is to create an environment in which parents begin to relax, show and tell me about themselves. How I approach this is discussed in detail in a companion volume (Scaife, 2024).

I prefer such interviews to be unconstrained by time limits since opening up emotionally sensitive areas requires the time and space for full exploration and a process of closure. A venue is selected over which the parent has a degree of control, be this at their home or in an office.

When we meet, after initial social niceties, running through the LOI provides a shared focus for the meeting, means that the parent does not have to speak at the outset, and gives an indication that I will manage the process of the interview. At this point it may also be appropriate to explain issues of confidentiality. This can be judged according to the parent's initial presentation. Some parents find it difficult to wait to begin their narrative and may struggle to pay attention to my concerns. Areas for exploration are prescribed by the questions in the LOI and by issues identified through the reading of the bundle. Whilst I prefer long loosely structured interviews, and often make use of just one, breaks can be scheduled or follow-ups arranged to guard against undue fatigue.

During such interviews, parents sometimes request that specific content be kept confidential. Confidentiality may have been discussed at the outset, but if it appeared likely to impact negatively on the establishment of rapport or engagement, I may have chosen instead to address it at a later point after the conversation was flowing. When such requests are made, I stop the interview and explain that anything shared with me has to be reported and will be seen by the other parties. Experts have an overriding duty of full and frank disclosure in all family proceedings.[1]

During interviews, parents not infrequently offer documents, texts, letters, videos or photographs as evidence supporting their assertions. Sometimes I ask for evidence. If parents wish to supply these, and they are relied upon by the expert in giving their opinion, they need to be submitted with the report so that all parties have access to them. Ideally, agreement to their inclusion should be sought from the other parties.

It is usually at the end of the interview that I ask the parent to complete formal measures in my presence. Many of the ones I use are self-report questionnaires. I am able to answer queries they may have about the meaning of some questions, ensure that they personally have completed them, and have not sought 'correct' answers through research on the internet. There are approaches that allow many of these measures to be completed remotely but they may require a specific standard of technology, such as a large screen or second remote camera, in order for this to be acceptable. Some sub-tests, such as block design, a feature of the commonly-used Wechsler Adult Intelligence Scale (WAIS-IV), are not available in digital form for remote administration unless there is a trained facilitator able to supervise use of the materials. Guidance on the remote use of tests for the assessment of specific learning difficulties (SpLD) is provided by the SpLD Assessment Standards Committee (SASC, 2021 updated 2023).

The selection of formal measures from the multitude available is a matter for the individual assessor, likely to be based on clinical experience, familiarity, validity, reliability, sensitivity and specificity, and their peer-reviewed research base. Psychometric measures, whilst having an extensive research base, present a number of problems when used in the family court. Fierce criticism has been levelled at the use of projective tests such as the Rorschach Inkblot Test in terms of reliability and validity and of the Bricklin Perceptual Scales and related others on the grounds that there are few or no peer-reviewed articles supporting their use (Erikson et al., 2007). The Millon Clinical Multiaxial Inventory-IV (MCMI-IV) and Millon Adolescent Clinical Inventory-II (MAC-II) are widely-used instruments in several forensic settings, particularly in the USA, but the peer-reviewed literature on these recent editions is virtually non-existent which leads to reliance on research relating to predecessor versions which is of questionable relevance. They are impacted by underreporting response styles in family court evaluations (Sellbom et al., 2022) and 'fail to meet the *Daubert v. Merrell Dow Pharmaceuticals, Inc.* (1993) criteria for admissibility into court testimony' (Sellbom et al., 2022: 204). Daubert[2] required that expert evidence meet the requirements of being based on a theory which could be tested and falsified, had been established through peer review and had achieved general acceptance in the relevant scientific community. The Kumho[3] case established that the Daubert principles applied not only to scientific evidence but to all expert testimony.

Letters of instruction typically contain questions about children, often beginning with a request to provide a psychological and personality profile, including consideration of their emotional, social and educational development, the impact of their life experiences upon their presentation and functioning, and, in public law, whether they have suffered significant harm as a result of the parenting they have received. Before arranging to see a child I generally prefer to explore a range of issues with their carers. In private law, parents often have very strong ideas about venue since they are concerned that the child will be influenced in their responses by the other parent. Schools and nurseries can be seen as relatively 'neutral' contexts where children have been socialised into generally cooperative behaviour. They may not be suitable when the child struggles with being out of the classroom under the scrutiny of their peers. CAFCASS or solicitors' offices also offer a degree of neutrality but may be less comfortable for the child. Contact venues are another option. Whilst their home may be suitable, it can be difficult to manage the many distractions that they offer and they are unlikely to be regarded by disputing parents as neutral.

I also like to ask carers about the child's interests which I may be able to explore with them as a way of settling into the meeting. Interviews with children and young people require flexibility and the use of age-appropriate activities. Many helpful exercises can be downloaded free from: https://www.socialworkerstoolbox.com/. Sessions may last from five minutes to three hours, so setting them up can be quite challenging. Children may benefit from the presence and support of a familiar adult who would need to understand and consent to the specific issues of confidentiality that apply in the family court.

Descriptions of many relevant tests, scales and questionnaires for adults and activities with children are given in Scaife (2024), where I counsel against dependence on measures designed for purposes other than assessments for the family court, and draw attention to the risks of undue reliance on numbers to represent individuals. Numbers in the domain of psychology are based on (sometimes hidden) assumptions that are used in their generation and interpretation. They have sometimes misrepresented whole populations (Ford, 2005). For most presenting psychological difficulties there are no 'tests' that provide a definitive result.

In addition to meetings with key protagonists, the assessment plan usually involves arranging discussions with others including professionals who have previously been involved with parents and children, substitute carers and some-times older children in the family who are not subjects of the proceedings. It is wise to ensure that all parties are agreeable to these discussions although time constraints can make this difficult. Experts are instructed to keep notes of all such conversations, and I prefer to send these to the people with whom I have had the conversation in order to check for accuracy before incorporating them into my report. Information in the bundle obtained from social work, medical and school records, police and probation may all contribute to a deeper understanding of the family.

In my experience, arranging appointments and creating an assessment plan can take an inordinate amount of time and effort. This can, to some extent, be expedited by asking for contact details from individual advocates ahead of receiving the LOI. Phone calls to schools, social workers, and CAFCASS officers in particular depend upon availability and may take many attempts before actually speaking to the person. Time taken for the conversations is funded by the LAA but administrative time taken to set them up is not. Nevertheless, I find the time well spent in order to set the assessment on a constructive path.

There comes a point where the next task is to collate the data generated, organ-ise thoughts about the functioning of the family and its members, and address the questions in the LOI. If data is missing, it is advisable to request it before finalising the report, and if it is not available for the filing date, to enter appropriate caveats in relation to the opinions expressed.

The process involves triangulation of the different kinds of data and decisions about what weight to accord them. If there is consistency between the inferences that are drawn from information that is obtained from different individuals, or dif-ferent sources, or that is of different types (documents, interviews, 'tests', ques-tionnaire measures, historical records), then more confidence can be placed in these understandings than if they are based on a single source, single individual or obtained through a single method. Explanatory accounts may draw on more than one theory.

The process of creating a provisional account of, 'how things seem to be, how they got this way and why they are continuing to be this way' is known as formu-lation or re-formulation. The process aims to create a description of a person's concerns, issues and problems, and by reference to theory and research findings make explanatory inferences about causes and maintaining factors so as to in-form interventions. It is a narrative which goes beyond description and includes provisional attempts to explain how problems have developed and are being maintained with a view to recommending interventions that have the potential to impact on the predisposing and maintaining mechanisms. This process of gathering together, sorting among and organising data, looking for patterns and discrepancies and hypothesising about the mechanisms that may account for client difficulties, is the skill of formulation. Whilst it takes place at the centre of the initial assessment process, it is continuously evolving, updated in light of further information and evidence. It is sometimes known as 're-formulation', a reminder for the practitioner to remain open to changing perspectives and understandings. The formulation or conceptualisation of the difficulties draws together material from and about the child and care-giver, linking with relevant theory and the research literature. The research process links theory and re-search with the personal story and idiosyncratic needs of each individual family member (Corie and Lane, 2006).

(Scaife, 2024: 295)

## Structure of the Report

Practice direction 5A (court documents – civil procedure) addresses the preparation of documents for court in general. It provides that documents should be on A4 paper with a margin not less than 3.5 cm, be fully legible and normally typed with consecutive page numbering, with numbered paragraphs, and have all numbers, including dates, expressed as figures. Paper bundles are now very unusual and reports become incorporated into large paginated PDF bundles.

For ease of reading, the font is best no smaller than size 11. If the report refers to other documents, cross-reference is made easier by giving an identifier such as page or paragraph number. Whilst reports benefit from being concise, this needs to be balanced against clarity of evidence and argument. When he was president of the family division Sir James Munby stated, '[E]xpert reports....should be more focused on *analysis* and *opinion* than on history and narrative. In short, expert reports must be *succinct, focused* and *analytical*. But they must also of course be *evidence based*' (Judiciary, 2013).

The procedure rules at PD 25B specify the content to be included in an expert report, and for ease of reference a logical structure is desirable. This is the structure that I use which owes a debt to Carter-Brown, a company providing referrals and support to professionals offering expert assessments:

### Front Page

This begins with the heading 'Confidential Psychologist's Report' below which the names and dates of birth of the family members are listed along with the case number, and my name, title and qualifications along with the date of the report. Other than on the front page, each page of the report is numbered and bears a footer listing the names of the people being assessed and the date of the report.

### Professional Qualifications and Experience

These are summarised in two paragraphs. A CV is attached as an appendix. The British Psychological Society (BPS), in conjunction with the Family Justice Council

(2023: 17), gives detailed guidance in appendix 6 on what should be included in the CV as follows:

- The psychologist expert witness's CV will clearly state under which code(s) of conduct they are governed, and any/all regulatory/professional body to which they belong, including their current registration details and the process by which such details can be verified, such as the website address.
- The psychologist's CV will provide relevant and verifiable details of qualifications, experience, other professional memberships, academic publications and post-qualification specialisations, including any matters in which they are competent.
- The psychologist will respond to questions on all aspects of their CV to ensure clarification with regard to regulation and professional competence in the relevant matter.

### Reason for the Report

This states the overall aim such as 'The proceedings concern the arrangements for the care of the named child/children with specific questions as follows:'. The questions from the LOI are then listed as provided.

### Basis of the Report

This lists all of the conversations, either in person, remotely or by phone, carried out during the course of the assessment, including dates, locations and duration.

### Background to the Report

This states that a bundle of documents was supplied and lists any additional information later provided by the lead solicitor, other professionals, carers or by family members. This is followed by a brief summary of the background, often provided in the LOI.

### General Observations and Procedures Used

Here, a list of any tests or questionnaires used is presented, with a brief description of what the instrument is designed to measure, and may include comments concerning validity, reliability and/or clinical usage.

### Meetings with Each Person Being Assessed

I afford each individual a separate section of the report. In order to assist readers, these are subdivided into sections which might be entitled 'history', 'history of relationship with child's other parent/s', 'issues arising from the bundle', 'mental health' etc. Courts prefer concise reports, but this needs to be weighed against giving a fair hearing to what each person has to say. A parent may consider that what they regard as important information has not been given a sufficient airing. I am particularly inclusive of what children express, in order to ensure that they have a voice. Children usually give consent for a recording to be made and I quote sections of these in order to ensure that carers are furnished with the child's exact words.

## Results of Formal Assessment Measures

This section gives results in terms of scores, or a range within which the specific result falls, may cite confidence intervals and offer brief interpretations of results. The BPS (2018a) advises that raw scores are not appropriately quoted in reports since they are not usually meaningful in themselves. Raw scores are contextualised by norm- or criterion-referencing and it is these scores, if any, that are appropriately communicated as standardised scores, T scores or percentiles. Neither does the BPS recommend communication of individual item responses although in certain situations they may be used qualitatively, as in examining the types of words that a child has misspelled in a test. Copyright law may be violated if materials such as score sheets marketed and supplied by commercial businesses are published in an expert report.

Some psychometric measures, such as IQ tests, are typically restricted in administration to registered psychologists. They contain information about reliability from which confidence levels have been derived. When citing such scores it is advised also to cite the associated confidence interval.

A danger of providing raw or over-detailed scores is that lay readers may make their own interpretations, in conflict with the purposes for which the test was devised. I have written elsewhere about caution in using psychometric measures devised for one population or purpose in assessments for the family court (Scaife, 2024). Norms have often been developed through comparison of populations which limits their relevance and meaning in relation to specific individuals, and minority cultures have traditionally been under-represented in standardisation samples.

## Conversations with Others Listed by Name and Title

These sections (one for each person) summarise information obtained from conversations with others who may be professionals, carers or other relevant people.

## Medical Records, Summary of Relevant Entries

I enclose these in a two-column table of date and a summary of consultation. I generally restrict them to consultations about mental health or previous and current proceedings. Sometimes physical health conditions may be relevant and reference made, but with an indication later in the opinion section of the report that they do not fall within my area of expertise. These, nevertheless, may be important to the wider consideration of issues, including constraints imposed on parental behaviour by physical ill health or incapacity.

Medical records vary greatly in legibility and the extent to which they record what may be regarded as facts and opinions. The latter, particularly in older records, can be expressed pejoratively. More recent records can be made very difficult to follow on account of zealous redaction of third-party information. I try to include only information that is pertinent to the proceedings. For example, terminations of pregnancies may be made without a partner's knowledge, and I would not include this unless it was relevant. Some entries may record data from questionnaires completed by a parent at the time of a consultation. Such results can be useful for purposes of comparison with current data, particularly if the same questionnaire has been completed.

Medical records can also be useful in reporting attitudes and behaviour expressed in the process of a consultation, such as hostility and aggression, warmth or distance in a parent's relationship with a child, repeated failure to attend, or they may give an indication in terms of number and frequency of appointments, of the demands that may be made on parents whose children have long-standing medical conditions.

### Opinion

In this section, I treat the questions in the LOI as headings and in what follows attempt to answer each question as fully as possible. In my experience, the questions can sometimes be repetitive and I tend to use the initial question regarding each individual to give a fairly extensive description of my opinion. In response to later questions I may then refer the reader to an earlier paragraph of the opinion section rather than reiterating what has already been stated.

### Summary

Here I attempt to summarise my opinion in a concise review of opinions expressed in the previous sections. I call it a 'summary' rather than 'conclusions' as it contains opinions, rather than conclusions from a research study and it is the judge's role to reach conclusions. Some experts place a summary early in their report, arguing that readers may study the detailed content later. My concern is that the detailed content may be overlooked although readers may anyway choose to read the summary first. It is always worth 'cross-examining' the report from the perspective of each party in order to ensure balance.

### Declaration

In this section, mandatory statements of compliance are specified as follows:

### Statement of Compliance

I understand my duty to the Court and have complied and will continue to comply with that duty. This Report includes all matters relevant to the issues on which my expert evidence is given. I have given details in this Report of any matters which might affect the validity of this Report. I have addressed this Report to the Court. I am aware of the requirements of Family Procedure Rules Part 25 and Practice Direction 25.

### Statement on Conflicts of Interest

I confirm that I:

a  have no conflict of interest of any kind, other than any conflict disclosed in my report;
b  do not consider that any interest disclosed affects my suitability as an expert witness on any issue on which I have given evidence;
c  will advise the instructing party if, between the date of my report and the final hearing, there is any change in circumstances which affects my answers to (a) or (b) above;

### Statement of Truth

I confirm that I have made clear which facts and matters referred to in this report are within my own knowledge and which are not. Those that are within my own knowledge I confirm to be true. The opinions I have expressed represent my true and complete professional opinions on the matters to which they refer.

I also confirm that I have complied with the Standards for Expert Witnesses in Children Proceedings in the Family Court which are set out in the Annex to Practice Direction 25B – The Duties of an Expert, the Expert's Report and Arrangements for an Expert to Attend Court.

Under these paragraphs the document needs to be signed and dated.

### References

Here I list all of the research papers and findings upon which I have relied in reaching an opinion. I cite them as I would at the conclusion of an academic paper.

### Appendices

These will include my CV and other documents that may help to clarify the basis of my opinion. It might include something that the child has drawn during my meeting with them, or pertinent emails or other communications provided by parents, although these may be provided separately rather than included in the report.

At times I have included details given to me by parents who are worried about these being available to all in the appendices so that if considered appropriate, that appendix can be removed from the report. This needs to be checked with the lead solicitor as confidentiality cannot be assured and the judge will make decisions about what is and is not shared. Parents understand that there cannot be confidentiality, but it may not be necessary for everyone involved to see this information. For the same reason, medical records may be excluded from the bundle by the lead solicitor and the full record made available only to those who have a need to know. I have seen test results included in appendices whilst caution needs to be exercised for reasons described above.

## Transparency, Accuracy, and Process for Distribution

Whilst the purpose of the report is to assist the court in making best decisions regarding the care of children, it is also a very personal account of family life. In writing reports I try to bear in mind how the readers, particularly the parents, may experience my analysis. Experts have a duty of care for the people whom they are tasked to assess. I try to express my opinion in a compassionate manner by attempting to explain how things may have got this way despite a parent's best efforts. I know that I am not always successful in this aim, through negative and sometimes hostile parental reactions. I am lucky in my professional career to have had only one complaint raised against me and this was dismissed through a lack of any evidence.

Particularly in the USA, where private law proceedings are sometimes called 'custody evaluations' or 'parenting plan evaluations', the literature warns would-be experts to anticipate a greater number of complaints than in their clinical work. Parents in private law proceedings can feel very bitter and angry, with a risk of this emerging against anyone whom they perceive to be 'the enemy'.

Opinions expressed by experts can be particularly influential on the judgments made. The adversarial process means that solicitors and barristers for each of the parties may seek to undermine expert evidence through the process of cross-examination. It is their job to test the evidence, seeking mistakes about facts, inconsistencies, questionable methodologies, discrepancies, or flaws in data or analysis. They may question degree of expertise, impartiality or potential biases. Expert witnesses need to be very careful and credible in reaching and expressing opinions in order to perform their duties to the court with respect to the welfare of children. This means expressing opinions clearly, accurately, and with a sound basis. In my experience, many reports submitted to the court contain grammatical errors, typos, inconsistencies around names, dates, places and events, and incorrect information which serves to undermine their credibility. My own are not immune. Even when reports are proofread, errors can creep through. Sufficient time needs to be made available to ensure accuracy and sound arguments for opinions expressed.

Credibility is also enhanced by ensuring the appropriate use of terminology. This requires constant updating of professional knowledge and awareness of current controversies. The term 'domestic abuse' is preferred to 'domestic violence' in order to give recognition to the insidious ways in which non-physical abuse, such as coercive and controlling behaviour, can erode people's sense of self. Use of the term 'failure to protect' has been impacted by a decision in L-W Children [2019][4] which concluded that: 'It cannot be said that any woman who fails to separate from a partner who has been violent in adult situations outside the home is failing to protect.' In the case of G-L-T Children [2019],[5] a child presented with medical issues which it was believed had been induced, inflicted and/or exaggerated by his mother. Following a move of house, the father reported that he had not observed the child to have any seizures. Within the original judgment this became translated into him knowing that the child had not had any seizures who in consequence continued to receive unnecessary medication and oxygen. Since the father had not reported this earlier to medical practitioners, he was accused of being guilty of 'failure to protect'. As this in itself would meet the threshold for significant harm, it carried serious consequences in terms of the overall assessment of the father. The appeal court argued that: 'Courts and LAs should approach allegations of "failure to protect" with assiduous care and keep to the forefront of their collective minds that this is a threshold finding that may have important consequences for subsequent assessments and decisions.'

Other language preferences involve choice of personal pronoun, with some people preferring 'they' and 'them' to binary terms, more accurately to express their gender identity. When reflecting a minority or 'social' model of disability, the term 'disabled parent' is preferred to 'parent with a disability' since the latter assumes that the disability lies within the individual rather than arising as a consequence of the non-adapted environment. Whilst a parent may have an impairment, the disablement arises from its context within society (Olsen and Clarke, 2003). However, the United Nations (2022) prefers 'person with a disability' in order to put the person first. It may be helpful instead to refer to a person's impairment, or as with any minority identity, politely to ask them for their own preferences about how they would like to be referenced.

## Ownership of the Report

Whilst there is no confidentiality for the family members being assessed, the findings and opinions expressed in the expert's report are confidential to the court. Nobody is allowed to share the contents of the report or any associated documents without the court's permission. The repercussions of disclosure include a fine and/or a prison sentence. A confidentiality warning is included on all court orders with the aim of avoiding accidental disclosure, as ignorance of the law is generally no defence. It is considered to be particularly serious in the family court since the papers contain the names and dates of birth of children and often details such as the schools they attend.

The confidentiality warning reads:

Until the conclusion of the proceedings no person shall publish to the public at large or any section of the public without the court's permission any material which is intended or likely to identify the child[ren] as being involved in these proceedings or an address or school as being that of the child[ren]. Any person who does so is guilty of an offence.

Further, during the proceedings or after they have concluded no person shall publish information related to the proceedings including accounts of what has gone on in front of the judge, documents filed in the proceedings, transcripts or notes of evidence and submissions, and transcripts and notes of judgments (including extracts, quotations, or summaries of such documents). Any person who does so may be in contempt of court.

Information related to the proceedings must not be communicated to any person other than as allowed by Rules 12.73 or 12.75 or Practice Direction 12G of the Family Procedure Rules 2010.

The first paragraph of the wording refers to Section 97 of the Children Act 1989 which concerns the privacy of children. The second paragraph summarises the law as stated in Section 12 of the Administration of Justice Act 1960. Posting information on social media is included in the definition of 'publishing'. Paragraph three refers to the rules for sharing information allowed within the Family Procedure Rules, such as sharing of documents with experts.

There are situations where information can be shared but it is wise to consult the lead solicitor if in any doubt. In recent years the courts have striven to balance confidentiality and transparency with the introduction and expansion of a reporting pilot, subsequently extended, which allows reporters and legal bloggers to attend and observe family proceedings and to report on them. 'Reporting must be subject to very clear rules to maintain both the anonymity of the children and family members who are before the court, and confidentiality with respect of intimate details of their private lives' (Judiciary, 2021a). Useful guidance is provided by HM Courts and Tribunals Service (2013, updated 2025) and HM Courts and Tribunals Service (2025). Chapter 5 explores the issue of confidentiality in more detail.

## Supervision

The codes of conduct for the British Psychological Society (BPS) and Health Care and Professions Council (HCPC) require that psychologists engage in regular supervision and/or peer review in relation to all of their professional practice (BPS and Family Justice Council, 2023). This is with the aim of ensuring that their practice is 'current, reflective, of an appropriate and consistent standard, and to obtain regular support, especially in relation to complex matters or new areas of application' (BPS and Family Justice Council, 2023: 16). However, they are not expected to require supervision of their opinion which would suggest a level of expertise inadequate for the task.

I have written extensively elsewhere about clinical supervision (Scaife, 2019). Participating in supervision seems to me to raise issues of confidentiality specific to the family court. Expert witnesses may not share documents without the court's permission, which implies that these may not be shared with a supervisor. Nor may client identifiers be disclosed. Nor may supervision be used to influence the supervisee's opinion. This means that certain methods, such as 'live' supervision or the use of recordings, are prohibited. What remains is constrained discussion.

Returning to first principles, supervision performs normative, formative and restorative functions. A useful definition for clinical contexts is provided by the Care Quality Commission (2013: 4):

> The purpose of clinical supervision is to provide a safe and confidential environment for staff to reflect on and discuss their work and their personal and professional responses to their work. The focus is on supporting staff in their personal and professional development and in reflecting on their practice.

As in any supervision, a contracting process at the outset and in review should ensure that the participants are in agreement about how they will fulfil the purposes. I find that work as an expert witness can generate many difficult feelings that benefit from support provided during supervision. For beginners, there is a great deal of learning to be accomplished, and remaining within the 'rules' both written and unwritten helps to ensure the safety and well-being of both clients and professionals.

## Key Points from this Chapter

- On receipt of the bundle and LOI it is advisable to create an assessment plan giving consideration to who is to be interviewed, what assessment measures are to be adopted, and what additional documents may be required.
- Family members need to understand that nothing they tell the expert can be kept confidential but will be shared with all of the other parties.
- It is wise to exercise caution in using assessment methods or materials that have been designed for purposes other than assessments for the family court.
- The BPS recommends that raw scores should not be quoted since these may be subject to misinterpretation. Copyright law may be violated if materials such as score sheets marketed and supplied by commercial businesses are published in an expert report.
- Parents engaged in the family court can feel very bitter and angry. Anyone who appears to be against them may find themselves the target of threats or formal complaints. Reports therefore benefit from being carefully constructed, coherent, consistent, credible and compassionate.
- The expert's findings, opinion and report are confidential to the court and must not be shared with anyone else either during or after the conclusion of the case.

- The BPS and HCPC require that practitioner psychologists engage in supervision and peer review for all of their professional practice. But experts are not expected to require supervision of their opinion since this would imply insufficient expertise.

## Notes

1 Practice Direction: Case Management [1995] 1 FLR 456.
2 Daubert v. Merrell Dow Pharmaceuticals, Inc., 509 U.S. 579, 588 (1993).
3 Kumho Tire Co. v. Carmichael, 119 S.Ct. 1167, 1171 (1999).
4 L-W Children [2019] EWCA Civ 159.
5 G-L-T Children [2019] EWCA Civ 717.

Chapter 5

# Data Protection, Costs and Invoicing

## Confidentiality within Proceedings

In the course of their assessments, expert witnesses become party to a great deal of sensitive personal information. Unlike the requirements in clinical contexts, none of this information may be kept confidential between the person providing it and the practitioner. Anything shared by each adult, child and involved professional must be made available to all. The reason behind this is one of fairness:

> ... it is a first principle of fairness that each party to a judicial process shall have an opportunity to answer by evidence and argument any adverse material which the tribunal may take into account when forming its opinion. This principle is lame if the party does not know the substance of what is said against him (or her), for what he does not know he cannot answer.
>
> (Lord Mustill in Re D at 603–604[1])

Whilst that may seem clear-cut, like most aspects of this work it is anything but. For example, in the case of A (A Child) UKSC 60,[2] which was heard in the appeal court, a disclosure had been made in confidence to the authorities by a vulnerable young woman that while she was a child she had been seriously sexually abused by the father of another child, then aged 10. Her treating physician and psychiatrist held that the stress of this being disclosed in the family court was likely to provoke a deterioration in her health. The mother of the ten-year-old had been informed by the local authority of the disclosure and on advice, had sought to vary a contact order such that family time between the child and the father became supervised. The allegations against the father could not be ignored but they could not be taken into account without proper investigation. This posed a dilemma not only in relation to these individuals, but also in terms of public interest regarding fair and open conduct of legal disputes, against the public interest of maintaining the confidentiality of this kind of communication and protecting both children and vulnerable adults from risk of harm. Lady Hale described this as being required to reconcile the irreconcilable.

DOI: 10.4324/9781003453390-5

In circumstances where one party is seeking to withhold disclosure from another, the court is required to balance competing principles including the general duty of disclosure and Article 6 of the Human Rights Act (1998) right to a fair trial, against the risk of harm to a child and Article 8 right to private and family life. In a more recent case example from private law,[3] which also went to appeal, the mother provided to the court a report from the school mental health nurse, noting the child had said that she did not want what she had discussed with the nurse shared with her father. The author of the report expressed concerns regarding the risk of harm to the child were the report to be shared (Whelan, 2024). The judgement concluded that,

> Non-disclosure should be the exception not the rule. The court should be rigorous in its examination of the risk and gravity of the feared harm to the child, and should order non-disclosure only when the case for doing so is compelling.
>
> (BAILII, 2024: no page numbers)

Experts therefore need ways of discussing issues of consent and confidentiality with parents and children, topics which are discussed elsewhere (Scaife, 2024).

Whilst information provided to the expert by the parties to the proceedings must be shared with all of them, it cannot be shared with anyone else other than the court. Expert reports are the property of the court. This and all the information provided to the expert in formulating and reaching an opinion must be kept securely according to data protection principles.

In some cases, extra care needs to be taken regarding the parties' contact details. Particularly where one parent has been the subject of domestic abuse and may have obtained a non-molestation order, it may be vital to keep addresses, email addresses and telephone numbers confidential. If in doubt, it is worth ensuring that this information is not shared with anyone other than the lead solicitor.

## Confidentiality Outside the Proceedings

Section 97 of the Children Act 1989 is quite clear that whilst a case is in progress the identity of a child is protected. This concerns their name, address, school, photographs of them and any other identifiers. It prevents people from making public that there is a court case about this child. Breaking this law is a criminal offence which may be punished with a fine or imprisonment. What is less clear is for how long this proscription is active after the end of the proceedings.

This is governed by Section 12 of the Administration of Justice Act 1960 which prohibits the publication of information relating to proceedings under the Children Act 1989 or the Adoption Act 2002. Section 12 deals with the detail of what is said and written in the family court, not the identity of the child or any other participants (including witnesses and professionals). There is no time limit, so the prohibition operates even after proceedings end. Running alongside these statutes is common law that has developed from decisions made in relation to individual cases. These laws apply automatically, without the need to make a specific order in an individual case. They can be changed by the judge – made more or less strict, disapplied or extended – but they come into effect automatically as soon as a court case about a child is begun.

When the proceedings have ended, these laws define that 'the nature of the dispute' may be published but not 'information relating to proceedings'. In most if not all family court cases there is not just one person's rights to consider (rights to freedom of expression, rights to privacy, etc.) but also the rights of other children, parents, and anyone else involved in the case. If a court is asked to rule on what is permitted, or to permit something that S12 (or the common law) prevents from being published, it will weigh all those rights in the balance before coming up with a solution. So, as soon as the question is put before a court, the Human Rights Act means that the common law has to be interpreted in light of the rights of anyone whose private information is involved (balanced with the rights of those who want to tell their/a story) (Transparency Project, 2024).

Experts are therefore advised to maintain confidentiality both during and after a case has concluded. Parents, however, are allowed to share information in order to assist them with mediation, to obtain counselling or healthcare for themselves and/or the child, and to pass the papers to certain complaints or regulatory bodies (Reed, 2022). Parents can show papers to certain supporters or to their MP only if it is for the purpose of seeking advice. These people must give an undertaking that they will not share it with anyone else, including posting on social media sites.

Experts are sometimes approached directly by parents who cannot ask an expert to prepare a report or show them any papers unless the court has given permission. In such a situation, the expert needs to advise the parent to seek permission rather than discuss the issues.

## Data Management and Data Protection

Aspiring expert witnesses will need to find ways of advertising their services and communicating with legal firms that represent clients involved in proceedings in the family court. Once established, in my experience referrals may come thick and fast, the rate being influenced by current preoccupations of the court. As I write, there are attempts to reduce the time that families, and children in particular, are waiting for hearings in order to expedite decisions within a 26-week timetable. This means that the appointment of experts may be seen as slowing down the process and is therefore limited to occasions when regarded as necessary to resolve proceedings justly (as defined in Part 25 of the Family Procedure Rules). This also means that experts who are able to provide a short timescale for producing reports are more likely to be instructed. Following receipt of an enquiry, the expert provides information about costs and timescales and may expect to hear within a reasonable timeframe whether or not their services are required. Some firms are assiduous in informing experts about this. In my experience, in order to manage the flow of work, it is advisable to give a date when the availability will expire. This can be within two weeks of the enquiry, for example, or, if provided by the referrer, on the day after the hearing on which the decision will be made.

Clinicians providing expert reports for the court will quickly accumulate large volumes of data, previously often in the form of paper bundles but more recently provided electronically. There may also be interview notes, medical records, test results, photographs, videos and other information provided by parents such as school reports, emails or certificates confirming attendance at relevant teaching and learning events. How the data is organised may be less important than whether it is organised since it will usually be the individual expert who needs to access and manipulate the data, so an idiosyncratic system could be adopted.

Personal data kept in relation to work for the family court, whether in paper or electronic records, are subject to UK General Data Protection Regulation (GDPR) which applies to all businesses including sole traders even if working with only a few families a year. They specify key principles that ensure that individuals know what data is held about them, that it is only held for specific purposes, that it is accurate, kept securely and only for as long as necessary. In order to comply with data protection regulations, experts need to register with the Information Commissioner's Office (ICO), for which there is an annual fee (https://ico.org.uk/for-organisations/data-protection-fee/register/).

Everyone responsible for using personal data is required to follow data-protection principles outlined in the Data Protection Act, 2018. They specify that the information is,

> used fairly, lawfully and transparently, used for specified, explicit purposes, used in a way that is adequate, relevant and limited to only what is necessary, accurate and, where necessary, kept up to date, kept for no longer than is necessary, handled in a way that ensures appropriate security, including protection against unlawful or unauthorised processing, access, loss, destruction or damage.
>
> (HM Government, undated)

There is stronger legal protection for more sensitive information, such as ethnicity, political opinions, religious beliefs, trade union membership, genetics, biometrics, health, and sex life and orientation. Organisations (including independent expert witnesses) are required to put in place appropriate security protections to make sure information is not accessed by hackers or accidentally leaked as part of a data breach. Whilst GDPR does not specify the nature of good security practices, proper access controls to information should be put in place, websites should be encrypted, and the use of pseudonyms is encouraged (Wired, 2024).

The UK GDPR requires that data protection concerns are integrated into every aspect of data processing activities. This approach is termed 'data protection by design and by default'. It is a key element of the UK GDPR's risk-based approach and its focus is on accountability, that is the organisation or individual's ability to demonstrate how compliance with its requirements is being accomplished. The ICO defines 'controllers' of data (including joint controllers) as the people who decide what personal data is collected and why, and exercise ultimate control over it. They have more obligations under the UK GDPR than do people defined as 'processors' who have day-to-day responsibility for managing the data.

Appropriate physical and technical measures need to be in place to protect personal data from unauthorised or unlawful processing including accidental loss, destruction or damage. Expert witnesses are advised to carry out a risk assessment to identify any vulnerabilities and mitigate against the risk using appropriate security measures or safeguards. The GDPR does not define the specific security measures needed, but they should be 'appropriate' and proportionate to the level of risk identified. What does this mean in practice?

## GDPR Security Measures

### Policy Management

Policies are of little if any use without understanding, consent and application. In my experience they can be like the terms and conditions that appear at the end of many electronic communications and which require a tick in order to proceed. But how many of us read them? It probably depends on our assessment of the risks involved in failing to do so. Ticking the box removes liability from the organisation that put them there. But to be useful in relation to GDPR, they need to state the purpose of the policy and ensure that everyone is familiar with and consents to it. In other contexts, I have found that they are most effective when created collaboratively by people who are able to see their value. But creating a policy is only the first step. To be useful they need to be revisited regularly, reviewed and updated, ideally without extending the length. Ongoing mandatory training could be an option for ensuring that new staff are aware of policies, existing employees reminded of them, and that they are not set in stone but repeatedly revised according to experience. It can help to make them concise, easy to understand, amenable to open dialogue and incentivised.

### Identity and Access Management (IDAM)

This refers to strategies that ensure access to data is only possible for those who need to know in order to carry out their job functions. Privacy training may be pertinent for those individuals who do have access in order to ensure that the intended purpose for the collection of personal data is maintained. Having worked in NHS settings where, out of curiosity rather than a need to know, staff have accessed health information about their neighbours or relatives, this seems to me to be a very beneficial requirement.

### Data Loss Prevention (DLP)

This refers to the need to keep data secure. Failures to do so in large organisations are not uncommonly reported in the media. Whether they are the controller or processor of personal information, organisations and individuals may be held liable for the loss of any personal data they collect. Data loss protection places controls (for example, encryption) around sensitive data. This means lockable spaces for paper and electronic records and devices; the use of secure processes for sending data electronically, such as secure email platforms which defend against advanced phishing attacks and data breaches; encryption with a password for documents; and a high level of data security on electronic devices with anti-virus and malware protection. Good passwords are at least eight characters and contain uppercase and lowercase letters, numbers, and symbols. Some devices may come with alternatives to passwords, for example fingerprint scanners or support for physical security keys which are even more secure than a password.

On Windows devices, the standard encryption system is called Bitlocker, and on Apple devices FileVault. In both cases *new* systems will have been enabled by default. Macs have been enabled by default since Apple started using their own CPU designs around 2020. Windows PCs have been enabled for devices that come with the '24H2' version of Windows 11 which was released in November 2024. For any device where it is not switched on, it can be turned on via a straightforward process. Devices should also be set to require a password if they are idle for a certain period (they should go to sleep and need a password after waking up). This will be the case by default. The national cyber security centre (part of the UK government) publishes recommendations regularly. These include recommendations about automatic updates, anti-virus/anti-malware and firewalls. Other governments offer similar sources of information and advice. In the USA this is the Cybersecurity and Infrastructure Security Agency (CISA) and also the Federal Communications Commission (FCC) and National Institute of Standards and Technology (NIST).

Larger organisations may employ a DLP tool which restricts the transmission of data outside the network. There needs to be a process for secure disposal/destruction of personal data, computers and IT equipment.

## Encryption & Pseudonymisation

Pseudonymisation is defined as 'the processing of personal data in such a way that the data can no longer be attributed to a specific data subject without the use of additional information' (ProcessUnity, 2020: no page numbers). This may include field-level encryption in databases, encryption of entire data stores at rest, and encryption for data in use and in transit. The purpose is to remove any personally identifiable information so that even if a breach were to occur, loss of personal data would be minimised.

Since the introduction of GDPR I have used initials rather than names on the result sheets completed for questionnaire or formal test measures. Better still would be a coding system with the coding manual kept securely in a separate place from the data. Many of the documents sent to expert witnesses contain names, addresses, dates of birth, medical history, schools, and other very personal data. As the documents already include these it is not possible to give pseudonyms at this stage, but instead there is a responsibility to ensure that they are kept securely.

## Incident Response Plan (IRP)

An Incident Response Plan specifies how to prepare for, identify, contain, mitigate and recover from a data breach. If an incident occurs and reaches the threshold for reporting, it has to be notified to the Data Protection Authority (ICO) within 72 hours wherever this is feasible. A breach is only reportable to the ICO if personal information is involved and it puts people at risk.

A personal data breach might involve an email sent to the wrong person, a laptop stolen from a car or files lost because of a flood. The ICO advises immediately to start a log of what has happened, who it involves and the investigative process. The facts need to be established as soon as possible and attempts made to contain the breach. If a message has been sent to someone by mistake they can be asked to delete it, send it back securely or have it ready to be collected. If a stolen laptop can be wiped remotely, it is advised to do so. Cyber incidents can be contained by making sure that staff passwords are changed immediately.

The next step is to assess the risk of harm to those affected through safeguarding issues, identity theft or significant distress. In a simple mix-up there may be little or no risk involved whereas a serious breach could have long-lasting repercussions. Good advice about the process is provided by the ICO (2023). Once what happened has been established, and if there is a high risk, there is a legal requirement to tell the affected people without delay. This allows them to take steps to protect themselves.

The ICO provides a self-assessment tool to help in making decisions about whether a breach is reportable. If the breach meets the criteria for reporting to the ICO, this can be done online with details such as what has happened and when, the assessment of risk and actions to contain the breach.

## Information Governance

Information governance determines the lifecycle of data held, how long an organisation retains the data, and its disposal. All documents copied to the expert should be retained by the original party. At the conclusion of the case, the expert may return these documents to the firm by whom they were originally supplied or, in the case of paper data, arrange for shredding as confidential waste. Documents supplied electronically can be deleted when the case concludes. Documents that are particular to the expert such as the expert's report, notes, raw data from test and questionnaire completion and recordings made by the expert need to be retained according to the rules of the court.

GDPR requirements need to be balanced against rules regarding retention and destruction of records. Regulations concerning retention and destruction of records differ according to organisation. The courts specify that in relation to the Family Law Act, which applies to private law, records need to be kept for three years from the expiry date of the final order and then destroyed. For Children Act cases (public law) they need to be kept for 18 years from the date of expiry of the final order, which would expire, if not revoked, when the child reaches the age of 18 years. Information can be found at: https://www.gov.uk/government/publications/record-retention-and-disposition-schedules.

This may seem straightforward but once the expert has provided a report, if they are not required to give evidence in court, there usually remains a deafening silence. Some firms are the exception and provide an update after the conclusion of the final hearing, but in my experience this is rare, despite it being a requirement within the Family Procedure Rules (Section 25: 19) which state:

> Within 10 business days after the final hearing, the party who instructed the expert or, in the case of a single joint expert, the party who was responsible for instructing the expert, must inform the expert in writing about the court's determination and the use made by the court of the expert's evidence.
>
> Unless the court directs otherwise, the party who instructed the expert or, in the case of the single joint expert, the party who was responsible for instructing the expert, must send to the expert a copy of the court's final order, any transcript or written record of the court's decision, and its reasons for reaching its decision, within 10 business days from the date when the party received the order and any such transcript or record.
>
> (Justice, 2022, Para 22.19)

Because of the long timescales, there needs to be a system for recording and monitoring record keeping and destruction. Determining when to destroy records may involve contacting the referring legal firm, but staff change, systems can be flaky, companies are taken over or closed. A best rule of thumb for private law may be to destroy records when the youngest child in the family reaches the age of 21 years and for public law when the youngest child reaches the age of 36 years. These figures make it clear how difficult it is to sustain a system that is compliant with the rules as the latter may well exceed the professional lifetime of an expert witness, and of the hardware or software on which data is stored and managed. Recordings made early in my career are held on cassettes for which there may eventually be no means of playing.

GDPR is relevant in relation to the professional indemnity cover that expert witnesses need to hold. Most, if not all, professional indemnity policies make it a condition of cover that the insured party keeps detailed records so that in the event of litigation, the business and the insurer can make a strong defence case based on solid documentary evidence (Professional Indemnity Insurance Brokers, 2018). The demands of the ICO and of the insurer may therefore be in conflict. Within the GDPR regulations, provision is made for businesses to retain data where it allows them to meet the conditions of their insurer and thereby carry out its responsibilities in the event of a claim for professional negligence.

Professional indemnity insurers usually provide what is termed 'run-off' cover when people take career breaks, retire or die. The period of this cover is in line with the Limitation Act 1980. These limitation periods vary according to when an issue arises which may be at the initial point of contact, but the damage caused may emerge at a later date. The issues are discussed in full in Professional Indemnity Insurance Brokers (2018).

## Subject Access Requests (SAR)

These are requests made under the Data Protection and Freedom of Information Acts that can be made by people on whom experts hold personal data. Such requests may be made for full disclosure including but not limited to all telephone records and logs, all official or clinical records, all case notes, all minutes of meetings and conferences, all personal notes, all emails, correspondence and text messages both to and from any private individuals or agencies, any photographic or audiovisual materials or recordings, any referrals and the responses, any statements or submissions gathered in evidence and any miscellaneous materials. Disclosure is required to be full, not partial. The ICO (2025) provides detailed information about how to respond to SARs, noting that further changes were due to come into effect later in 2025.

A SAR only entitles individuals making the SAR to information that constitutes their own personal data. But information that falls within this category could simultaneously be the personal data of another person. For example, the statement, 'John said Jane attacked Charlie with a knife' is the personal data of both John and Jane, as it conveys information about each of them. If Jane then issues a SAR seeking to know who said she had attacked Charlie, it is important to know whether revelation of John's identity is required.

The ICO's guidance on supplying third-party information is that because the obligation is to provide information rather than documents, names may be deleted or documents edited if the third-party information does not form part of the requested information. The ICO advise that a blanket policy of withholding the identities of other individuals should not be applied but that a detailed assessment of the issue should be made, including asking involved individuals whether they would consent to the disclosure. In the case of expert witnesses, it is likely that John would already have been identified in the report. In fact, the bulk of the information obtained by the expert should in any case be accessible by family members as it will have been incorporated into the final report.

Requests may be made for hand-written notes, recordings or raw data. Issues with the disclosure of notes and recordings are unlikely to arise but psychologists are advised, given the risks of misinterpretation, not to make raw test data available to those outside the profession. The British Psychological Society (2019a) advises that psychologists and those in training, under supervision, and test users should not release raw test data, other than to another appropriately competent professional/test user directly, *and* with the consent of the test taker.

Demands for the release of raw test data set into motion ethical and legal challenges for the practitioners involved. Ethical, because of the risk of misinterpretation by unqualified individuals, and legal because many test report forms are subject to copyright and the user has entered into an agreement with the provider that they will protect the integrity of the test. 'Test publishers, such as Pearson consider its secured tests to be trade secrets' (Morel, 2009: 641 cited in Bütz et al., 2023).

Experts who are just starting out are advised to consider these issues in detail in order at the outset to establish data storage systems that weave a safe path through the sometimes conflicting demands of retaining and destroying data. For those who have been carrying out this work for a substantial period of time, it may be necessary to carry out a thorough review and update of systems that are no longer fit for purpose.

## Recordings and Notes Taken during Interviews

I have had interviewees (both adults and children) request to make a recording of our session/s. And with contemporary devices, anyone can make a covert recording without the consent of the professional who may have no awareness that one is being made. When requested, I always agree to a recording being made whilst enquiring into the purpose and intent with regard to sharing of the data. But clients do not need my consent, and because they are only processing their own personal information they are exempt from data protection principles (Zack, 2014).

Given the possibilities of instant communication and online posts, recordings have the potential to 'go viral'. Sections may be taken out of context and distort the overall picture. But such a recording is likely to qualify as material that cannot be published whilst the case is ongoing.

It is possible that a parent may make a recording of an interview with a view to contesting the accuracy of the expert's report. In the case of F (A Minor) [2016] EWHC 2149 (Fam), a consultant clinical psychologist was instructed to assess a mother. Unbeknownst to the psychologist, the mother recorded their sessions and transcribed them later to show that the psychologist had been inaccurate in reporting her words (Reed, 2022). At Paragraph 26 of the judgement, it was reported that

> The overall impression is of an expert who is overreaching his material, in the sense that whilst much of it is rooted in genuine reliable secure evidence, it is represented in such a way that it is designed to give it its maximum forensic impact. That involves a manipulation of material which is wholly unacceptable and, at very least, falls far below the standard that any Court is entitled to expect of any expert witness…
>
> Moreover, it is manifestly unfair to the mother, who it should be emphasised is battling to achieve the care of her children whilst trying to manage life with diagnosed PTSD. Ipso facto this is a case of unique gravity and importance. Common law principles of fairness and justice demand, as do Articles 6 & 8 of the ECHR, a process in which both the children and the parents can properly participate in a real sense which respects their autonomy.

Dr Harper's professional failure here compromised the fairness of the process for both Mother and children.[4]

## Costs and Invoicing

Unlike the public sector, work for the courts involves the clinician in generating invoices which have to be set out in specific ways, with the costs divided amongst the parties, although reports are sent to a specific individual to be distributed to the parties and lodged with the court. Fees are defined by the Legal Aid Agency (LAA) who may require supporting evidence for costs incurred.

I have found it useful to keep a running log of time spent on each aspect of the work involved in producing a report. This is started as soon as I begin to read the letter of instruction and background information in the bundle. The LAA provides a benchmark breakdown of the number of hours that they expect an expert to spend on specific aspects of the work. For psychological services it is as follows: reading five hours, attending adult five hours, attending child three hours, psychological adult testing three hours, psychological child testing 1.5 hours, observing contact (where appropriate) per parent three hours (Legal Aid Agency, 2025: 12).

The total hours specified by the LAA for carrying out psychological assessments are 25 hours for one person, 35 for two, 45 for three and an additional ten hours per additional person assessed. There are activities that are not listed in this LAA table, such as scoring and interpreting test results. The LAA also requires detailed documentation of travelling time and costs which I find helpful to log at the time the journeys are undertaken. This is an example of an activity log from my own practice (with fictitious post codes and dates) with thanks to Carter Brown for providing the original table (Table 5.1).

If journeys are completed on public transport the actual costs are logged instead of the mileage. Tickets and receipts need to be retained. Whilst taxi fares are payable, I have had these challenged but nevertheless accepted. This makes sense as journeys by public transport are sometimes almost impossible and would incur greater costs in time taken than the taxi fare itself. The LAA pays 45p a mile and £40 an hour for travel costs. Guidance rates for overnight stays when it is considered unreasonable to travel back and forth to home are £85.25 in London and £55.25 elsewhere.

At the time of writing, hourly rates for assessments for civil cases are £100.80 for child psychologists and £93.60 for psychologists. These rates have been extant since 2013. The rates for criminal proceedings were revised in 2022 to £116 for child psychologists and £107.64 for psychologists (Legal Aid Agency, 2025). There is no protected title of 'child psychologist'. If a child is assessed as one of the family members, the higher rate applies for the whole report, but the lower rate if only adults are assessed. If solicitors suggest charging different rates for proportions of a single report this should be rejected as LAA rates refer to the title of the assessor, not specific aspects of a single report. Rates for other disciplines are published by the LAA (2025).

Table 5.1 Example of an Activity Log

| Date | Activity | Prof. time | Travel time | Mileage |
|---|---|---|---|---|
| 13.4.25 | Writing report | ½ hour | | |
| 13.4.25 | Reading background | ¾ hour | | |
| 30.5.25 | Observation of contact | 1 hour | 1½ hours | B20 4JF to GR 4 1PF 65 miles |
| " | Meeting with father | 3¾ hours | 5 mins<br>1 hour | GR4 1PF to GR4 1PY 1 mile GR4 1PY to B20 4JF 65 miles |
| 31.5.25 | Meeting with mother | 3 hours | 3 hours | B20 4JF to GR4 1PY and return 130 miles |
| 7.6.25 | T/C support worker | 20 mins | | |
| " | Writing report | 1 hour | | |
| " | Scoring and interpreting test results | ¾ hour | | |
| 8.6.25 | T/C social worker | 20 mins | | |
| " | Writing report | 4 hours | | |
| 9.6.25 | " | 2 hours | | |
| " | T/C to leaving care worker | 20 mins | | |
| 11.6.25 | Writing report | 1¾ hours | | |
| 12.6.25 | " | 2 hours | | |
| " | T/C mother | 10 mins | | |
| " | Writing report | 1 hour | | |
| 16.6.25 | T/C advocate | 5 mins | | |
| 23.6.25 | T/C drug tests service | 15 mins | | |
| " | Reading and summarising medical records/ analysing drugs test results | 2 hours | | |
| 25.7.25 | Reading and summarising medical records | 3¼ hours | | |
| 26.7.25 | Reading additional documents | ¾ hours | | |
| 27.7.25 | Writing report | 1 hour | | |

Whilst these are the defined rates, the LAA specifies conditions under which fees may be exceeded. In order to invoice these, the additional rates or hours have to be agreed in advance in a process termed 'prior authority'. This is obtained through a request to the lead solicitor. Prior authority for higher hourly rates may be sought when the

> complexity of the material is such that an expert with a high level of seniority is required or the material is of such a specialised and unusual nature that only very few experts are available to provide the necessary evidence.
>
> (LAA, 2025: 6)

Sometimes the amount of material that the expert is required to read and consider can take many hours to digest. I have been provided with medical records that run into thousands of pages and in these cases it is reasonable to give an estimate of costs that exceeds LAA estimated hours. In such cases, prior authority has been sought and obtained.

Although this work often requires much administrative time in making appointments, following up requests for information, and consulting back and forth between various parties and representatives, the LAA will not pay for time spent on such tasks. I ask the referrer to provide contact details for the parties and any other individuals with whom I am likely to want to speak, such as social workers or staff who supervise family time, in order to minimise the hours spent in trying to locate these. Neither will the LAA pay for anything designated as therapy or intervention.

Whilst in public law all of the parties are publicly funded, this is not the case in private law, where increasingly, parents are acting in person. Even when they are represented, there is no guarantee that a parent will pay for an expert report, particularly if they find it is not to their liking.

When a request is made for an expert report, the letter of instruction will define the apportionment of costs. Most often, the costs are shared equally between the parties. In public law this will be between a number of parties, one of whom will be the child, and the local authority. In private law this may be shared equally between parties, but, if requested by the guardian, the expert fee may be apportioned entirely to the child's legal aid certificate. The LAA states that

> in public law cases an unequal apportionment of costs will not always be unusual. For example, a party may be an intervener in a case and have limited involvement and it would not be appropriate for them to bear an equal share of an expert report. Another example is where there may be several children involved in proceedings with different fathers and there is an issue only in relation to one child.
>
> (LAA, 2025: 7)

The process for submitting costs is to create an overarching invoice of the total fee and expenses, to divide this into the number of shares and present an invoice to each of the parties for their share. The LAA advises that it is sufficient to create a single invoice that contains all the information required including all of the parties' names. Each solicitor should submit a copy of the invoice. All invoices are sent with the report to the lead solicitor with a request to distribute to the parties and to lodge the report with the court. This is all very well in most instances, but solicitors, like any other profession, vary in the assiduousness with which they treat the invoices. My experience is that a very efficient system is necessary in order to follow up outstanding invoices at regular intervals. The follow-up usually needs to be with each of the parties' advocates, or directly if they are not represented. Hurdles are created by failure of the lead solicitor to distribute to the other parties, by solicitors moving firms in the middle of the process, possibly taking their cases with them, and by staff leaving all together.

A major potential hurdle is a parent's failure to pay. The cost of an expert report can be a major strain on already tight finances. I have agreed at times for a parent to pay in instalments over a number of months. A company for which I sometimes work pre-empts defaults by requesting payment in advance and refusing to release a report until payment is received. This can conflict with the agreed timescales for the report and may not be in the child's best interests. It is usually possible to tell from an initial reading of the bundle whether there may be issues with parents being able or willing to pay for their share of the report and this can be raised with the lead solicitor at the outset, before much time has been spent, and a strategy agreed.

The format of the invoice needs to include the name and address of the expert (PO Box or only the first half of the post code for confidentiality purposes), the name of the individual (and firm) to whom it is addressed, the date, case names and number, itemised costs summarised by type of activity, summary of travel costs and time, name of expert and bank details for payment. There are specialist firms for whom individual experts may prefer to work as self-employed associates. They will undertake the majority of the administrative tasks described in this section, deducting their fee for the service from the overall cost of the report. They may also offer additional services such as proofreading, training events and contact with a community of other experts. They can provide a regular supply of work suited to the skills and experience of each individual practitioner.

Some experts provide not only assessments for the court, but also therapeutic and other intervention services. Care needs to be taken to ensure that there is no conflict of interest. The Family Justice Council argues that the court should be extremely cautious when asked to consider assessment and treatment packages offered by the same or a linked provider. Guidance created in conjunction with the British Psychological Society states,

> This is particularly relevant when a psychologist expert recommends an intervention or therapy that they or an associate would benefit financially from delivering. Whilst this may be experienced as helpful and facilitative to the court, this would be a clear conflict of interest and threat to the independence of their expert evidence.
>
> (BPS, 2023: 17)

## Summary of Safeguards When Commencing Work as an Expert Witness

As I review this chapter I note that it is very heavy on administrative tasks, which may not be a motivating factor for people who like to work with people. Establishing functional systems and completing necessary administrative tasks at the outset, or on review, probably makes these tasks easier later on. Drawing on topics discussed in earlier chapters, this is a summary of what needs to be established and regularly reviewed in order to ensure safe practice:

- Register with an appropriate professional body such as HCPC
- Register with the ICO
- Obtain professional indemnity insurance
- Obtain an enhanced DBS certificate
- Set up regular supervision sessions
- Set up systems to record personal data, maintain its security, remove the data once it is no longer required and enable investigation of breaches
- Set up systems to enable invoicing and follow-up of unpaid bills
- Set up systems to keep track of initial enquiries with dates by which availability to carry out the assessment expires

---

### Key Points from this Chapter

- The confidentiality of information obtained during an assessment and the content of the expert's report are essential for the protection of children and young people whose details must not be disclosed. Breaking this proscription is punishable with a fine or imprisonment. For experts, this prohibition generally operates without a time limit, even after the proceedings conclude.
- Experts approached by a parent with a request for a report or an offer to show documents from family court proceedings should be directed to a legal representative for advice.
- In order to manage workloads and large quantities of data, comply with GDPR and schedule appointments and accounts, experts need to set up and regularly review effective and flexible systems.
- All personal data is subject to GDPR under the key principles that individuals should know what data is held about them, for what purposes, is accurate and kept securely only for as long as is necessary.
- Even if they are sole traders, experts need to register with the ICO, ensuring that they have secure systems in place for managing both paper and electronic records.
- GDPR rules need to be balanced against those covering retention and destruction of records. The courts specify the duration for which records about children need to be kept under the Family Law Act (1996) for private law proceedings, and under the Children Act for public law proceedings.

- SARs may be made under the Data Protection and Freedom of Information Acts for full disclosure of any personal data held, even if this may simultaneously be the personal data of another person.
- If parents or children request to make a recording of their session with the expert, my advice is to explore their reasons for this request and to agree, since they are in any case entitled to make such a record and may do so covertly.
- Experts need to keep a detailed time and costs log in order to facilitate invoicing and meet the requirements of the LAA.
- The hours and fees specified by the LAA may only be exceeded by request from the lead solicitor for prior authority which must be obtained before invoices are submitted.

## Notes

1  Re D (Minors) [1996] AC 593 at 603–604.
2  On appeal from: [2012] EWCA Civ 1084; [2012] EWCA Civ 1204.
3  Re T (Children: Non-Disclosure) [2024] EWCA Civ 241.
4  F (A Minor), Re England and Wales High Court (Family) Aug 18, 2016.

Chapter 6

# Giving Evidence

## Introduction

UK Government statistics (Department for Work and Pensions, 2024a) reported that in 2023 there were 2.4 million separated families in Great Britain and 3.8 million children in those separated families. Many will have parted company without recourse to the family court but 23% of parents with whom children reside, and 27% of non-resident parents have been reported to use the family courts, most often to try and resolve disputes about the arrangements for looking after the children (Dabhi et al., 2022). Earlier work suggested that about 11% of separating parents obtain court orders following a contested hearing (Office for National Statistics, 2008), but I could not locate data about how many of these involved an expert witness. Statistics relating to public law cases are harder to come by. A study by CAFCASS reported in Community Care (2013) suggested that the number of cases in which an expert was appointed had fallen to 80% since the imperative to use experts only when necessary had been introduced. But between 2013 and 2016/2017 there was a 33% rise in the number of experts instructed (Courts and Tribunals Judiciary, 2022). In August 2024, the president of the family law division, Sir Andrew McFarlane, reiterated the intention to 'reinvigorate' the Public Law Outline (PLO) in an attempt once more to reduce the unacceptable backlog of public law cases (Fouzder, 2024a). The PLO lays out the steps that a local authority needs to take when concerns about a child's well-being lead them to consider an application to the court for an order. In the most recent reiteration, the delay does not appear to have been attributed to the appointment of experts.

Although experts seem to be in demand, being invited to give evidence at a final hearing is a much more infrequent requirement. As this increases costs and may extend the timescale, attendance is only required if it is in the interests of justice (Part 25.9 of the Family Procedure Rules). This means that when experts are invited to provide oral evidence, there are likely to be significant areas of disagreement between the parties.

Practice Direction 25B, Paragraphs 10.1 and 10.2 set out the arrangements that must be made. When expert witnesses are to be called, areas of disagreement are likely to have been identified by the parties and their advocates, but it has not been

DOI: 10.4324/9781003453390-6

my experience that these are necessarily communicated to the expert in advance. Nevertheless, it is usually reasonably clear from the investigations undertaken where conflicts are likely to lie.

Sometimes, a finding of fact and final hearing take place during the one court session although this may take place over several days. On occasion, rather than be examined on the evidence in my report, I have been asked for my opinion on local authority plans in light of the findings of fact which are immutable. In one family matter, a mother was found, as a finding of fact, to have coached the child to fabricate an allegation of sexual abuse against the father. Under the mother's influence, the child had made the allegation, and as a result had been subjected to unnecessary intrusive medical examination and multiple occasions of having to repeat the fabrication to professionals. I was asked to comment on the local authority's plans to increase contact with the father whilst the child remained in the care of the mother. My opinion was that the plan was a good one except that the likelihood of its success was negligible. There had been many previous attempts to increase the father's contact without success. The difficulty in such scenarios is that whilst the expert has had time to reflect on the evidence and opinions in their report, they are presented at short notice with the outcome of the finding of fact hearing, and asked to give an opinion with minimal time for reflection. Much more typically, the hearing focuses on the content of the expert's report.

## Standards of Dress and Behaviour

Family courts follow strict procedural guidelines but can be seen as somewhat less formal than other courts. There are no wigs or robes; the standard of dress is smart with lawyers and advocates generally preferring suits. The people involved sit rather than stand, magistrates or judges speak directly to parents, and parents may or may not be represented by a lawyer. While there are no specific laws or penalties related to court etiquette and manners, it is generally expected that all participants in the court system, including judges, barristers, solicitors, and members of the public, behave in a professional and respectful manner. This includes standing up when the judge enters or leaves the courtroom and addressing them appropriately, depending on the level of the court. Senior judges in the high court are addressed as 'my lord' or 'my lady', circuit judges as 'your honour', and district judges, recorders and assistant recorders as 'madam' or 'sir'. The best advice is to follow what others call them, as the same judge may be addressed differently when acting in a different court. But in most cases I have not found it necessary to use a title at all.

## Reporting Restrictions

Up until 2009, family proceedings were generally held in private. Since 2009, accredited media representatives and, more recently, legal bloggers have been allowed to attend most family court hearings within strict reporting constraints. The Children, Schools and Families Act (2010) changed the law, allowing experts in individual cases to be named. The purpose of the changes was to increase transparency, accountability, and inspire greater public confidence in the functioning of the family court, whilst still protecting the privacy of the children and families involved. The drive for more openness is responsive to arguments that the removal of children from their parents' care is amongst the most draconian interventions of the state in family life. Campaigners argued that in the interests of justice, proceedings should be subject to public scrutiny.

A pilot scheme to extend the reporting rights of accredited journalists and legal bloggers into family courts began in England and Wales in 2023 in Cardiff, Carlisle and Leeds with the proviso that they continue to protect the anonymity of the families involved. It has since been extended to courts in other jurisdictions. Until this time, reporters could attend hearings but only publish details of what they observed if the judge agreed to vary the automatic reporting restrictions. In the pilot scheme, journalists were provided with key court documents. They were proscribed from publishing any details that could identify the family involved but were able to name local authorities and high-level individuals involved in a case, such as court-appointed experts. Lay parties were also permitted to talk to journalists and give interviews anonymously; under the previous law, they could be found in contempt of court for doing so.

## People Present in Court

Each party may be represented by a solicitor and/or barrister. Solicitors primarily engage in legal work outside of court, providing advice and preparing cases, whilst barristers specialise in courtroom advocacy. Some act in both capacities. In public law proceedings, a social worker, possibly their manager and their legal representatives will be present. In private law, if parents are representing themselves (acting in person) they may be accompanied by a lay representative who can speak for them or a McKenzie Friend, a person experienced in family court issues who can provide moral support. A McKenzie Friend can advise on different questions a litigant can ask and other legal points. They can take notes and organise essential documents.

If the case involves children, domestic abuse or forced marriage, people for whom English is not a first language may be provided with an interpreter, as may those who are deaf or otherwise struggle with hearing. It is the responsibility of the court to appoint interpreters who attend hearings. Solicitors may also arrange for an interpreter to be present specifically for their client in order that they are able accurately to take instructions.

Although it must be deemed necessary for upholding the court user's Article 6 Human Rights to a fair trial, intermediaries may be appointed for vulnerable witnesses including people with learning difficulties, people who have been subjects of domestic abuse, those who suffer from mental health problems, are under the age of 18 years or who have a physical impairment. The role of intermediaries is to assist vulnerable clients in understanding information and the court process, and in expressing their own thoughts and feelings.

A number of other people may be asked to give evidence on issues relevant to the decision-making process. They may be witnesses of fact, who may not give an opinion, but provide evidence about what they have observed first-hand, and expert witnesses who are invited to provide an opinion on matters likely to be beyond the knowledge and experience of the representing legal practitioners and the judge.

This means that the courtroom may be very full of people. Expert witnesses are normally present only if giving evidence, when there is a process of examination and cross-examination. At times the expert is invited to hear other evidence prior to giving their own. Having given their evidence they are released from the court and play no further part in the process. The court will not direct an expert to attend a hearing unless it is necessary to do so 'in the interests of justice' (Family Procedure Rules, 25.9). This is usually when there are significant areas of disagreement. Although quite frequently expert witnesses are not asked to attend court hearings, they need to be available to do so. Hearings are tightly timetabled from the outset and it is critical that the expert meets the filing (submission) date for their report in order not to cause delay in the proceedings. Court dates will usually be provided in good time and the expert's availability established. Court appearance may be in person or remote

## Preparation

Whilst it may seem obvious, in order to feel 'on top of' what is contained in my report, I read it thoroughly and carefully before the hearing as there is often a great deal to remember and it is not necessarily clear at this stage what the foci of the different advocates will be. In a text directed towards parents, Lucy Reed (2022: 65) gives good advice about how to prepare for attending court. These suggestions may seem obvious but bear repeating here. She advises to settle nerves by visiting the court building in advance so as not to worry about getting lost when attending on the actual day. It is prudent to arrive half an hour early and check in advance the location of the family court which may be in the County Court or Magistrates' Court building. The Crown Court is usually in a separate building and deals only with criminal matters. The lead solicitor can be a good source of information regarding the specific location and transport means to get there. I have found that dedicated parking is not usually available. Lucy Reed has made three YouTube videos entitled, 'The Family Court Without a Lawyer' intended to help parents in private law proceedings prepare for the experience of going to court. They usefully show examples of the family court and some of the procedures that take place. The third one in the series can be found at: https://www.youtube.com/watch?v=FdjYtbOVS-Q.

Entrances to the court building are staffed by security personnel and many have a security arch that scans visitors and their possessions. Bags are checked visually and security officers may use a handheld detector after visitors pass through the arch. Certain items are proscribed including weapons, sharp objects, glass, metal cutlery, syringes, toy guns, tools, ropes, chains, alcohol and liquids that are not drinks or prescription medicine. Visitors may be asked to take a sip of any drink they bring into the building.

Once in the building, the next task is to identify the location of the specific hearing as many cases will have been listed to be heard on the day. Court buildings typically house a number of different courts and consultation rooms. In some cases, there is an entrance desk where enquiries can be made. In addition to the names of the parties which, for the purposes of confidentiality may not be listed, it is necessary to know the case number. Sometimes, instead of a desk, reference needs to be made to a list posted on a wall somewhere near the entrance. Court buildings do not usually have maps to show locations of the different courts, so it may be necessary to locate them by navigating the building. There are usually court officials present who typically wear black gowns and will direct visitors to the correct court. It is important to let an official know that you have arrived and then I usually sit down outside the specific court and wait. I also turn off my mobile phone in case I fail to remember to do this after being invited to give evidence.

At this stage, the parties and their representatives may be in the building, but engaged in discussions in some of the consultation rooms, or may even be presenting a different case in a different courtroom on the same day. My experience is that someone will eventually come and introduce themselves and explain the stage that the hearing has reached. Final hearings can be listed to take place over several days, although experts are usually invited to appear early in the timetable. There is invariably some waiting involved before being requested to enter the courtroom. This time may be free, in which case I tend to use it to rehearse factors that I consider to be important and likely to be contested. On occasion, additional documents are handed over which need to be considered and on which the expert may be questioned, sometimes as to whether this has led to a change of opinion expressed in the assessment report. At other times, the expert is formally invited into discussions taking place outside the courtroom. It is wise to be circumspect about entering into any other conversations, particularly related to the case, and ensure that these are authorised. Sometimes parents will greet me and I will respond to them socially but not enter into discussions about the issues. When under oath, talking to anyone about the case is prohibited. Often experts will continue to be under oath during lunch and other breaks when it is not permitted to talk to anyone, including advocates or the parties. If so invited, it is appropriate politelyto refuse on the basis of being under oath. This is easy to forget, and on occasion I have had to be reminded.

## In Court

When invited into the courtroom, I usually take a seat at the back. When they enter the room, the judge sits at the front of the court facing the other benches where the parties and their representatives sit in groups. Sitting in front of the judge will be a member of court staff who is there to assist and carry out administrative duties. Close to the judge's bench and to one side of the court will be the witness box or table to which the expert will be called when their evidence is due to be heard. On

*Figure 6.1* Example of Family Court Layout. Courtesy of Napper Architects Ltd.

the box there is usually a cup, supply of water and a copy of the bundle. It is worth taking water with you in case of a dry mouth and because giving evidence can take a substantial period of time.

When the judge enters the court, everyone stands up and usually lowers their head, similarly when the judge departs. With little preamble experts are typically invited into the witness box and required to take an oath to tell the truth either on a religious book such as the bible, or by affirming. The court official will ask which is preferred and then tell the witness what to repeat after them or sometimes hand them a card to read out. Witnesses stand at the beginning but are usually invited to sit down whilst giving evidence.

The first lawyer to ask questions is the lead solicitor or their barrister. They will ask the witness to describe their title, qualifications and address. This does not need to be a long statement, but just a summary such as, 'I am a clinical psychologist based at...'. The lead solicitor then directs the expert to the location of their report/s in the bundle and asks for confirmation that a report was provided on a specific date, and for similar confirmation regarding any addendum reports that have been provided.

Although questions are being asked by the various parties' representatives or by the parties themselves if they are acting 'in person' without representation, answers are directed towards the judge, so it is appropriate to orient oneself in that direction. There is no requirement to look at the person asking the questions, and I find that it can help concentration to look at the bundle instead. The process can be disconcerting, and neophytes to the court may find it useful to practice these unusual interpersonal interactions. If attending remotely, responses will be impacted by what is being shown on screen.

Expert witnesses firstly give 'evidence in chief', responding to questions asked by the lead solicitor or their barrister, where they are asked to confirm issues on which they have reported or to clarify their opinion. Questions are then posed in cross-examination by the advocates of the other parties in turn, or in the case of litigants in person, by a lay family member. Before posing questions, each of the advocates will usually introduce themselves and explain for whom they are acting.

Because the process is primarily adversarial, each of the representatives will ask questions intended to further their client's position. Judges often ask helpful clarificatory questions, or seek explanations of technical terms. They may also ask challenging questions in order to test the robustness of the opinion and data on which it is based. Barristers vary in their questioning style, from calm and curious, to seemingly hostile and challenging. This is part of the drama of the courtroom but can be disconcerting when unfamiliar. If the opinion cannot be undermined, then the status of the expert may be the focus of attack.

> If you are cross-examined, do not take such probing personally. No one is on trial in a family court. Testing evidence is an important part of court procedure: it allows judges to establish the facts and reach a fair verdict quickly.
>
> (Major Family Law, 2022)

Often, a 'yes' or 'no' reply is sought but I find it advisable to qualify the answer at the beginning of the response, as many questions relating to children and families do not yield such definitive positions.

When asking questions, advocates often direct the expert to relevant pages in their report or other evidence in the bundle. Experts are expected to present their opinion based on a comprehensive understanding of the case from memory but can be prompted with such references to the bundle. It is not advised to take notes into court unless, in the interests of transparency and fairness, these have been made available to all of the parties in advance. Requests may be made for copies of academic papers on which the opinion is based, and whilst it may be advisable to make these available to all parties, if multiple copies are supplied, this is quite likely to constitute a violation of copyright. If it is critical to their argument, advocates could have sought a copy themselves in advance of the hearing. Similarly, unless experts are happy to have their informal notes and test results shared with all parties, it is unwise to take them into court, since what the expert references needs to be shared with all.

It is critical not to be rushed, to stay calm, polite and able to think. If more time is needed to consider a question, there is no harm in asking for it to be repeated or to ask for a few moments. It is also acceptable to ask for a moment to consult your report in order to be precise in your response. Particularly when very long questions are asked, the repeated question may differ from the original and is usually more concise and easier to remember. I am not aware of any proscription about taking notes if a question is particularly long or complex, although it may be difficult to anticipate this. Taking a drink of water before answering may also give more time to respond. The questions are helpfully regarded as opportunities to elaborate on the expert's opinions expressed in their report. This may occasionally mean answering a question linked to the one that was posed, whilst also responding to the original. If the advocate is unhappy with the answer, they can say so and ask their question again. I have never been interrupted when speaking, so it is possible to give a long answer that covers many aspects of the issue being interrogated and to make clear the nuances of the opinion.

Experts need to be particularly aware of the danger of straying from their areas of expertise. They should always be prepared to decline to give an opinion when this is appropriate, and to remind the lawyers or judge of the limits of their expertise and remit of instruction. I have sometimes been asked questions about a person, maybe assessed by someone else, who was not included in my instructions. It is important to be clear about this and not be drawn into giving an opinion about a person who was not a subject of the assessment.

Whilst it is not possible to provide information about specific questions that may be asked, lawyers will seek to further their client's position through a number of strategies which their questions aim to elaborate. If an advocate is fully prepared they will have examined the expert's report in detail, including interrogating their CV for evidence that they are remaining within their area of expertise. Questions about the following may be anticipated:

- Do the expert's qualifications and experience make them eligible to give an opinion on the questions in the LOI? This is where it will have been important to give consideration to suitability before accepting the instruction and/or when studying the letter of instruction in case it contains questions that are outside areas of expertise.
- Are the methods used to address the questions evidence-based and congruent with those used within the community of experts? Experts may be asked to

provide information about the validity, reliability and credibility of any tests or measures used, particularly if these are unusual or controversial within the discipline. I have rarely found this to be a focus of exploration, as experts are, by definition, experts in the subject matter. More often I have experienced attempts to undermine an opinion by referencing the results of a single measure, whereas this will have formed only one element in reaching the overall opinion, which needs to be made clear.

• Is the expert biased in any way? Do they have any other connections with the parties or their advocates? Do their publications show evidence of a bias in favour of a particular methodology or controversial diagnosis?

• Is the expert showing consistency in cross-examination with the content of their written report? Unless well prepared, it is possible to be led into making assertions in the witness box that are not warranted by the opinions expressed in the report. Changes of opinion in light of new evidence are welcomed by the court, but in the absence of such, credibility will be undermined by differences between what is written and what is said under cross-examination.

• Inconsistencies between opinions expressed in the evidence and in the expert's own published papers may similarly undermine credibility.

• Experts need to be familiar not only with their own report but also with the rest of the bundle. Questions may reference particular information from other sources which the expert has asserted that they have studied in reaching their position. Credibility will be undermined if the expert has missed some evidence, particularly when it has a significant bearing on the matters at hand.

It is at final hearings that expert witnesses may be invited to provide evidence. During the final hearing the judge assesses all of the evidence in conjunction with the welfare checklist to make a decision based on the best interests of the child in question. This will result in a judgment and the making (or not) of an order. Some judgments are published and these can be very helpful in clarifying aspects of law and how these pertain to specific families.

## Remote Hearings

Remote hearings have become commonplace since the Covid-19 pandemic, and the expert may be offered the choice of providing their evidence this way. A stable internet connection is required, and a quiet location in which to participate, allowing confidentiality to be maintained. Courts tend to use Microsoft Teams or Cloud Video Platform (CVP) for hosting these hearings. An invitation to join the hearing may be sent in advance with a request to test the platform, or may be sent moments before the hearing is due to commence. As the expert is often referred to specific pages of the bundle relating to the questions being asked, I have found it essential to have two devices in front of me, one for following the hearing and responding to questions, and the other to access court documents.

Whilst it could be argued that attending remotely is more cost-effective, and is more flexible with regard to the expert's other commitments, there can be issues with technology, and in-person interaction tends to be richer because it involves body language, the use of inflection and rubato: variations in pace and phrasing which often carry momentum. Conversely, it could be argued that this carries the advantage of reducing unintended bias arising from assumptions about appearance or mannerisms. Conventions and patterns of interpersonal interaction in the courtroom differ from those in other contexts, so remote communication could be seen as offering a better fit and may help people to feel less anxious or intimidated as they are in their own familiar surroundings.

The unintended experiment with remote hearings during the Covid-19 pandemic provided an opportunity to consider the role of physical courts in the family justice system and whether anything was lost by taking family court hearings into a virtual world (George and Marsh, 2024). These authors argued that taking instructions from clients who are vulnerable in some way (such as by virtue of limited English language skills, physical or cognitive impairments, or anxiety) demands great care and affects a large proportion of parents who find themselves in court.

> Barristers are also duty-bound by their regulator to 'try to avoid any unnecessary distress for [their lay] client' which is 'particularly important where [they] are dealing with a vulnerable [lay] client' (Bar Standards Board, Code of Conduct, gC41). The means open to a barrister to try to reduce a client's distress and offer support differ hugely depending on whether they are sitting next to their client or only in contact with them digitally.
>
> (George and Marsh, 2024: 62)

Whilst the family court's legal activity is to make orders, it is also seen as carrying out persuasive and conciliatory functions. It is not making administrative adjudications in the absence of humanitarian considerations, but is attempting to help people resolve their painful disputes through empathy, negotiation and invocation of its moral authority.

> In care proceedings, for example, it is common for judges to impress on parents the importance of engaging with the local authority while social workers conduct assessments. Do those messages carry the same impact if conveyed by telephone while the parent is at home or in their car? Similarly, it is common for judges to seek to steer a local authority; do social workers and their managers feel more able to 'disappoint' the judge if they are not physically in the judge's courtroom?
>
> (George and Marsh, 2024: 65)

These authors concluded that:

> While legal advice can still be given remotely – and instructions taken, negotiations had, evidence weighed, and decisions made – part of the 'magic' is

lost when physical proximity to one's lawyer, the 'other side', and the ultimate decision-maker is not part of the process. Face-to-face hearings keep interpersonal, human interactions at the core of the court process, which after all is primarily concerned with interpersonal relationships and their consequences, in the interests of children, human welfare and fairness. In doing so, physical family courts maintain the legitimacy of the court process, by making plain the moral authority of the family court to intrude into family life. Physical family courts are therefore an essential part of the family justice system.

(George and Marsh, 2024: 77)

In private law, if a parent fails to comply with a child arrangements order, the court can order unpaid work, a fine or imprison them for contempt of court (M v M, 2005),[1] but this is a rare occurrence. In research by Trinder et al. (2013), the family court overwhelmingly took a non-punitive problem-solving approach, seeking compliance through punitive measures in only 9% of enforcement proceedings. Lady Hale (1998: 133) pointed out that 'the law is not good at enforcing personal relationships'. The court's functions in assisting parents to understand why their child is being removed from their care, or impressing upon them the unbearable position of the child between parents at war with each other seem to me to be critical central purposes. As well as everything else there is to remember when giving evidence, it behoves us as experts to respond in ways that acknowledge the harrowing experiences that such parents have had to bear. Sometimes parents have begun to sob when hearing what I have said in the witness box, and I think that the more I can frame it in non-blaming and compassionate terms, the better.

---

## Key Points from this Chapter

- Experts are only required to give evidence at final hearings if it is in the interests of justice and there are outstanding areas of disagreement.
- The primary focus of questioning of the expert is usually the opinions expressed in their report.
- Findings of fact hearings may take place during the same hearing as the final hearing, in which case questions may be addressed to the expert's opinion in light of the findings which are immutable.
- The family court is not overly formal, but standards of dress are smart and all participants are expected to behave in a polite and respectful manner.
- Changes to reporting restrictions mean that experts may now be named in the press.
- Present in court will be the parties, their advocates and others such as interpreters and/or intermediaries where these are required.
- Preparation is key. Experts need to arrive at the correct court in good time and be fully conversant with the content of their report and the contents of the bundle.

- When invited to give evidence, the expert will be required to take an oath to tell the truth. When under oath, which may continue through lunch and other breaks, the case should not be discussed with anyone.
- Following the oath, the expert is asked to give their name, qualifications and professional address.
- Examination in chief follows, usually undertaken by the lead solicitor or their barrister, followed by cross-examination by the other parties or their advocates.
- Although the parties ask the questions, answers are directed towards the judge.
- Solicitors and barristers employ different questioning styles which vary from calm and considered to assertive and challenging.
- Questioning takes place in the context of an adversarial approach intended to challenge the opinion, evidence on which it is based, and establish whether the expert is qualified to give their opinion on the specific matter.
- It is critical to remain within one's area of expertise.
- Remote hearings have highlighted the multiple purposes of in-person hearings in keeping interpersonal human interactions at the heart of the court process. This is best kept in mind when framing evidence and expressing opinions.

## Note

1  *M v M* [2005] EWCA Civ 1722.

Chapter 7

# Domestic Abuse and Alienation

This chapter is the first of those exploring special issues arising in the family court, some of which I have found particularly challenging. They may be the subject of debate and differing opinion. Some are raised in referrals or letters of instruction, but may not become apparent until after the assessment has begun. If, when they arise, they are outside the expert's current experience, the lead solicitor needs to be alerted in the event that it would be advisable to appoint a different expert.

I have focused here on domestic abuse and 'alienation' (a child's reluctance or refusal to communicate or spend time with a parent) or 'alienating behaviours' as these often feature together in private proceedings. Whilst in my clinical experience of working in Children and Young People's Mental Health Services (CYPMHS) domestic abuse has not infrequently been raised as an issue, this is not so for the more contentious label of 'parental alienation'. Statistics concerning children referred to CYPMHS (NHS England, 2023) do not track referrals based on either category but in 2023 over 827,000 children in England and Wales are estimated to have been present in a household where partner abuse occurred (Foundations, 2023a). This was calculated by multiplying the number of domestic abuse cases recorded by the Office for National Statistics Labour Force Survey by the average number of dependent children per household.

Some specialist services such as the Attachment and Trauma team at Great Ormond Street Children's Hospital may accept referrals highlighting 'parental alienation' but it is unlikely to come to the attention of mainstream NHS services other than in the more general category of children's emotional needs. Although the category 'parental alienation' appears largely to be confined to the family court, practitioners working in CYPMHS will have significant expertise in working with children experiencing emotional difficulties.

Both of these issues are culturally situated which means that they are understood within a context in which values change and the pendulum swings under the political and social influences of the times. Participants in the family court, including experts, advocates and judges, need to keep abreast of these changes in order to

DOI: 10.4324/9781003453390-7

reflect contemporary values. In the case below from the 1980s, the judge was seen on appeal as failing to have done so. In his judgment, he stated:

> My concern about this occasion centres on the idea that the mother did nothing physically to stop the father. In particular, given the position in which intercourse was occurring, because the mother was not in any sense pinned down on this occasion, but could easily, physically, have made life harder for the father. She did not do so. I do not find that the father was in any way on this occasion so physically forcing her as to cause her not to be able to take preventative measures, nor, in fact, is that case alleged. Following the event, as I have already said, the mother took no immediate action to report the matter to the police, or indeed to anyone else. Her description, of course, does not indicate that the circumstances were such that she might in any way have been thought wise to seek medical advice.[1]

The appeal judge commented:

> This judgment is flawed. This is a senior judge, a Designated Family Judge, a leadership judge in the Family Court, expressing a view that, in his judgment, it is not only permissible but also acceptable for penetration to continue after the complainant has said no (by asking the perpetrator to stop) but also that a complainant must and should physically resist penetration, in order to establish a lack of consent. This would place the responsibility for establishing consent or lack thereof firmly and solely with the complainant or potential victim.
>
> The judge in the instant case should have considered the likelihood that the Appellant had submitted to sexual intercourse; he singularly and comprehensively failed to do so instead employing obsolescent concepts concerning the issue of consent.

## Domestic Abuse

### Domestic Abuse Statistics

The Crime Survey for England and Wales estimated that 6.6% of women and 3.0% of men aged 16 years or over experienced domestic abuse in 2024. This equates to an estimated 2.3 million adults (1.6 million women and 712,000 men) (Office for National Statistics (ONS), 2024). The ONS defines domestic abuse as 'any incidence of threatening behaviour, violence or abuse (psychological, physical, sexual, financial or emotional) between adults, aged 16 years and over, who are or have been intimate partners or family members, regardless of gender or sexuality'.

- Approximately one in five (20.5%) people aged 16 years and over (9.9 million) had experienced domestic abuse at some point since the age of 16 years.
- A higher percentage of people aged 16 years and over experienced domestic abuse by a partner or ex-partner (3.2%) than by a family member (1.9%) in the last year.

- Women were disproportionately represented among victims of domestic abuse-related crimes, as in previous years, with 72.5% of all victims being female in the last year.
- The Crown Prosecution Service (CPS) recorded 51,183 domestic abuse-related prosecutions in the last year. Of these, 38,776 resulted in convictions and 12,407 resulted in non-convictions.
- Of the cases that did not result in a conviction 6,005 were a result of complainant-related issues (including victim retractions, victim non-attendance at trial or where the evidence of the complainant did not support the case) and 1,949 were because of acquittals.

(Office for National Statistics, 2024)

The Criminal Injuries Helpline (2023) reported that 48.4% of women and 48.8% of men who contacted the helpline reported facing emotional aggression from a partner, making it the predominant form of intimate partner violence (IPV). From the same source, 58.9% of men who called the charity ManKind helpline had never spoken to anyone about the abuse and 64% would not have called the helpline had it not been anonymous. Mankind created a YouTube video of an individual case with two scenes depicting the man as perpetrator and an equivalent with the woman as perpetrator. Passers-by reacted in very different ways to the two scenarios (https://www.youtube.com/watch?v=u3PgH86OyEM), threatening to call the police in one instance and laughing in the other.

There are what may appear to be conflicting views about the interpretation of this data. Some argue that the stigma of reporting such experiences leads to understatement of the extent of male victimisation, others that it is a gendered crime which is deeply rooted in societal inequality between men and women (Women's Aid, 2024b). It can be argued that both arise from social constructs that reinforce traditional gender roles and relationships. Because IPV has been recognised as a gendered issue, disproportionately affecting women (World Health Organization, 2024), much of what is currently known about IPV comes from samples of women and, in particular, cisgender heterosexual women in relationships with men (Scott-Storey et al., 2022).

Political, personal and professional agendas have the potential to be misleading and harmful. What the data does portray is how widespread is the experience of domestic abuse, much of which is between intimate partners, and that it can affect anyone, irrespective of age, gender, sexuality, ethnicity or other social factors.

## The Changing Conception of Domestic Abuse in the Family Court

Over the course of my lifetime there have been significant changes to the understanding and public conception of domestic abuse which have been, and continue to be, reflected in modifications to approaches within the family court. The Domestic Violence and Matrimonial Homes Act 1976 (DVMA, 1976) introduced the concept of 'domestic violence' which allowed the court to make an injunction restraining a party in the relationship from using violence against the applicant, or a child living with the applicant. A power of arrest could be attached to the injunction only if the judge was satisfied that actual bodily harm had been caused (The National Archives, undated a).

By the 1980s domestic violence was regarded within the family court as an issue exclusively between the adults, not relevant to questions concerning the welfare of children. It was only later that this became a consideration of the court in a seminal judgment made in 2000 of four court of appeal cases involving expert testimony providing evidence of the consequences for children of exposure to 'domestic violence' between parents and other partners (re: L and Ors, 2000).[2] In each of the cases, direct contact between a father and his children had been denied against a background of domestic violence between the spouses or partners. In each case the appeal court upheld the original judgment. The four cases included one in which the extent of the domestic abuse had led to a custodial sentence for the father who showed no remorse. In another, the father successfully had set about addressing his behaviour but the child continued to resist contact despite the mother's encouragement. In particular, the case of the H children in L & Ors described above illustrates how complicated such decisions can be. The mother of the two children in question had parents of English and Pakistani heritage. They divorced and she was brought up by her mother and step-father in a relaxed household until, following the death of her step-father, her birth father returned when she was aged 11. Subsequently her life was led in a circumscribed Muslim tradition. As an adult she experienced an arranged marriage with a man who adhered to strict Islamic law and with whom she resided in Germany where the two children were born.

She alleged violence by the father which appears to have been the result of her refusal to continue to conform to the strict requirements of her faith. The centre of the conflict in the last few months of cohabitation was her failure to keep her head covered. Actual violence was minor but the threats of violence were extreme. The father made repeated threats to kill her if she did not wear a headscarf. He threatened to cut her up into little pieces and put her down the lavatory. He twice threatened her with a knife and once that he would cut her up with an electric saw... She fled with the children to a women's refuge in Germany and from there to England... She went to great lengths to prevent the father from finding out her whereabouts. She changed her name and the names of the children...

The mother is no longer a practising Muslim. The children have been brought up... outside the Muslim faith in a Westernised style of life and have not seen their father since they left Germany... The father discovered their address... and applied for defined contact and a prohibited steps order. The mother applied for residence and that there should be no contact to the father... The judge made findings as to the violence alleged by the mother. He found that she was obviously frightened in describing the threats of violence and that, despite some discrepancies, she was telling the truth. He said "I have come to the conclusion, therefore, that the father did threaten violence in the way the mother describes and she is very frightened of him, as the welfare officer confirms. I am also satisfied that she fears, on reasonable grounds that he may attempt to remove the children from the jurisdiction."

(BAILII, 2000)

The appeal judges called for evidence from two child psychiatrists, Dr Claire Sturge and Dr Danya Glaser. They identified a number of risks of direct contact where domestic abuse pertains, including escalating the climate of conflict, resulting in a tug of loyalty and a sense of responsibility which would affect the relationships of children with both parents. There might be direct abusive experiences, including emotional abuse by denigration of a child or a child's other carer. There might be continuation of dominant or bullying relationships involving fear, bribes or emotional blackmail, which would serve to undermine a child's sense of stability and continuity. They nevertheless reiterated the advantages to children of sustaining relationships with both parents. Showing remorse and addressing abusive behaviours were seen as necessary if the non-resident parent were fully to support a child and play a part in undoing the harm caused. They suggested creative ways of encouraging reluctant children to meet with their other parent safely such as using a one-way screen with an interviewer discussing the matter with the parent on the other side.

The judgment concluded that such allegations ought to be addressed by the court at the earliest opportunity and findings of fact made so as to establish the truth or otherwise of the allegations and then to consider the effect of these findings on decisions regarding contact.

There should be no presumption against contact simply because domestic violence is alleged or proved; domestic violence is not to be elevated to some special category; it is one highly material factor amongst many which may offset the assumption in favour of contact when the difficult balancing exercise is carried out by the judge applying the welfare principle and the welfare check list.

(BAILII, 2000: no page numbers)

However, Lord Justice Thorpe commented that:

Whilst the mother's attachments to Islam did not match the father's, she is half-Pakistani and was brought up and married as a Moslem. Whatever her reasons, her rejection of Islam was achieved by unheralded flight and the subsequent endeavour to obliterate the traces of flight. Had she been childless the principal person affected would have been her husband. But to include the children was to deprive them of their father, their settled home, their culture and their heritage. The decision to replace that with an environment and culture of Anglicised agnosticism and assimilation was done, of course without reference to the father, but more seriously without reference to any independent power or authority that might have investigated the proposal or the fait accompli to ensure that what met her needs was compatible with the welfare of her children...

But this was a mother whose determination to assimilate had extended to replacing the children's Moslem names and to including pork on the family menu. Where the unilateral action of one parent has severed children's links with their home, the other parent, and the culture and tradition of their birth then the first task of the family justice system is to investigate the possibility of restoring the children's loss to the extent that is realistic in the circumstances obtaining at the date of judgment. If they cannot be returned to their former home and to shared life with their parents then the least the court will ordinarily ensure is that the loss is mitigated by productive contact with the lost parent and by conditions and requirements to ensure that the parent providing the primary home does not use the opportunity to obliterate the culture and religion into which they were born and which she herself affirmed at marriage.

(BAILII, 2000)

Lord Justice Thorpe argued that it was not only Muslims who might conclude that the mother had impoverished the children's experience of childhood by choices that she had made for herself.

He regarded the outcome of the proceedings as quite atypical and only justified by the exceptional facts and circumstances. He pointed to the much-publicised situations in which English mothers had experienced the total loss of their children by paternal abduction into an Islamic society. In those circumstances he argued that a minimum expectation of the religious courts in Islamic society would be to ensure generous contact with the mother within the Islamic state. He was concerned that the applicant was left as bereft as might any Christian applicant be to a Sharia court.

I have assessed families with elements in common with this case. The parents are from different cultural and ethnic backgrounds and have contrasting views about the upbringing of children. Parents flee, taking children with them and failing to reveal their whereabouts. The children are confused and have to make rapid adjustments to changes of circumstance, removal from their home, school, extended family and friends. Parents hold such contrasting views that it is difficult to see how they can come together. They are unable to recall the love that they held for each other when the relationship began. Almost all of the behaviours of each of the ex-partners come to be seen as efforts to exercise control and in the midst of this, the children struggle.

Since this decision, there have been further developments in the understanding and construction of domestic abuse in the family court (Re: H-N and Others).[3] Four different women were striving to reverse decisions made by the family courts concerning their allegations of rape and coercive control. Their appeal was heard in 2021 by Lord Justice MacFarlane, Lady Justice King and Lord Justice Holroyde who addressed whether the focus in some cases should be on a pattern of behaviour rather than on specific incidents of domestic abuse. They judged that abusive, coercive and controlling behaviour is likely to have a cumulative impact upon its victims which would not be identified simply by separate and isolated consideration of individual incidents through a Scott Schedule (a table which clearly sets out the allegations in dispute). The Harm Panel (Ministry of Justice, 2020) had reached a similar conclusion that 'reducing a long and complicated history of abuse into neat and discrete descriptions is challenging and can itself result in minimisation of the abuse' (Chapter 5.4), and that by limiting the number of allegations the court is not exposed to 'more subtle and persistent patterns of behaviour' (Chapter 7.5.1).

At that time, it was thought that at least 40% (around 22,000) of private law children cases involved allegations of domestic abuse. In such cases, the court needs to consider the impact that abuse has had on both the child and parent and thereafter determine what orders are to be made for the future protection and welfare of parent and child in light of those findings. 'Depending upon the circumstances, such orders may substantially restrict, or even close down, the continuing relationship between the abusive parent and their child' (Judiciary, 2021b: Para 4, no page numbers).

Practice Direction 12J (PD12J) makes clear the range of behaviours that are encompassed in the term 'domestic abuse' which refers to a pattern of acts or incidents (Judiciary, 2021b: Para 26):

> 'domestic abuse' includes any incident or pattern of incidents of controlling, coercive or threatening behaviour, violence or abuse between those aged 16 or over who are or have been intimate partners or family members regardless of gender or sexuality. This can encompass, but is not limited to, psychological, physical, sexual, financial, or emotional abuse. Domestic abuse also includes culturally specific forms of abuse including, but not limited to, forced marriage, honour-based violence, dowry-related abuse and transnational marriage abandonment;
>
> 'abandonment' refers to the practice whereby a husband in England or Wales deliberately abandons or 'strands' his foreign national wife abroad, usually without financial resources, in order to prevent her from asserting matrimonial and/or residence rights [and/or rights in relation to childcare] in England and Wales. It may involve children who are either abandoned with or separated from, their mother;
>
> 'coercive behaviour' means an act or a pattern of acts of assault, threats, humiliation and intimidation or other abuse that is used to harm, punish, or frighten the victim; 'controlling behaviour' means an act or pattern of acts designed to make a person subordinate and/or dependent by isolating them from sources of support, exploiting their resources and capacities for personal gain, depriving them of the means needed for independence, resistance and escape and regulating their everyday behaviour.

In my experience, people who are subject to such treatment in their adult partnerships have sometimes experienced trauma during their formative years. Their already-fragile self-esteem is easily undermined and the court process itself may be too daunting to contemplate or may serve to re-traumatise those who have been subject to abusive behaviour, a finding made by Nicole Jacobs, the Domestic Abuse Commissioner (2023). In her study of a survey of 138 legal practitioners, 80% felt that the family courts were likely to re-traumatise those who had experienced domestic abuse. The following is typical of accounts given to expert witnesses when assessing families in which domestic abuse has featured:

> When I met David he was so kind and I felt really lucky. He was working and things were going well but he started spending more time with his mates down the pub and when he came home he would have a go at me. I was walking on eggshells. He was swearing and going ballistic at me, 'You fucking slag, you're a whore, shagging loads of guys.' He'd walk out and then call the next day over and over saying sorry and that he would get help. I'd get 50 messages a day. He would call Bethany and I realised he was just trying to see if there was anyone else in the background. I asked social services for help and it ended up going to court and I felt as if I had lost all my parental rights. I thought that I was making slow progress but it just evaporated. I couldn't show that I was angry or upset. I knew it would be held against me as more evidence that I was incapable of looking after Bethany. I still have days when I feel very very sad and dissociate. I close the curtains and I can't go out. My head is spinning, I sink into myself and when I look at the clock, 4 hours may have passed. I ask myself what's the point but I don't want to do what my mother did and take an overdose or cut myself. Some days I feel really broken and don't think I can ever live a normal life.

This vulnerability is now addressed through the Domestic Abuse Act (2021) and recognised by the family court which may make participation directives that allow for the provision of special measures ensuring that the contribution of vulnerable witnesses is not diminished. The Act introduced a ban on direct questioning of a subject of domestic abuse by the perpetrator. Special measures may also include screens in the courtroom to prevent a party from being seen by another, separate entrances and exits in the court building, separate waiting areas and/or waiting rooms and/or attending court via video link instead of in person.

In response to changing conceptions of domestic abuse PD12J has undergone a number of revisions. The 2024 version (Justice, 2024) states:

> domestic abuse having otherwise been established, the court should apply the individual matters in the welfare checklist with reference to the domestic abuse which has occurred and any expert risk assessment obtained. In particular, the court should in every case consider any harm which the child as a victim of domestic abuse, and the parent with whom the child is living, has suffered as a consequence of that domestic abuse; and which the child and the parent with whom the child is living is at risk of suffering, if a child arrangements order is

made. The court should make an order for contact only if it is satisfied that the physical and emotional safety of the child and the parent with whom the child is living can, as far as possible, be secured before, during and after contact; and that the parent with whom the child is living will not be subjected to further domestic abuse by the other parent.

### The Impact of Domestic Abuse on Children

Studies described by Barnett (2020) have reported that between 75 and 95% of children living in abusive households witness or overhear abusive incidents directly. Even if children are not present they are typically aware of the aftermath of the abuse and distorted inter-partner relationships, communications and behaviours. Callaghan and Alexander (2015) found that children have a sophisticated understanding of control dynamics and subtle controlling behaviours. There is a plethora of research summarised by Barnett that reports both short- and long-term negative sequelae for children and young people living with domestic abuse, be it openly physical and verbal or more subtly coercive and controlling.

The courts have been subject to criticism that they have been slow to respond to societal changes in the conception of domestic abuse, continuing to privilege sustaining the child's relationship with both parents over ensuring safety of the child and resident parent (Walsh, 2023).

Changing perspectives are reflected in a practice policy published by CAFCASS (2024). The policy listed 22 directives that needed to be followed by CAFCASS officers when parents described experiences of domestic abuse. These included a prescription to use a person's own words in describing abuse, counselling against 'rape' being re-interpreted as 'non-consensual sex' or 'unwanted sexual attention'. Where a parent is being investigated by the police for a sexual offence, has a conviction for a sexual offence and/or has served a prison sentence for a sexual offence, children not spending time with that parent should be a starting assumption. The policy cautioned that in trauma-informed practice, there is no such thing as 'historical' abuse since the impact is ongoing and dismissing it in this way contributes to the trauma. Practitioners were urged to understand that feelings of anxiety and fear and related behaviour and actions may be a trauma response to the experience of abuse rather than being defined as mental ill-health unless clinically diagnosed. The practice policy published in 2024 was subsequently replaced by a version which has removed all reference to 'starting points' and broadened the section on sexual abuse to include domestic abuse of all kinds. The new policy directive put the onus back onto the CAFCASS Officer to assess the individual case before them with reference to Section 1(2A) of the Children Act 1989 and the relevant paragraphs of PD12J, rather than relying on a generalised 'starting point' (CAFCASS, 2025b).

Whilst these policy decisions are critical in protecting parents and children who have been subject to domestic abuse, I do have serious reservations about an assumption of no contact, particularly as once terminated, it is typically very difficult to reinstate. Most important are the child's safety and the option to sustain relationships that are of benefit to them. Because a parent has such a conviction, does it mean that they cannot provide input of benefit to their children? Do not such circumstances deserve thorough investigation and risk assessment rather than a blanket one-size-fits-all response?

December 2024 saw the introduction of new Domestic Abuse Protection Orders and Domestic Abuse Protection Notices in trial areas (Chaloner, 2024). These enable recognition of the courage needed by victims of domestic abuse to disclose what is happening. Domestic Abuse Protection Notices can be issued by the police immediately following any incident of abuse, as an interim measure whilst longer term protection is put in place. The new orders have no time restrictions and breaching them is punishable by up to five years in prison. Friends and family are able to apply for these orders on behalf of the victim, enabling them to avoid the daunting process of seeking an order themselves. Requirements to attend behaviour change programmes can be mandated for protagonists. Family courts can also impose tagging on perpetrators.

Sophie Francis-Cansfield, Head of Policy at Women's Aid (2024a) noted that if family and friends are to apply for these orders, this needs to be in collaboration with the victim/survivor in order that they develop and sustain their autonomy and voice. She also cautioned against discrimination arising from over-surveillance, which disproportionately impacts Black and Minoritised communities.

I am heartened that domestic abuse, including in its more subtle forms, is beginning to be addressed with the seriousness and understanding of its long-term and insidious impacts that it deserves. As a psychologist, I am also interested in its origins. What leads people to engage in such behaviours? The literature focused on such understanding is sparse, although it might help in preventing and addressing such a widespread phenomenon.

## The Role of Domestic Abuse in Contested Private Law Proceedings

A literature review by Adrienne Barnett (2020) for the Ministry of Justice, indicated

> that the prevalence of allegations of domestic abuse in private law children cases is considerably higher than in the general population, with findings and estimates ranging from 49% to 62%. In the vast majority of cases, the alleged or proven perpetrator was the father (CAFCASS and Women's Aid, 2017; Harding and Newnham, 2015).
>
> (Barnett, 2020: 20)

In some cases of warring ex-partners, and these may be more likely to be referred to an expert witness, allegations of domestic abuse take central place on the battleground alongside counter-allegations of 'parental alienation', and the role of victim *may* be acted. One mother's self-described strengths were 'accuracy, challenging injustice, truthfulness and obstinance' (Child Protection Resource, undated) but on advice from her barrister, she enacted the part he told her that the judge needed to see – 'an exhausted, working mum who has been driven to seek to need the court's help to deal with an utterly uncooperative parent'. She likened the processes of the family court to playing a game of chess.

In other cases, fathers have been found to attempt to manipulate the court:[4]

> [T]he evidence before the Court leads to the clear conclusion that the father has sought consistently, systematically and falsely to manipulate the mother, the children, professionals and the Court into believing that he is the victim of domestic abuse perpetrated by the mother. His pernicious actions alone have resulted in both children rejecting him. Both children are now refusing a relationship with him for reasons that are justifiable. The children have both aligned themselves fully with their mother, with whom they are living, by way of a normal and justifiable response to the father's negative attitudes, communications and beliefs that have sought to denigrate, demean, vilify, malign, ridicule and dismiss the mother, persistently seeking to convey false beliefs about her.
> (The National Archives, 2024b: Para 168)

More invidious is the engagement of children in a parent's combat strategy. In Doncaster MBC v Haigh, Tune and X,[5] the local authority appealed to the court to put the facts of what had begun as private law proceedings into the public domain in order to counteract misleading information disseminated by the mother and others. The mother, being unhappy with a court hearing of the original dispute, made allegations that the father had sexually assaulted the child. At a fact-finding hearing the judge concluded that the child had not been abused and that she had been coached into a disclosure by her mother. The mother's views about the alleged abuse then hardened to become a certainty which she expressed dogmatically and in public. The judge concluded that the mother had continued to manipulate the child's feelings and that it was contrary to the child's best interest to live with her (Family Law Week, 2011).

These three cases illustrate the lengths to which parents may go when engaged in a legal battle over arrangements for the care of the children, being capable of losing a perspective that privileges the well-being of the children. I have assessed families where fact finding hearings have established that a parent has required a child to make false allegations to numerous professionals and undergone unnecessary intrusive medical examinations, told their partner's employer falsehoods that threaten their continued livelihood, propagated misinformation to the children's school and other parents, and/or has published such extensive details of the case that the child is readily identifiable.

## Legal Representation in Private Law Cases

In April 2013 the removal, by The Legal Aid, Sentencing and Punishment of Offenders Act 2012 (LASPO), of legal aid for many private law cases resulted in a significant increase in parents representing themselves (litigants in person). Cases in which both parents represented themselves increased from14% in March 2013 to 40% in June 2024. Over the same timescale the percentage of cases where both parties had legal representation decreased from 41 to 19% (Ministry of Justice, 2024). 'Most children live with their mothers after separation and spend time with their fathers, a gendered pattern reflected in court users: most applications are from fathers wishing to spend time with their children' (Cusworth et al., 2021: 9).

LASPO was intended to encourage litigants to resolve their private family law issues out of court and to increase the uptake of mediation. Between 2012–2013 and 2016–2017 the number of cases fell by only 2% and the uptake of mediation fell significantly as previously 80% of clients were referred by their legal representative (Organ and Sigafoos, 2018).

## Gender Distribution in Relation to Legal Aid on the Basis of Domestic Abuse

To understand the gender distribution of legal aid relating to domestic abuse in private law proceedings, I have searched the literature in vain. I cannot find statistics that record the proportion of cases by gender of parents who apply for legal aid on the basis of being subject to domestic abuse, let alone take account of contemporary non-binary understandings of gender. Barnett (2020) was unable to identify any studies which explored victim/survivors' experiences of fathering in the context of domestic abuse whilst a wide range of studies investigated victim/survivors' experiences of mothering in the context of domestic abuse. The UK government recognises that the majority of victims/survivors are women, dealing with male victims/survivors under the umbrella of the Tackling Violence Against Women and Girls (VAWG) Strategy, 2021 and Domestic Abuse Plan, 2022 (Home Office, 2023). Given the prevalence of applications to the family court from fathers, and official statistics evidencing the experience of domestic abuse by people of all genders, it has puzzled me as to why I have not encountered any fathers supported by legal aid on these grounds.

Unravelling allegations and counter-allegations in assessments for the family court is something that experts need to tackle, bearing in mind that it will be the judge who determines the facts of the matter.

## Pathfinder Courts

In March 2022 family courts in Dorset and North Wales began piloting a new approach to private law proceedings, particularly those involving reports of domestic abuse. In 2024 this was extended to SE Wales and Birmingham, and in

2025 to West Yorkshire and all of Wales. Pathfinder courts take an investigative problem-solving approach, and there is a presumption that children will have the opportunity to be seen and heard at an early stage. Whilst prioritising the safety and well-being of family members, parents are encouraged to focus on the needs of the children rather than on each other. Where there are concerns about domestic abuse, families are referred to specialist agencies for a risk assessment and ongoing support. CAFCASS and CAFCASS Cymru are at the core of the investigation, producing a Child Impact Report which involves coordinating information from local authorities, the police and support services at an early stage in order to clarify the issues and avoid, where possible, the need to resolve the matter through the court. The government provides couples with a £500 voucher to assist them in reaching agreement about the care of the children through mediation. The Ministry of Justice (2025b) reported that this project has led to the completion of cases sooner and halved the number waiting to be heard. In North Wales the time to taken for a case to progress through the system reduced on average from 29 to 18 weeks. Survivors and perpetrators have fed back that the process is much less brutal and unkind than standard adversarial family law proceedings. More details of the approach can be found in Herbert (2025).

The next section addresses the topic of alienation, usually known as 'parental alienation' although it is the child who becomes alienated from a parent, sometimes by a deliberately alienating other parent, but for many other reasons as well. In my experience 'domestic abuse' and 'parental alienation' are often referenced in the same referral, along with other vocabulary such as 'implacable hostility', all of which need unravelling in order to understand what is going on in *this* family. In a previous publication (Scaife, 2024) I asked the question, 'Is the increase in allegations of domestic abuse fuelling reciprocal accusations of parental alienation or implacable hostility?' I am not the only one to ask this question.

## Alienation

In the course of my assessments in private law proceedings, I have encountered many children who have shown reluctance, and often abject refusal, to communicate or spend time with one of their parents, invariably the one that they do not live with. Sometimes this reluctance attracts the controversial term 'parental alienation'. The term originated in publications by Richard Gardner in the USA as a syndrome, 'parental alienation syndrome' which is not recognised as a medical condition and not accepted in the family court.

But some children do become alienated from one of their parents after separation or divorce, and it is these parents who may appeal to the family court for resolution. It is not uncommon for such parents to have been unable to resolve conflicts during the course of their relationship and, not surprisingly, on separation their failure to resolve differences of opinion continues. Whether or not parents are overtly hostile towards each other and/or outwardly critical of the other parent, children cannot but be aware of the disharmony within the relationship. In my opinion it is difficult for anyone to live in a conflict zone without being drawn into taking a 'side'. This is particularly the case for children who have not yet gained sufficient maturity in the development of mental processes to be able to weigh up and balance their experiences or to manage the attendant tension and anxiety. Externalising (behavioural) and internalising (emotional) adjustment problems often arise (Rhoades (2008) reported in van Eldik et al., 2020). These meta-analytic studies report that the negative impacts of parental conflict on children's functioning endure over time. The UK government also cites a strong body of evidence that damaging inter-parental conflict can put children at more risk of having problems with school and learning, negative peer relationships, physical health problems, smoking and substance misuse, mental health and wellbeing challenges. The risks can also have an effect on long-term life outcomes such as poor future relationships, reduced academic attainment, lower employability, heightened interpersonal violence, depression and anxiety (Department for Work and Pensions, 2021).

When children attempt to manage their anxiety by aligning with one parent and rejecting the other this may be with or without any explicit action on the part of either to draw them in. The psychological process is sometimes known as 'splitting', in which children tend to view their world in an 'all or nothing' way. Such polarised thinking helps them to make sense of the storm that they are in (Rudkin, 2024). This may become entrenched in their efforts to maintain psychological stability and cohesion (Kernberg (1975) reported in Gould et al., 1996). Alienation from a parent is then the result, arising explicitly from the interpersonal conflict, and not necessarily from parental actions designed to achieve this end. In this process, children's attention tends to be drawn to experiences that confirm negative feelings towards one parent and warmth towards the other. Their confidence in the parent from whom they are estranged decreases. Alienation is thus appropriately understood as a process not a condition, and the problem to be addressed is the parental conflict that underlies it. Unfortunately, I have often found it very difficult to assist disputing parents in understanding the harm that the conflict itself is causing to the children, as they are often locked in battle, convinced, and attempting to convince all around them that the fault lies with the other parent, either as a result of domestic abuse or 'parental alienation'.

My analyses suggest that there are many additional reasons why children resist contact, many of which do not warrant the term 'alienation'. It has been argued that there is a need to distinguish alienation from 'justifiable estrangement' or 'Appropriate Justified Reaction' (Family Justice Council, 2024) arising from abuse or impaired parenting. In my experience a diagnostic or other label is unnecessary and unhelpful, as a description of the dynamics in individual families has been sufficient to inform judgments, and the dynamics are typically much more complex than a simple 'either-or' position can reflect. This was also a finding in research by Kelly and Johnston (2001: 251):

> These reasons include resistance rooted in normal developmental processes (e.g., normal separation anxieties in the very young child), resistance rooted primarily in the high-conflict marriage and divorce (e.g., fear or inability to cope

with the high-conflict transition), resistance in response to a parent's parenting style (e.g., rigidity, anger, or insensitivity to the child), resistance arising from the child's concern about an emotionally fragile custodial parent (e.g., fear of leaving this parent alone), and resistance arising from the remarriage of a parent (e.g., behaviors of the parent or stepparent that alter willingness to visit).

This statement is unlikely to generate much controversy, but when reluctance to see a parent is labelled as 'parental alienation' it appears to engender strident and hostile reactions from both supporters and opponents, whose views may be taken up by pressure groups and the press. It even divides barristers. As children resort to the defence of 'splitting', so it appears that one parent must be labelled 'bad' and the other 'good' in accounts of such families in the press. The alignment of the media changes with the current zeitgeist.

The Guardian (14 July 2016) described 'parental alienation' as 'a phenomenon where one parent poisons their child against the other parent... Distinct from the all-too-common acrimony between divorcing parents, the syndrome is an internationally recognised phenomenon.' In contrast, five years later Charlotte Proudman in the Guardian (21 July 2021) under the heading of 'The discredited legal tactic that's putting abused UK children in danger' stated that 'The dangerous label of parental alienation is now the single biggest threat to the credibility of victims of domestic abuse, and to the voices of children. It gives validation, power and control to perpetrators.' In Family Law Week dated 8 March 2024, Howe et al. ask 'Alienation and Domestic Abuse-What on Earth is Going On?' They state:

Do parents seek to alienate children from their other parent? Is parental alienation a real issue for the court to address in family law proceedings in England and Wales? Our answer is yes – it exists and is deeply harmful to children and families...Anyone undermining a child's relationship with a parent for their own ends is as responsible for domestic abuse as those who emotionally and physically undermine an adult partner in an intimate relationship. It is just a different form of abuse.

(Howe et al., 2024: no page numbers)

A UK study (Hine et al., 2024) of parents who had separated from a partner with whom they had at least one child reported that around four in ten people (39.2%) felt their ex-partner had tried to turn their child against them and when asked about specific behaviours this increased to 59.1%. The survey also reported that those affected by parental alienating behaviours showed greater signs of serious mental stress, such as PTSD symptoms, depression and suicidal thoughts. Although participants did not report many manifestations of alienation in children the authors concluded that this did not mean that children were not impacted by these behaviours.

Although some parents deliberately coach children to reject a parent, alienation more often arises as a result of the manner in which the wider family interacts without any explicit intent on the part of the parent. Janet Johnston and Matthew Sullivan (2020) argued that a single-factor model that explains a child's alienation from a parent as arising from the behaviour of a vindictive parent is overly simplistic and misleading.

Sometimes a child's resistance and hostility towards a parent has been influenced by deliberate actions of the other. What that parent does could be termed alienating behaviours and these can be described without recourse to the label of 'parental alienation'. In such cases, the Family Justice Council (2024) suggests that the term 'Alienating Behaviours' is capitalised. Another way to describe a parent's attitudes and actions that impact the quality of the other parent's relationship – whether positively or negatively – is with the term 'gate-keeping'. Attitudes and actions that discourage the relationship are classified as 'restrictive gate-keeping' (Austin et al., 2013). Such behaviours include withholding information about the child's school, medical appointments, or activities from the other parent; disparaging the other parent in front of the child; removing any reminders of the relationship between the child and other parent from the home; blocking the receipt of gifts, cards, letters or other communications; deliberately scheduling activities during the other parent's contact time; refusing to answer phone calls or messages; making false accusations of abuse or neglect against the other parent; or coercing the child into making such allegations. 'Facilitative gatekeeping is defined as proactive, constructive attitudes and behaviors that are supportive of the other parent-child relationship' (Austin et al., 2013: 488). Gate-keeping can be conceptualised as on a continuum of attitudes and behaviour, rather than being understood in categorical terms. Whilst restrictive attitudes and behaviours may be expressed by both resident and/or non-resident parents, typically children align with the parent with whom they currently live.

Restrictive gate-keeping behaviours can be adaptive, particularly where there are evidenced concerns about the other parent's drug or alcohol misuse, quality of parenting knowledge and skills, history of offending or domestic abuse. These factors do not necessarily preclude the child from having a relationship with that parent; rather, the context needs to ensure the child's safety.

Children subjected to a parent's maladaptive restrictive gate-keeping may develop unremitting negativity towards the targeted parent, a poor rationale for the negativity, strong assertions that they have come to their views independently, use of mimicked 'adult' phrases, the description of scenarios of which they could not have memories or for which they are unable to provide any detail, and extension of negativity to the targeted parent's extended family and friendship network. Parents with whom the child resides assure me that the child is being encouraged to enjoy contact but through their behaviour endorses the child's refusal. At its worst, I have found it very distressing to experience children squirming in extreme discomfort having been pressured to fabricate an incident involving the other parent. I have found such positions to be intractable.

When a child is hostile towards and refusing to see a parent with whom they previously experienced a warm and affectionate relationship, I ask the targeted parent to provide me with photographs of happy times spent together, with a view to observing the child's responses to these events. Reactions vary from an outright refusal to look at the material to enthusiastic and excited commentary about what was happening, even though a few minutes earlier the child may have been telling me how much they hated this parent. I have had a child look at a photo that included them and both parents, still to deny that the rejected parent had been present.

There is evidence that the impact on children of being subject to negative manipulation of their relationship with a non-resident parent is lifelong. In a phone-in on BBC Radio Five (BBC, 2009), people in late middle age spoke in tears about the continuing impact of their parents' battles. A number of qualitative studies of adults who were impacted in childhood (Baker, 2005; Bentley and Matthewson, 2020; Verhaar et al., 2022) reported consequent mental health issues including anxiety, panic attacks, depression, emotion dysregulation, attention problems, post-traumatic stress disorder, disassociation, eating disorders, suicidal ideation, self-harm and substance misuse. Low self-esteem was common:

> One woman in the current study reported gluing her ears to the side of her head so that they looked less like the "sticking out ears" of her father. In general, the participants said that they could not distinguish between the parent's hatred of the other parent and the parent's hatred for those parts of the child that were like the targeted parent. As children they naturally concluded that the alienating parent hated them as well. Because the alienation campaign against the targeted parent started when the child was relatively young (for many it went as far back as they could remember) the negative self-feelings seemed to be incorporated into the very core of their self-identity and sense of self-worth.
>
> (Baker, 2005: 294)

> When you have somebody like my mother who is constantly sitting there telling you this person who is your dad and is a part of you is such a bad person and he is going to do all these terrible things and it is like if he is so bad and I am a part of him then doesn't that sort of make me like that too?
>
> (Baker, 2005: 294)

Some respondents harboured varying degrees of anger towards the parent who had turned them against the other and some forgot about their relationship with the other parent as it had become so distant:

> I blame my mother and fuck you, fuck you, you fucked it for a fucking long time, you fucked it love. And there's a part of me that has such major resentment, major, you know…if she wasn't so old, if I could drag her into court to sue for that, I would do it.
>
> (Verhaar et al., 2022: 9)

> I stopped talking about Mum and all the memories and all the good things and stuff, so all the good things were just put away, they were just stored, completely stored, it was like as if, it got to the point I almost couldn't remember them, just so distant'.
>
> (Bentley and Matthewson, 2020: 516)

When children have been subjected to the unremitting negativity of a parent, ascertaining their wishes and feelings can be very tricky. Particularly as they grow older, children can be very guarded and may have learned that above all they need to protect the main carer from distress. In my experience, when an expert witness provides an entirely plausible analysis of the dynamics, parents usually struggle to accept any other account than their own. In a study by Trinder et al. (2005), applications for court orders often appeared to exacerbate rather than resolve parental disputes.

But it is not the expert who makes judgments about the allegations and counter-allegations; that is the province of the judge. 'There is now clear authority that the decision about whether or not a child has been alienated is a question of fact to be resolved by the court, and not a diagnosis to be offered by a psychologist' (Howe et al., 2024: no page numbers). They went on to say:

> We should need no reminding of the fundamental principles which apply during a fact-finding exercise in the Family Court – the burden of proof lies with the party making the allegations, the standard of proof is the balance of probabilities, findings must be based on evidence not suspicions or speculation (*Re A* [2011] EWCA Civ 12) and, crucially, for the purposes of this article, the court must take into account all the evidence and consider each piece of evidence in the context of all the other evidence (*Re T* [2004] EWCA Civ 558). These principles apply whether the court is considering allegations of domestic abuse or alienating behaviours, whether the allegations come from the mother or from the father.

In light of the conflicting opinions regarding the counter allegations of domestic abuse and parental alienation, the Family Justice Council (2024) has issued guidance to assist the courts when allegations of parental alienation are made:

> This guidance will therefore refer to a child's unexplained 'reluctance, resistance and refusal' to spend time with a parent (RRR)…wherever possible. However, because it addresses calls from across the sector for practical guidance on how allegations of Alienating Behaviours are responded to, this term will also be used for necessary clarity where psychological manipulation by a parent has resulted in RRR.
> This guidance acknowledges that where found the harm of Alienating Behaviours to a child can be significant and enduring, akin to other forms of emotional/psychological child abuse. Alienating Behaviours range in intensity and their impact on children, but these harms can be far reaching. They can affect a child's emotional, social and psychological development. Severed relationships and growing up with a false narrative can also have a harmful impact on a child's identity, self-worth and sense of safety in the world.
>
> (Family Justice Council, 2024: 6)

The Council helpfully defines terms to be used when issues of alienation are brought before the court:

- Attachment, affinity and alignment (AAA) – reasons why children may favour one parent over another, or reject a parent, which are typical emotional responses to parenting experiences and not the result of psychological manipulation by a parent.
- Appropriate justified rejection (AJR) – situation where a child's rejection of a parent is an understandable response to that parent's behaviour towards the child and/or the other parent.
- Alienating Behaviours (AB) – psychologically manipulative behaviours, intended or otherwise, by a parent towards a child which have resulted in the child's reluctance, resistance or refusal to spend time with the other parent. *[This term is capitalised throughout the guidance to refer to this definition]*
- Protective behaviours (PB) – behaviours by a parent towards a child in order to protect the child from exposure to abuse by the other parent, or from suffering harm (or greater harm) as a consequence of the other parent's abuse.
- Reluctance, resistance or refusal (RRR) – behaviours by a child concerning their relationship with, or spending time with, a parent, which may have a variety of potential causes.

(Family Justice Council, 2024: 4)

The Council argues that

In light of their respective prevalence, and the relative harm to children and adult survivors, allegations of domestic abuse and 'parental alienation' cannot be equated. The risk, relevance and weight attached to 'parental alienation' and domestic abuse should not automatically be considered equal.

(Family Justice Council, 2024: 9)

Rather than take their complaints to court, parents are now encouraged to engage in alternative forms of dispute resolution (ADR). These include mediation, arbitration and collaborative practice. But these are costly and beyond the means of many parents. In England and Wales, before making an application to court, parents are required to attend a Mediation Information and Assessment Meeting (MIAM) although this does not invariably take place. In England, CAFCASS has developed a four-session Positive Co-Parenting Programme for parents within proceedings which encourages them to place themselves in their children's shoes and to improve communication between them. A systematic review (Templer et al., 2017) concluded that changes to residential arrangements in favour of the targeted parent, specialised family therapy, and a coordinated approach from legal practitioners and therapists could be effective in restoring family relationships and functioning.

The longer the duration of a pattern of non-contact, the more difficult it becomes to reintroduce parent and child. In a case heard Re D by Munby J the previous two years of litigation were described by him as, 'an exercise in futility…The system has failed him… I feel desperately, desperately sorry for him. I am very sad that the system is as it is'.[6]

## Implications for Expert Witnesses

High-conflict parental separations taken to the family court have been amongst the most challenging and distressing of any with which I have worked over many years. Professionals can be drawn into the support of one parent or the other. Parents are often angry and closed to any other perspective on the issues. Meanwhile the children are harmed by the emotional cauldron in which they flounder. No matter how much they may try to explain that it is the conflict with which they struggle, sometimes appealing for help from teachers and other adults, their anguish often falls on deaf parental ears.

No matter how sensitively experts express their opinions, they may also become the butt of parental rage and hostility. But when such families appeal to the family court for assistance, experts can sometimes act as a catalyst for change. Some parents are able to change their minds and actions. Joyful reunions do take place and this is what makes the work worthwhile.

---

### Key Points from this Chapter

- Private law proceedings typically take place in a context of parental hostility towards and anger with the child's other parent.
- Proceedings in private law are often characterised by allegations of domestic abuse and/or 'parental alienation'.
- Perspectives on both of these topics are socially and politically situated and change over time.
- Social and political groups align themselves in relation to these two issues which are reflected in the media, often with dramatic headlines.
- Parents' descriptions of behaviours categorised under these headings are necessarily perspectival and motivation arising from the hostile environment may play a part in their construction.
- In these contests, children tend to suffer, may attempt to manage tension and anxiety by polarised thinking, may be engaged as allies by one parent, and sometimes are required to support that parent at all costs.
- These are the most intractable cases that experts are likely to encounter. Experts may also become the butt of parental hostility and anger themselves.

## Notes

1  JH-v-MF [2020] EWHC 86 (Fam).
2  L & Ors (children), Re [2000] EWCA Civ 194 (19 June 2000).
3  H-N And Others (Children) (Domestic Abuse: Finding of Fact Hearings) (Rev 2) [2021] EWCA Civ 448 (30 March 2021).
4  GB (Parental Alienation: Factual Findings), Re [2024] EWFC 75 (B).
5  Doncaster MBC v Haigh, Tune and X [2011] EWHC B16 (Fam).
6  F v M in the matter of D [2004] EWHC 727 (Fam).

Chapter 8

# Vulnerable Families

## Introduction

In a study by Ireland et al. (2024), two data sets were linked in order to explore the characteristics of mothers in first care proceedings. Hospital admission records for England were used in one of the studies, and in the other, records from mental health services provided by the South London and Maudsley (SLaM) NHS Trust which serves four local authorities. The study aimed to propose preventive interventions that might foster a reduction in the burgeoning number of public law proceedings described by MacAlister (2022).

The records for England indicated that compared with peers, health problems occurred disproportionately in the mothers who were involved care proceedings after a first birth: any health problem (39.1% among those involved in proceedings vs 13.8% not involved); mental health (18.4% vs 4.7%); intellectual disability (5.5% vs 1.2%); physical or sensory disability (15.6% vs 1.4%); chronic health condition (13.5% vs 7.9%), and adversity-related admission (related to self-harm, drug or alcohol misuse or violence; 15.6% vs 1.4%). In the SLaM Trust data, the majority of mothers involved in care proceedings (54.2%) had been diagnosed with a mental illness requiring secondary or tertiary mental health services, more than one-third had two or more diagnoses (34.0%) and one-fifth (22.1%) had substance use problems.

This chapter explores the legal implications of some of these factors as they contribute to the vulnerability of parents in family proceedings. They have been addressed in a previous publication (Scaife, 2024) in terms of adapting approaches when conducting assessments for the family court. Here, the focus is on the construction of them in a legal context which can be a rapidly-changing landscape.

## Practice Direction 3AA

The Family Procedure rules (FPR) Part 3A place a duty on the court to consider whether the quality of evidence given by a party or witness is likely to be diminished by reason of vulnerability and, if so, whether it is necessary to make one or more participation directions. Practice direction 3AA (Justice, 2023b) sets out the procedure and practice to be followed to achieve a fair hearing involving vulnerable

DOI: 10.4324/9781003453390-8

witnesses by providing for appropriate measures to be put in place. It is advised that this should be accomplished as early as possible within the proceedings at a 'ground rules hearing' defining the nature of the support that will be provided and participation directions implemented regarding conduct of the advocates and the parents in respect of the evidence being given. When needs become apparent at a later stage in the proceedings, these ground rules may need to be revisited.

FPR 3.8 provides for the following participation directions: prevention of a party or witness from seeing another party or witness; allowing the giving of evidence by live link; providing for use of a device to help communication; providing for a party or witness to participate in proceedings with the assistance of an intermediary; providing for a party or witness to be questioned in court with the assistance of an intermediary; or do anything else which is set out in Practice Direction 3AA.

### Vulnerable Witness Toolkits

The Advocate's Gateway (TAG) (2024) was founded in 2012 and provides free access to practical, evidence-based guidance on communicating with vulnerable witnesses in the form of toolkits. These address general issues and principles and provide specific advice in relation to particular impairments including autism, hearing impairment, learning disabilities, 'hidden' disabilities such as dyslexia, dyspraxia and ADHD, mental health difficulties and trauma. Toolkit 2 describes general principles for questioning a vulnerable witness including people with communication needs. Toolkit 13 is focused specifically on vulnerable witnesses in the family court.

Toolkit 2 points out that vulnerable people are not a homogeneous group and not everyone with a disability will automatically feel vulnerable or would wish to be regarded as such. Parents who appear to be robust or resistant to assistance may fear that disclosure of a learning disability or mental health history could negatively impact assessment of their parenting. Such vulnerabilities may be hidden or masked out of fear, embarrassment or feelings of shame.

Advocates are advised that for vulnerable people it is almost always necessary to take regular breaks with sufficient time to explain what has happened and what is about to happen ('explanation time') in addition to time for a proper break ('rest time'). The toolkits give extensive advice about appropriate questioning, tone and body language, pace, the use of non-verbal communication aids, awareness of loss of concentration, use of clear and simple language, avoidance of metaphors and non-literal language, avoidance of abstract concepts, keeping questions short, awareness of a tendency towards compliance, avoidance of questions containing one or more negatives and closed questions.

### Intermediaries

Intermediaries are impartial communication specialists, whose primary responsibility is to facilitate communication between all parties, ensuring that vulnerable people are able to understand and participate in the proceedings. This includes making an assessment and reporting to the court, orally, in writing, or both, about the communication needs of the vulnerable person, and the steps that need to be taken to meet those needs (Blatt, 2024). Vulnerability is not enough to argue the case for appointment of an intermediary; it must be shown that no other special measures can be put in place sufficiently to alleviate the communication difficulties. The test is not centred on what is in the child's best interests, but on what will ensure a fair process.

Whilst they may assist parents to participate more generally in proceedings, the primary function of an intermediary is limited to the process of explaining questions and communicating answers to the court. Even when an intermediary is necessary, it is rare for them to be appointed for the entirety of the hearing. Consideration has to be given to alternative measures to enable participation in the hearing (Courts and Tribunals Judiciary, 2025a). 'The decision to appoint an intermediary is always one for the judge. The conclusions of either a cognitive assessment and/or an intermediary assessment, whilst informative, are not definitive on this issue' (Courts and Tribunals Judiciary, 2025a: no page numbers). Sir Andrew McFarlane, in the advice in the paragraph above, was at pains to argue that only towards the far end of the spectrum of vulnerability will there be people for whom an intermediary is necessary. When they are appointed:

> Their presence ensures that the court can consider the needs and viewpoints of all parties, fostering a more inclusive and compassionate legal environment. Intermediaries play a crucial role in reducing barriers to access justice. By assisting individuals with communication challenges or specific needs, they contribute to a more level playing field in family court proceedings. This commitment to inclusivity ensures that all individuals, regardless of their abilities or disabilities, can actively participate in and understand the process their family is going through. In family court proceedings, where emotions run high and the stakes are deeply personal, the role of the intermediaries is indispensable. They act as bridges, fostering effective communication, providing support to vulnerable individuals, and contributing to a more inclusive legal environment.
>
> (Gowen, 2025: no page numbers)

Being assessed can, at the best of times, be nerve-wracking. Appearing in the family court is an unfamiliar experience which is daunting to anyone unused to the procedures and language. Despite the legislation, parents with disabilities in particular are likely to struggle with the whole process and feel that professionals are 'against' them. Parents' accounts illustrate the variability of their experience of the extent to which helpful adjustments were made, their participation assured, and a fair process achieved (Hunter et al., 2024)

> I would be physically shaking, like, you could see it. I would be terrified. And I'm not even scared to admit that I was… I had no idea what was going on…I

didn't feel like I had a say. I just had to sit there, say my name, and listen to what they were saying. I wasn't allowed to talk.

(Erin)

You have to explain things to me in layman's terms, because I'm not used to all those big words, and that is the biggest struggle when it's in court and you get all those letters and stuff through. I don't understand none of it. I did not understand what the words meant.

(Hannah)

[The judge was] Pointing at my legal team, to ask, 'Does he understand?' [lawyer] turns around and asks me, 'Do you understand? I'm like, 'Yeah, I understand,' I'm nodding my head. Because obviously we're not allowed to speak in family court unless we're obviously instructed by the judge to speak.

(David)

You feel lonely anyway and so vulnerable. And you are alone... And there are all these people that are high up in the world doing these things... Like I said, if you've got, like me, dyslexia and stuff, you don't really understand exactly what they're saying and what's going on. You're just in this bubble. I just expected I would go all through that and get my children back, because I never done nothing wrong. So, obviously, at the end to say, 'Oh, you're not having your children back'... it just ripped me apart.

(Amber)

They [social services] tried to adopt my first [child]... and [the judge] wouldn't go for it. She actually fought for the SGO [Special Guardianship Order]. And she let me have breaks through the process. She let me take my time when being questioned, and certain things I didn't understand – when the local authority was- because they go at you, and they shout at you. They make you nervous, and things.

(Nancy)

She phones me regularly, emails regularly, sends over documents quite fast. Helps me break down all the legal paraphrases, as I don't really understand some parts of the legal framework. Always makes sure that she's half an hour, 45 minutes, early before court, so she can talk to me about X, Y and Z. And then we're ready to go, we're ready to fight together, fight my corner.

(David)

## Disability

In the UK, a definition of disability is enshrined in the Equality Act, 2010: 'A person is considered to have a disability if they have a physical or mental impairment that has 'substantial' and 'long term' negative effects on their ability to do normal daily activities' (Department for Work and Pensions, 2024b: no page numbers). This definition is wide-ranging and may include visual impairments, hearing loss, mental health problems, medical conditions including HIV infection, cancer, multiple sclerosis, progressive conditions, and 'hidden' disabilities that involve impaired communication, information processing speeds and interpretation of social situations. Disabled people are regarded as vulnerable witnesses and therefore entitled to assistance with communication and understanding of the proceedings in order to ensure that justice is served. Dependency on non-prescribed drugs or alcohol is not included although these parents are also likely to be vulnerable.

The Family Resources Survey (2024) reported that for working-age adults, the proportion of disabled people has risen gradually from 16% in 2012/2013 to 23% in 2022/2023, the most recent survey year at the time of writing, an increase of seven percentage points, resulting in a total of 16.1 million working-age adults with a disability. Of these, 47% reported a mental health impairment, the most prevalent category among this age group, closely followed by a mobility impairment, at 41%. The third most likely impairment type was to do with stamina, breathing or fatigue, at 34%. Those reporting a learning disability amounted to 16% of the working-age total. The totals amount to greater than 100% as a result of people reporting more than one type of impairment. The 2022 survey reported that since 2013 the number of disabled people with mental health difficulties had increased by around 1.1 million (Powell and Francis-Devine, 2022) and was thus responsible for the largest proportion of the increase.

In addition to laws concerning the welfare of children in the Children Acts (1989, 2004) and the Children and Families Act (2014), there is a raft of additional legislation that applies to disabled parents. Article 8 of the Human Rights Act (1998) requires that all steps be taken to facilitate the maintenance or reunification of children and their parents and to enjoy family life without interference from public authorities. Articles 3 and 14 encompass the right to freedom from discrimination and degrading treatment. Research data suggest that disabled people are more likely than non-disabled people to report feeling unsafe when walking alone and to worry about physical attack and theft. In England and Wales, disability is reported to be the second most common motivator for hate crime incidents (Hackett et al., 2020). Over half of disabled respondents in a UK survey reported worrying about being insulted or harassed in public places, and a similar proportion reported being mistreated because of their disability (Allen et al., 2021).

The Disability Discrimination Act (1995) made it unlawful to discriminate against disabled people in connection with employment, the provision of goods, facilities and services or the disposal or management of premises. It continues to apply in Northern Ireland but in the rest of the UK has been replaced by the Equality Act (2010) in which disability is one of the protected characteristics along with other personal attributes, such as age, gender, gender reassignment, marriage and civil partnership, pregnancy and maternity, 'race', religion or belief, sex, or sexual orientation, which cannot be used as a basis for discrimination under the law. The

Act prohibits direct and indirect discrimination, harassment and victimisation. It also prohibits discrimination in relation to something arising from a person's disability and creates a duty to make reasonable adjustments for disabled people in various scenarios, including at work, in education and in the provision of services and public functions. Public authorities are subject to a Public Sector Equality Duty which means they must 'have due regard' to equality considerations when exercising public functions (Pyper and Uwazuruike, 2025).

The Mental Capacity Act (2005) applies in England and Wales, providing a framework to protect and empower people who lack the capacity to make certain decisions for themselves. The Act makes a presumption of capacity unless assessed otherwise and asserts that people should be supported to make decisions themselves. Decisions should be based on a person's best interests and the first consideration should be the least restrictive option. Advice on conducting assessments of capacity is provided by the BPS (2019b).

The Care Act 2014 states that in all their social care work and decision-making local authorities must take into account a person's wellbeing. This Act shifted the focus away from determining what services are to be provided to how an individual's needs can best be met. Local authorities are required to treat disabled people with respect, to consider their holistic needs, to protect them from abuse or neglect, to encourage autonomous decision-making and support involvement in society through work, education and leisure activities.

Despite the extensive legislation there is evidence to suggest that its aims and purposes are not always achieved. A study of disability in Iceland (Sigurjónsdóttir and Rice, 2018) reported a surprising preponderance of strange or even absurd evidence presented by practitioners purporting to show neglectful caring by parents with intellectual disabilities (ID):

This included such things as the observation there was a cat on the bed in a parent's home, with no explanation as to its significance or relevance for an investigation of parenting neglect. Or that there were fingerprint smudges on a window pane, which one would normally expect in a household with children. Or a comment from an anonymous source that a child's teeth were broken and in poor shape, yet a report from a healthcare worker from the same time period made no such observation. Or a comment that there was a dresser in a child's bedroom full of small toys that the child had been rooting through, with no further explanation of its import and leaving the reader adrift as to why this was problematic and what it had to do with the matter at hand. Or the observation that there was a 'Russian lightbulb' in the parent's living room, which in Iceland refers to a naked lightbulb without a cover; we later discovered that this 'Russian lightbulb' was merely part of a lighting system in place when the parent moved in and never used. We could easily fill an entire article with these kinds of mundane, seemingly unimportant, sometimes contradictory and most certainly odd observations that we routinely encountered in our project data. We initially left this kind of 'evidence' of parenting neglect unanalysed, reserving it for humorous anecdotes to be used in classrooms and conference presentations about the difficulties that parents with ID in Iceland faced during their encounters with the child protection system. However, as we continued to find more examples of this kind of material we began to ponder its significance.

(Sigurjónsdóttir and Rice, 2018: 68)

The authors went on to describe a case example of a couple with mild learning disabilities who lost their child to the care system as a result of a lack of professional knowledge, prejudiced attitudes and a failure of inter-agency cooperation.

In another example (Re: C),[1] a local authority in the UK was adjudged to have failed to deal equitably with hearing-impaired parents. The mother was of Turkish Cypriot origin. She was said to have a low level of cognitive functioning and a degree of speech and hearing impairment, although she could communicate in English without the need of an interpreter. The father originated from the Angolan Portuguese community but came to the UK when he was seven and was profoundly deaf. He was educated to degree level and communicated in British Sign Language (BSL). Staff at the hospital where their child was born immediately identified deficits in the couple's day-to-day care of the infant. When the child was six days old social workers, communicating as best they could, sought consent under Section 20 of the Children Act 1989 for the child to be accommodated by the local authority. No interpreter was present and the mother was the only person who could explain to the father what was going on. When the parents later withdrew their consent, the local authority sought a care order which was granted but later successfully appealed. The appeal judge made clear that 'translation', as of one verbal language to another, was insufficient to ensure a fair hearing, and that 'interpretation' was necessary:

Communication between a profoundly deaf individual and professionals for the purpose of assessment and court proceedings involves a sophisticated, and to a degree bespoke, understanding of both the process of such communication and the level and character of the deaf person's comprehension of the issues which those in the hearing population simply take as commonplace. For a profoundly deaf person, the "commonplace" may not be readily understood or accessible simply because of their inability to be exposed to ordinary communication in the course of their everyday life. What is required is expert and insightful analysis and support from a suitably qualified professional… "Interpretation is not merely a matter of word for sign equivalence; cultural brokerage is required which is far more effective if the hearing professional has some knowledge and experience of the Deaf community."

(Conn, 2014)

Deaf and hearing-impaired parents may use a range of methods to aid communication including BSL, lip reading, Sign Supported English (SSE), the combination of lip patterns with hand gestures (cued speech), finger spelling, tactile signing, sign systems such as Makaton or Signalong, and written text. In a hearing before HHJ Nasser Patel, it was adjudged that the local authority had failed to make adequate adjustments or provide appropriate support for hearing-impaired parents.[2] The expert psychologist who had assessed the parents advised that lip-reading is incredibly difficult. Estimates typically report up to around 30–40% effectiveness but there is evidence that at a sentence level people accurately identify as little as 12% of what they see (Altieri et al., 2011). The expert drew attention to a text that she recommended professionals working with the deaf community are advised to read which highlights the implications of using only oral communication with a deaf parent (Austen and Holmes, 2021). HHJ Patel concluded that

> simply allowing a parent who says they can lip read to indeed attempt to lip read and rely on oral communication in the context of professionals from social care engaging with them (which is likely to be anxiety invoking) massively risks the exchanges, the delivery of information and/or intervention to cause change, being at best ineffective, or at worst, a complete waste of time.

## Learning Disabilities

'People with learning disabilities have the right to receive care and support that is dignified and respectful' (Learning Disability Allies, undated: no page numbers). An investigation by Channel 5 News in 2024 reported that of the 72,154 children who entered the care system between April 2020 and April 2022, 8.1% had parents assessed as learning disabled, this being a factor of concern leading up to the removal of the children (Nicole, 2023). The investigation claimed that 0.15% of adults with a learning disability were parents, concluding that they were 54 times more likely to have their child removed than other parents. In my opinion, this claim cannot be defended in the absence of equivalent data relating to parents without a learning disability.

Other authors (Baum, 2014) argue that there are no reliable estimates of the number of parents with a learning disability due to variations in the definition of learning disabilities over time and cross-nationally (Whitman and Accardo, 1990) and the fact that relatively few parents with learning disabilities are known to the relevant services (McGaw and Sturmey, 1993). The most robust estimate is regarded as that from the National Survey of adults with learning disabilities in England which stated that one in fifteen of the nearly 3,000 (6.6%) people interviewed had a child, but of these only 52% looked after them (Emerson et al., 2005). At that time there were an estimated 796,000 adults aged over 20 years with learning disabilities in England. If one in fifteen were parents (as in the National Survey), this would suggest that there were about 53,000 parents with learning disabilities in England alone. Based on data from MENCAP, prevalence rates from Public Health England (2016) and population data from the Office for National Statistics

(2020), the Office for Health Improvement and Disparities (2025) calculated that there are over 950,000 learning disabled adults aged 18 or over in England. If the one in fifteen figure still applies, this would mean an increase since 2005 to over 63,000 parents with a learning disability, with a correspondingly greater number of children of parents with a learning disability not looked after by their birth parents.

It has long been reported that parents with a learning disability are disproportionately represented in care proceedings and are much more likely to have children removed from their care (Booth, 2003; Booth et al., 2005). A more recent study which included parents with a learning disability or specific learning difficulties (Burch et al., 2024) stated that in 45% of cases, parents' learning disabilities or difficulties were not identified until the care proceedings were instigated, while in a further 30%, they had been registered during a previous set of court proceedings involving the parent. Professionals interviewed for Burch's research said that parents' difficulties were identified far too late with frequently-missed opportunities to recognise these earlier. Children's social workers lacked the necessary experience and expertise or had limited face-to-face time with parents which did not allow them effectively to identify learning disabilities or difficulties. These factors undermined the quality of practitioners' communication with parents, thereby adversely affecting parental engagement.

Cost was seen as a significant factor in the failure to identify parental needs sooner. Pre-proceedings investigations are funded in full by cash-strapped local authorities rather than being shared between parties as is typically the case once proceedings begin.

> But …those are parents that are slipping through a net …whether it's because when the lawyers go to the pre-proceedings meetings they don't get paid that much and they frequently send their paralegals and perhaps have less experience of picking up on these matters, as opposed to an experienced solicitor who might very quickly ascertain that something is not quite as would be expected (Judge).
>
> (Burch et al., 2024: 38)

Mothers interviewed for the research reported that practitioners' communications were not tailored to their needs, while they also criticised the turnover of social workers, which meant they had repeatedly to retell their stories.

## Definitions of Learning Disability and Difficulties

A learning disability is defined by the Department of Health and Social Care (DHSC) (2001) and cited in the Office for Health Disparities and Improvements (OHDI) (2025: no page numbers) as:

> A significantly reduced ability to understand new or complex information, to learn new skills (impaired intelligence), with a reduced ability to cope independently (impaired social functioning), which started before adulthood.

A learning difficulty is defined within OHDI (2025: no page numbers) as:

> A reduced ability for a specific form of learning and includes conditions such as dyslexia (reading), dyspraxia (affecting physical co-ordination) and attention deficit hyperactivity disorder (ADHD). A person with a learning disability may also have one or more learning difficulties. Additionally, there are a number of conditions and neurological disorders that often involve or cause some type of learning disability, including Down's syndrome, autism, meningitis, epilepsy or cerebral palsy. A learning disability is not a physical disability.

These definitions tend to be deficit-based and do not specifically relate to parenting, but do provide a starting point for identifying those parents who may need significant support in order to provide adequate care for their children.

### Lack of Reasonable Adjustments

More broadly, the Burch et al. (2024) report identified a failure to make reasonable adjustments for parents prior to the care proceedings stage, which runs counter to councils' duties to make such adjustments to avoid disabled people being put at a substantial disadvantage (Section 20 of the Equality Act 2010). This was evident both in parenting capacity assessments and the provision of parenting support. In just under two-thirds of cases (64%), parenting support was 'poorly or not at all tailored to the parent's needs'; in most of these circumstances, the parent's learning disability or difficulty had not been identified. Problems included parents being given inappropriate worksheet-based learning materials, having pre-birth sessions that covered far too many topics or being referred to non-tailored parenting classes. In their study, where parental learning disabilities or difficulties were suspected prior to court proceedings, a cognitive assessment undertaken by an expert during proceedings (invariably including an IQ testing element) often provided much more focus and depth of understanding.

I would caution against relying exclusively on IQ testing to identify and describe specialist needs. These usually generate significant anxiety in the test taker. They contain tasks that can be associated with schooling and previous failure. Testing continues until people are unable to accomplish the level of task involved and therefore have an inbuilt experience of failure. I have described elsewhere (Scaife, 2024) how they also suffer from design characteristics that make their validity questionable for people who obtain particularly low scores

> At low IQ levels the 'normal' distribution on which the tests are based does not hold, as there are more people with severe and profound learning difficulties than would be predicted by the normal curve. Finally, the sets of instructions for some of the sub-tests require greater understanding than the test itself. Whitaker gives the example of Letter-Number Sequencing which has an 80-word set of instructions requiring understanding of 'in alphabetical order'.
>
> (Scaife, 2024: 101)

The British Psychological Society has acknowledged the damaging legacy of intelligence testing in the UK (BPS, 2025), in this case as a result of culturally biased IQ tests leading to thousands of children of the Windrush generation being incorrectly labelled 'educationally subnormal'.

In Burch et al.'s study, adult social care services were rarely involved, contributing to an assessment in only 15% of cases, despite this having been requested in 27%. Professionals reported that support from adult social care was 'often unattainable' for parents with learning disabilities or difficulties because of long waiting times or high thresholds. This is despite people with learning disabilities being eligible for care and support under the Care Act 2014 if, as a result of needs arising from their condition, they are unable to achieve at least two of 10 outcomes – including caring for a child and maintaining family relationships – with significant impact on their wellbeing.

When Sir James Munby was President of the Family Division of the High Court of England and Wales, various cases that appeared before him led him to issue new guidance on family proceedings that involve parents with a learning disability.[3] He also spoke about this in 2023 (Courts and Tribunals Judiciary, 2023). He endorsed key points made in a judgment by J Gillen in Northern Ireland[4]:

1   People with a learning disability are individuals first and foremost and each has a right to be treated as an equal citizen... courts must take all steps possible to ensure that people with a learning disability are able to actively participate in decisions affecting their lives. [164.2]
2   Parents with learning disabilities can often be '*good enough*' parents when provided with the ongoing... support they need. The concept of '*parenting with support*' must underpin the way in which the courts and professionals approach... parents with learning disabilities. [164.4]
3   Judges must make absolutely certain that parents with learning disabilities are not at risk of having their parental responsibilities terminated on the basis of evidence that would not hold up against other parents. Their competences must not be judged against stricter criteria or harsher standards than other parents. [164.4]
4   Too narrow a focus must not be placed exclusively on the child's welfare, with an accompanying failure to address parents' needs arising from their disability which might impact adversely on their parenting capacity. [164.5]
5   The court must also take steps to ensure there are no barriers to justice within the process itself. Judges and magistrates must recognise that parents with learning disabilities need extra time with solicitors so that everything can be carefully explained to them... The process necessarily has to be slowed down to give such parents a better chance to understand and participate. This approach should be echoed throughout the whole system, including LAC reviews. [164.6]
6   All parts of the Family justice system should take care as to the language and vocabulary that is utilised. [164.6]
7   The courts must be careful to ensure that the supposed inability of parents to change might itself be an artefact of professionals' ineffectiveness in engaging with the parents in appropriate terms. [164.6]

8  A shift must be made from the old assumption that adults with learning disabilities could not parent to a process of questioning why appropriate levels of support are not provided to them so that they can parent successfully... The concept of '*parenting with support*' must move from the margins to the mainstream in court determinations. [164.7]

(Richardson, 2016: no page numbers)

The main principle expressed in these eight paragraphs is the importance of the concept of '*parenting with support*'. Sir James Munby argued that the concept is '*crucial*', reflecting the positive and broad obligation upon the state to provide the precise support that is necessary for parents with learning disabilities to retain care of their child(ren).

Sir James Munby heard counsel for the parents acknowledging that they *needed* help and made the case that this was no different from parents with other disabilities such as those physically disabled by Thalidomide, who were blind, or had a brain injury. Counsel argued that such parents need a reasonable adjustment for the deficits in their parenting which arise from their own inherent difficulties rather than from neglect or failure or indifference. Such parents may be receiving a high level of help and support but this does not mean that they are not bringing up their children. The judge argued that at some point the level of support offered goes beyond what is reasonable or appropriate, to the extent that professionals providing that support become substitute parents, for example, where the level of support offered involves visiting all day every day.

In 'substituted parenting', the bulk of parenting would be provided by professionals and other carers with presumed adverse consequences for the child's emotional development. Subsequently, Tilbury and Tarleton (2023) investigated how 'substituted parenting' was being used in care proceedings because the use of this term appeared to result in children being removed from their parents. Respondents confirmed that there was no clear understanding of when support became 'substituted parenting', but that it applied when social workers or other professionals would be 'doing the parenting' and hence children would develop problems with attachment, which would significantly harm their welfare. Questions have been asked about how 'substituted parenting' in the context of learning disability compares with situations where children are cared for most of the time by nannies or placed at an early age in boarding schools (Tilbury and Tarleton, 2023). Where it was argued that 'substituted parenting' would be necessary, there was no analysis of the perceived risks that might arise from a high level of support, nor was any thought given to how these risks might be addressed, managed or even eliminated.

When it is argued that children be removed on the grounds of unrealistic levels of support being required, it is important to know that the arguments being raised against providing support are legitimate and not based on cost, prejudice or other inappropriate factors. The current lack of this analysis raises concerns around the fairness and transparency of the family court system in relation to cases involving parents with learning disabilities/difficulties.

(Nuffield Family Justice Observatory, 2025a: 9)

The Working Together with Parents Network (WTPN) supports professionals working with parents with learning difficulties and their children. It is recommended that professionals be familiar with Care and Support Statutory Guidance issued by the Department of Health and Social Care (2024b), the Good Practice Guidance for Clinical Psychologists when Assessing Parents with Learning Disabilities (British Psychological Society, 2011), Good Practice Guidance on Working with Parents with a Learning Disability, WTPN (2021) and person-centred planning guidance (Social Care Institute for Excellence, 2017). The following are described as key elements of good practice

1   Assessors should be knowledgeable about both their statutory responsibilities and about parents' legal rights, including their entitlements under relevant legislation.
2   Where learning disability is suspected, an initial screening tool should be used in order to determine whether a specialist assessment is required.
3   Assessors should be sensitive to the stigma attached to a learning disability label. Every effort should be made to frame the issue as one of identifying particular support needs.
4   Psychometric assessments should not be relied on as the sole or primary measure of parenting capacity.
5   Out-of-home assessments should be avoided if at all possible, unless the home environment is disempowering to the parent.
6   Parents should be told, in plain language, what the assessment is, what it is for, what it will involve, and what will happen afterwards. They may need to be told more than once, for example, a parent may need to be reminded what happened at the last meeting.
7   Close attention should be paid to parents' access needs (this is a legal requirement). These may include putting written material into an accessible format, avoiding the use of jargon, taking more time to explain things, telling parents things more than once. Beware, however, of the risk of sounding patronising.
8   Assessments should include the role of significant adults in the parent's life, to establish positive and/or negative contributions to the parenting role and effects on children's welfare.
9   Assessors should be aware that previous experiences may create significant fear about the role of children's social care services. Parents may be hostile and anxious, and considerable effort may be required to prevent this fear becoming a real barrier to a comprehensive assessment.
10   Assessors should generally be wary of misinterpreting the effects of cognitive impairment.

11 Advice and specialist input should always be sought when parental learning disability is suspected.

(Working Together With Parents' Network, 2021)

A number of approaches have been developed to aid parents with learning disabilities in expressing their parenting skills in interview. These include the Parent Assessment Manual (PAM) devised by Sue McGaw et al. (1998) and regularly updated until August 2023. ParentAssess is a framework that was developed by Sarah Lowe in 2016 specifically for the assessment of parents with learning disabilities and other additional needs whose children are the subjects of care proceedings (https://parentassess.com/). A third framework termed CUBAS (Cubas, 2023) has been created by Geraldine Wetherell and Clair Chamberlain. These are described in more detail in Scaife (2024). More recently, a further framework termed 'MALD' (Making Assessments Accessible for those with Learning Disabilities, Difficulties and Other Additional Needs) has been developed by Danielle Hoskinson and Nichola Doyle, described at: https://maldassessment.co.uk/. Whilst these approaches have face validity, I could find only very limited (PAMS) or no evidence of their efficacy compared with standard parenting assessments.

Supporting texts with pictorial information can help to clarify any information provided. Illustrated texts have been written by David Hawkins and Sarah Jane Lynch for the purpose of explaining the court process to parents with a learning disability. They address both public and private law proceedings and can be downloaded free from the Courts and Tribunals Judiciary website at: https://www.judiciary.uk/related-offices-and-bodies/advisory-bodies/family-justice-council/litigants-in-person-in-the-family-justice-system/the-court-and-your-child/ and are available in a number of languages.

I would like to end this section with stories told by parents with learning disabilities about their experiences of parenting and of being assessed.

Ian talked about frustrations about others *'always look[ing] at us like we're different'* possibly *'lesser'*, than others without learning disabilities, and that professionals were *'just too eager to take the child away' (Ian)* from parents with learning disabilities:

*They prey on our disability and our vulnerability ... it's just unfair, 'cause we've got learning disabilities ... but we want to be parents like everybody else. We want to have the opportunity; we want support from the beginning like everybody else. Parents without learning disabilities can be bad parents too, but they get support ... if you've got a learning disability you get judged you can't parent. (Ian)*

(Theodore et al., 2018: 190)

Shared Lives care is a service for adults who have a long-term condition and want to live independently in their community alongside someone else in a supportive house-share. Half of the 10,000 people using Shared Lives move in with their cho-sen carer to live as a member of their household; half visit for day support or over-night breaks. People are provided with safe, personal care and support, in a place which feels like home. This is Abby's story (Shared Lives Plus, 2025):

> It all started when I was in hospital. During pregnancy everything was fine. The hospital contacted social services and I had a several visits a day, health visitor, midwifery team, specialist parenting team, but it wasn't working. They had con-cerns about leaving Isabella with me. They had a right to be worried. Isabella was in a vulnerable position, because no one had taught me to do things.
>
> They wanted to send me to a mother and baby centre, in an area I didn't know anyone and wouldn't have been able to see my family. My social worker had worked for Shared Lives in the past and helped me get in. At first it was a bit daunting but I met my Shared Lives carer, Mel, and she was lovely. We just laughed a lot. It was a fresh start, a fresh opportunity.
>
> I always looked after Isabella, I just needed Mel to guide me along, just hav-ing someone to be there. Mel offered suggestions, like the need for routine. We come up with ideas together like what's a good time for the baby to go to bed, reading stories to her.
>
> Isabella is so clever. She goes to nursery, she really likes it. She has made friends, she's always happy and cheerful. There have been lots of firsts, I took Isabella to parks, to see animals. We have a laugh at home, do game nights and karaoke. Before Shared Lives I wasn't always happy, I didn't do a lot. I have a full life now and Isabella is thriving.
>
> (Shared Lives Plus, 2025: no page numbers)

The Intellectual Disability Rights Service which operates in New South Wales helps people with intellectual or cognitive disabilities. Parents tell their stories in a video recording on YouTube which can be accessed at: http://www.idrs.org.au/support-parents/cnp-stories.php.

## Mental Health

Despite the high prevalence of serious mental health difficulties noted by Ireland et al. (2024), mothers involved in care proceedings were more likely than other users to have referrals rejected and to be discharged for failure to engage. Pat-terns of service contact before and after care proceedings also suggested unmet needs for some mothers. Service contacts increased before care proceedings for one-third (34.1%) of mothers who were accessing mental health services but declined steeply after proceedings started in one-quarter of mothers (25.6%). Just over half (53.8%) of all mothers in care proceedings who were known to mental health services had very little contact in the two years before or one year after care proceedings. These findings are consistent with qualitative research reporting that mothers feel abandoned and struggle to access social care or mental health support once the process of removing their children has begun.

In a Welsh study of private law proceedings (Cusworth et al., 2020, 2021), more than four in ten female (41.7%) and three in ten male (31.2%) parents had at least one mental health-related GP contact or hospital admission in the year prior to court which represented one and a half times the level for men and women in the comparison group. Common mental health conditions were between two and a half and three times more likely among adults involved in private law applications. In the year prior to proceedings, 13% of women and 9% of men had a diagnosis of depression, with 12 and 7%, respectively, being given a diagnosis of anxiety. The prevalence of diagnoses of more serious mental illnesses such as bipolar disorder and schizophrenia was at least twice as high as in the comparison group. The incidence of 'hidden' conditions such as ADHD or eating disorder was between one and a half and two and a half times those in the comparison group.

Not only may parents suffering from mental health difficulties have experienced such symptoms prior to the involvement of the court, but it has been argued that the proceedings themselves can exacerbate or cause such harm to parents' well-being (Dalgarno et al., 2024). Dalgarno et al.'s study was of 45 self-selected mothers who reported abuse by their ex-partners. They told the researchers they attributed psychological conditions including suicidal ideation, memory loss, depression and flashbacks to their experiences in court. Physical conditions such as Crohn's Disease, cancer, psoriasis, heart palpitations and miscarriage were reported either to have been exacerbated by or directly associated with the proceedings. This chimes with my own experience of parents engaged in family court proceedings who, virtually without exception, whatever their gender or prior experience of their relationship with the child's other parent, find them stressful and often utterly harrowing.

Dalgarno et al.'s study was supported by pressure groups highlighting the plight of women impacted by domestic abuse. The selection process of the participants limits the extent to which the conclusions can be generalised to a wider population but usefully illuminates some consequences of being a litigant, and particularly a respondent, in the family court. In an online survey of 171 fathers reporting alienation from their children after separation from the child's mother, substantial negative impacts on mental health including suicidal ideation, were described. They reported unbearable feelings of 'living grief' about the loss of their children and a sense that their lives had been destroyed (Hine and Bates, 2023). The research is referenced on the 'Both Parents Matter' charity website. In my opinion, neither piece of research can be interpreted without reference to contemporary societal values within a range of different world views reflecting gender, ethnicity, social class, age, sexuality and other visible and invisible differences in beliefs, power and lifestyle. 'Descriptions, understandings and treatments of human suffering are fraught with contention because they are socially and politically situated manifestations of the values and vested interests of the time' (Scaife, 2024: 84).

Parents in proceedings may be assessed by professionals who understand these symptoms within different explanatory frameworks which prescribe different approaches to treatment such as medication and/or a variety of 'talking' therapies. Experts are requested to be as specific as possible in describing these interventions and where they may be sourced. They are also requested to give an opinion about the prognosis and the period over which intervention is needed if adequate change is to be accomplished. In reaching an opinion, I have found the Stages of Change model (Prochaska et al., 2013) to be invaluable in assessing indicators of enduring change.

Trauma-informed perspectives on mental health acknowledge the impact of difficult life experiences and the danger that treatment within systems and services may readily re-traumatise. It does not surprise me that parents experiencing separation, abuse, those being threatened with local authority intervention and the court processes themselves are likely to experience varying degrees of mental health difficulties. Not all of these will have trouble in caring for their children, but many will, and experts may be requested to give an opinion on such matters.

Parents struggling with their mental health may have short-term or enduring, complex or more straightforward difficulties which they are more or less successful in managing. There may be a reluctance to disclose such issues to the court for fear of the stigma with which they continue to be associated and fear of a negative influence on outcomes.

Children are often the most informative respondents to aid a professional in opinions about the capability of a parent battling mental health issues. This child gave a clear account of her mother's struggles:

> I'd get up in a morning and ask my mum to please get up and make me some food. She would always say that she would get up in a minute but then when I asked again she would say, 'In five minutes,' and after five minutes it would be ten minutes and then it never got done. I just got a chair and climbed up to get the cereals down and I got some for my little brother too. Sometimes there would be milk and sometimes we had them dry. And she used to put my school uniform in the washer but forget about it and in the morning I'd get it out and put it on the radiator but it was never dry and I had to put it on wet. The teachers would brush my hair and make sure my teeth were cleaned. My mum loved me very much and used to like me to cuddle her in bed and I loved to do that but she was always tired and it was so sad.

Although mental health difficulties are a protected characteristic under the Equality Act (2010), I cannot say that I have always experienced effort expended in making adjustments for afflicted parents. To do so is complicated by the over-arching concern for children's welfare. Undoubtedly, despite their best intentions, some parents' long-standing issues make it almost impossible for them to provide adequate parenting. Mental health services are seriously over-stretched with people having to wait months or years for treatment. Without recourse to private funding, access to such services is typically managed by the NHS which is not 'joined up' to local authority provision. How can parents then make the necessary changes within the 26-week timetable for public law proceedings? This can be extended, but meanwhile the child may languish in unsuitable circumstances without ongoing stability and security. The conflict of interest between the needs of the child and the needs of the parent can be difficult to navigate because ultimately the child's best interests often lie in the effective functioning of their birth parents, provided that this can be achieved.

Mental health issues may come into play in many different ways in the family court. In these private law proceedings[5] brought by the children's American father, the privileging of the mother's mental health stability enabled her to retain care of her children after she relocated to the UK. The judgment included the following paragraph, in which M refers to the mother and F to the father:

> My focus remains squarely on the children and the situation they would face on a return to Iowa. Whilst Dr McClintock considers it unlikely that M's response to being required to return to Iowa would impact significantly on her parenting capacity, he is clear in his view that the precise nature and severity of M's likely symptoms cannot be predicted. Given this unpredictability and the seriousness of M's allegations, I am satisfied that I cannot confidently discount the possibility that a return order would expose these two young children to a grave risk of harm. In my judgment, the protective measures proposed by F do not, and could not, adequately address that risk. Even if F were to obtain a consent order in Iowa and abide by his undertakings, there is still the possibility that M may suffer a significant deterioration in her mental health. Whilst that possibility may be low (but cannot be predicted), the consequences for these children would be grave.

Mental health difficulties may have a variety of direct and indirect impacts on the quality of care that children receive but one condition that has an insidious and sometimes irreversible negative impact on children's wellbeing is that of Fabricated or Induced Illness (FII) which is a rare form of child abuse. A parent or carer exaggerates or deliberately causes symptoms of illness in the child whilst presenting as particularly caring and solicitous of the child's well-being. Because it is so rare, it can easily go undetected and the parent/carer, usually the mother, tends to make positive and close relationships with involved professionals. The parent's behaviour typically exposes the child to unnecessary treatments, other interventions or tests. Children may come to see themselves as invalids and their education may be disrupted. A wide range of symptoms and conditions have been presented by parents which may involve exaggeration or fabrication of symptoms, manipulation of test results, for example, by putting glucose in urine to suggest that a child had diabetes, or deliberate poisoning of the child. Incorrect reporting or exaggeration of symptoms is much more common than directly inducing an illness.

Here I cite in detail the findings in Re: N[6] (Honeyman, 2024) in relation to children A and B because not only can children in the most severe cases be seriously harmed, but professionals can become inadvertently complicit in the abuse unless they recognise when they are being drawn beyond their regular professional and ethical conduct. Key findings include:

- In May 2022 M put B at grave risk of harm by administering morphine, chlorphenamine and trimethoprim to B whilst she was in hospital to sedate her, reduce her respiratory rate and complicate her presentation;
- M covertly siphoned blood from B on multiple occasions between 2020 and 2022, which caused B's perplexing anaemia;
- M fabricated and/or exaggerated apnoeic incidents to convince doctors that B had a chronic respiratory condition, deliberately damaged her CPAP machine after being told that medics needed to analyse the data within it and, over a period of years, increased the usage and settings of the CPAP machine contrary to the ventilation plan. In fact, B either did not need CPAP at all or not to the degree sought by M;
- M engaged in "doctor shopping" and manipulation, playing professionals off against each other;
- M falsely reported or exaggerated diarrhoea in B, leading to concerns that she might have Pancreatic Exocrine Insufficiency and to B being medicated for that condition, for which in fact there is no evidence;
- As a result of M's portrayal of B as chronically ill, she has been wrongly brought up as a child with Shwachman-Diamond Syndrome, a rare and serious condition which was considered by medics but never diagnosed;
- A suffered from a number of minor conditions which would all have either resolved or been amenable to treatment in the community and she did not need the regular hospitalisations, invasive treatments and other interventions that she received as a result of M fabricating and/or exaggerating reports of apnoeic episodes and diarrhoea, the latter leading to treatment for possible Pancreatic Enzyme Insufficiency which she did not have;
- M made false or exaggerated claims about A's feeding difficulties and vomiting, leading to A being unnecessarily fed for a long time via nasogastric tube;
- A's over-medicalisation, including repeated prescriptions of oral steroids for her cough and long-term prophylactic antibiotics, as well as unnecessary adenoidectomy and tonsillectomy, exposed her to numerous risks;
- A became very distressed by medical procedures, including shouting in distress during injections, requiring restraint to access her port and screaming in pain when it was accessed. She became emotional when her Hickman line was used and said the medicine made her feel "*weird and sad*".

At [157], the judge made findings against Dr K:

- Dr K was one of a number of professionals manipulated by M;
- Their relationship was unusually and inappropriately close: she gave M her personal number, shared personal details, exchanged personal messages and allowed M to "friend" her on Facebook.

- She permitted M to take the children in and out of hospital for intravenous anti-biotics rather than remaining on the ward.
- She relied on M's accounts of the children's presentation, and blurred boundaries affected her ability to keep an open mind and look objectively at the potential causes of their presentation.
- She preferred M's accounts at times to the diagnoses and recommendations of the tertiary treating hospitals.
- Her communication with those hospitals was at times limited.
- She failed to coordinate an early multi-disciplinary meeting across all treating hospitals.
- She was abrasive and abrupt towards nurses who raised concerns about M's behaviour, on several occasions shouting at them.
- Dr K's conduct hindered professionals' ability to uncover the true cause of the children's presentation.

(Honeyman, 2024: no page numbers)

At [147] the judge paid tribute to four nurses who had raised concerns, commenting that *Without them, the future prospects for these children would have been very bleak.* At [158], the judge set out a detailed list of practice points and practical steps which should be taken by paediatricians and other professionals in order to avoid pitfalls that hinder the early identification of safeguarding issues. The list includes:

- Being fully aware of the guidance of the Royal College of Paediatrics and Child Health about Perplexing Presentation/ FII in children.
- Everybody involved in treating and caring for the children is likely to make important contributions to the professional discussions. It is essential that those who work in less senior roles feel valued and are able to freely contribute to the discussions. These individuals can have a greater insight into the day-to-day life of the family and the patient.
- Correspondence and notes should be consistent and accurate. The history should be accurately reported.
- Perplexing presentation raises FII as a point for consideration, even if it is to be considered and dismissed. Where FII has been discounted, it should remain under consideration until it can be properly dismissed.
- At all times to establish and maintain professional boundaries with the patients and their families. To do otherwise would be a disservice to the patient and their family at a time when they are likely to need the professional around them most
- Always keep an open mind.

## Drug and Alcohol Misuse

One night I remember, my dad came home drunk. I think he came back from the pub at half past ten, storming in, just then he was in a temper then mum called the police. He was just grabbing her, pushing her. It was arguing. I just ignored it. I went in my room 'cos I don't want to be a part of it. I just shut the door in my room. When the police came my heart was racing like mad 'cos he's my dad. I don't want him to go to prison.

Some children endure a great deal of alcohol- or illicit drug-fuelled parental disharmony which at times transmutes into physical violence, bloodshed and broken bones. It can be terrifying and some children live in environments where they are constantly on the alert for signs of danger, a state which can continue into adulthood as hyperarousal and post-traumatic stress. Even when the abuse is verbal and emotional, parents and children describe 'walking on eggshells', aiming to avoid any behaviour that acts as provocation to the misusing parent.

According to the Children's Commissioner for England's data on childhood vulnerability, there were 478,000 children living with an alcohol or drug dependent parent in 2019 to 2020, that is a rate of 40 children per 1,000 parents (Public Health England, 2021). Problem alcohol and drug use can negatively impact parenting capacity and is a factor in some cases of child maltreatment. In 2019 to 2020, the Department for Education (DfE, 2020) reported that parental drug use was relevant in around 17% of child in need cases, and parental alcohol use was a factor in 16%. In DfE statistics for 2011–2014 (DfE, 2016), parental alcohol or drug use was recorded in 36% of serious case reviews.

Whilst these figures reference public law proceedings, in my experience, substance misuse is not infrequently alleged in private law, affecting every social stratum of society. Non-prescription drug and alcohol use is widespread, and does not automatically disqualify parents from providing adequate care for their children. What matters is the extent to which the pattern of use is 'maladaptive' or 'harmful', when the priority given to it interferes with the fulfilment of major role obligations, when its use impairs functioning and judgement, and when persistent or recurrent social or interpersonal problems result.

Whilst drugs are used for multiple purposes including experimentation and recreation, substance misuse refers to the use of a psychoactive substance in a way for which it was not intended and which causes physical, social, and/or psychological harm (Rassool, 2009). The Diagnostic and Statistical Manual (DSM-5-TR) (USA) and International Classification of Disorders (ICD-11) (World Health Organization) are global standards for classifying diseases and related health conditions (World Health Organization, 2022). DSM-5-TR uses the term 'substance use disorder', combining the categories in previous DSM versions of 'substance dependence' and 'substance abuse' for drug misuse problems, listing 11 defining criteria which can be grouped into four primary categories of physical dependence, risky use, social problems, and impaired control. ICD-11 identifies such difficulties as 'substance dependence' based on the presence of two out of three criteria of impaired control over substance use, an increase in its priority in life, and physiological features such as tolerance and withdrawal (Basicmedical Key, 2020).

The World Health Organization (WHO) (1994) has used the terms 'hazardous' to refer to use of a drug that increases the risk of harmful consequences for the user despite the absence of any current disorder, 'dysfunctional use' when it is leading to impaired psychological or social functioning such as loss of employment or marital problems, and 'harmful use' when drug use is causing harm to health through tissue damage or psychiatric disorders (WHO, 1994). The Alcohol Use Disorders Identification Test (AUDIT) is a ten-item screening tool developed by the WHO to assess alcohol consumption, drinking behaviours, and alcohol-related problems. This self-report questionnaire is designed to indicate whether a person's drinking is harmful, hazardous or dependent, categories which I find useful as non-medical terminology.

> For parents in children's proceedings, my experience is that problematic substance use has often begun in people's teen years and has developed into a way of escaping strong negative emotions. This can lead to the development of a lifestyle in which the drug takes centre stage. It dictates relationships, demands funding, involves deception, and supports avoidance of difficult issues or life histories. It serves to protect the user from thinking about painful and difficult experiences and may lead to physiological and/or psychological dependence. Chaos tends to result because judgement is impaired and priorities are distorted.
>
> (Scaife, 2024: 91)

Where drug or alcohol misuse is implicated in proceedings, testing may be ordered. Urine tests give results about recent use up to a few hours or days, depending on the substance. Immunoassay tests are relatively cheap but are susceptible to false positives or false negatives. Gas chromatography – mass spectrometry tests (GC-MS) are more reliable and can detect more substances but are also more expensive and the results take longer to produce. Blood analysis or breath tests may be used in situations when it is suspected that a person is actively under the influence of drugs or alcohol, but they are rapidly metabolised and eliminated from the body, typically being detectable only within minutes to hours, depending upon the drug and dose. Oral fluid (saliva) drug testing can be used to detect very recent drug use of up to 48 hours after drugs were first consumed. SCRAM bracelets, which continuously sample perspiration every 30 minutes to monitor for alcohol use, may be worn on the ankle.

The most common drug and alcohol testing ordered within the family court is hair strand and/or nail analysis. These tests are regarded as being able to provide evidence of patterns of use over a time period of several months. They provide a historical record of consumption and changes in patterns of usage over time. Reports from laboratories that carry out these assessments typically include significant detail of the analyses carried out, with the overall findings summarised in a relatively brief and straightforward conclusion, often with reference to a cut-off point. Sometimes, in my experience, the summaries fail fully to reflect the detail and can appear to give a misleading result. This was the case in a judgment made in 2024 Re: D[7] which was heard in the High Court. The children had been placed with their maternal grandmother. The local authority sought to remove them on the grounds that the children's hair strand analysis tested positive for exposure to a range of Class A drugs. Various issues were raised in the appeal, one of which was that the report summaries were misleading

> The general summary section of Report #2 in relation to A, for example, indicated that she had experienced passive exposure to cannabis during the period from around February to late October 2023 and passive exposure to cocaine and MDMA during the period from around October 2022 to October 2023; this was said to be "*regular passive exposure* to cannabis during the period from around February to *late October 2023*" (emphasis added: i.e., three months after placement with the maternal grandmother), and "close contact with cocaine users" or "cocaine residues" and "close contact with MDMA users" in the period up to and including late-October 2023 without any identification of the source. However, on reviewing more carefully the specific data findings in relation to A, it appears that *no* traces of cocaine were found in the hair sample from May 2023, and *no* trace of MDMA in the hair sample from March 2023; *no* traces of cannabis were found in the hair sample at all, and *diminishing* quantities of cannabinoid (compounds found in cannabis) were found in the period up to August 2023, and none thereafter; these specific data were not reflected in the general summary.

There are additional grounds for caution in the interpretation of hair strand testing. In Re: D an independent expert toxicologist recommended re-testing of the initial hair samples because results from various providers can vary. Duplicate analyses can provide vital additional evidence. I have also found this to be the case when samples taken during overlapping timescales by different laboratories have given conflicting results.

In Re: H,[8] HHJ Peter Jackson gave the opinion that

> the variability of findings from hair strand testing does not call into question the underlying science, but underlines the need to treat numerical data with proper caution. The extraction of chemicals from a solid matrix such as human hair is inevitably accompanied by margins of variability... A very high result may amount to compelling evidence, but in the lower range numerical information must be set alongside evidence of other kinds.

He noted that test results are usually reported as being within the high/medium/low ranges but this categorisation is calculated by varying procedures in different testing laboratories.

Multiple factors confound hair strand analysis results (Branson and Hunter, 2023) including environmental contaminants, hair treatments, exposure to UV, individual differences in drug absorption, application of heat to hair as in the creation of dreadlocks, pregnancy and hair colour and type. '[T]he application of hair dye or bleach can remove an average of around 60% of the drug from the hair sample and multiple use can remove all detectable levels' (Branson and Hunter, 2023: 671). More insidious is the difference between dark and light hair. A study reported by Rollins (2003) involved standardised administration of the opiate codeine to participants with a range of hair colours. The levels of the drug in the hair of participants with black hair were ten times that for blonde hair and over 15 times higher than for those with red hair. Asian black hair results showed higher drug levels than Caucasian black hair. The issues are discussed in a podcast hosted by Opie (2025a).

Cut-off levels, above the threshold at which a person is considered to be a drug user, were developed by the Society of Hair Testing almost 30 years ago, before research established the impact of these influencing factors on drug absorption (Summers, 2024). Two people who have consumed the same amount of a substance may obtain quite different results, and two people with the same result may have consumed quite different quantities of the substance.

One lab (Hackett, 2025) looked at 3,000 cases from their own historical data where other evidence such as nail testing and declared usage were available, then applied standard cut-off levels to them. They reported that in 12% of cases where heroin was not used and in 18% where cocaine was not used, the cut-off gave positive results. Amongst chronic heroin users, 22% came back negative and amongst chronic cocaine users, 20% returned negative results. Of chronic cannabis users, 60% returned negative results.

Along with others, I have concluded that hair strand test results are best used as an indicator of changes in use over time, although that is not necessarily how the conclusions are reported, and that the application of cut-off levels can be particularly misleading. Interpretation of the data requires consideration of context and great care in order to avoid results producing the 'pseudo-certainty' that numbers tend to generate. Consideration needs to be given to hair colour, lifestyle, passive exposure and hair treatments.

In recognition of these concerns, a campaign by 'Taking a Strand' (Birth Companions, 2024), supported by practitioners from across the legal, voluntary, technical and academic sectors, urged the Family Division and Family Justice Board to commission a wholescale review of the way hair strand testing evidence is instructed, reported and interpreted in the family courts. The Family Justice Council began a review at the time of writing.

Whilst it sometimes appears obvious that drug or alcohol use is creating chaos in a family, some medical conditions can masquerade as intoxication, producing behaviours such as staggering and slurring of speech when no alcohol has been consumed. In this case, chemical analysis can lend credibility to a parent's claims of sobriety.

### Family Drug and Alcohol Courts

Family Drug and Alcohol Courts (FDACs) offer an alternative approach to public law care proceedings, specially designed to assist parents who struggle with substance misuse (FDAC, 2025). The aim of these courts is to assist parents to turn their lives around and address the presenting issues, which often include poor mental health and domestic abuse as well as substance misuse. The same judge reviews progress every two weeks at an informal hearing with carers who speak directly to the judge. Alongside the judge, a team of professionals from a range of specialisms work closely with the family during what is termed a 'trial for change'. The aims and timescales of the intervention are clear to all parties and towards the end of the proceedings the team makes a recommendation to the local authority regarding the possibility of family reunification.

Since FDAC was first piloted in the UK in 2008, the Department for Education has invested in increasing the number of FDACs across England and Wales. They have been implemented in 19 courts serving families in 35 local authorities. Research commissioned by Foundations (2023b) reported that children with a primary carer in FDAC care proceedings were more likely to be reunified with them compared to children with a primary carer in non-FDAC proceedings (52.0% vs 12.5%). A higher proportion of parents in FDAC has ceased to misuse drugs or alcohol by the end of the proceedings (36% vs 8.1%). A lower proportion of FDAC cases instructed expert witnesses (7.7% vs 96.1%). But 'due to limitations with the methodology and data collection in this evaluation, we cannot attribute the effects found entirely to FDAC and we are unable to draw firm conclusions about the impact of FDAC based on this study' (Foundations, 2023b: no page numbers).

A study review by What Works for Children's Care was based on research by Zhang et al. (2019). That study reported that family reunification was substantially more likely with this approach without increasing the risk of subsequent return to substitute care or reports of further harm. In contrast, the Foundations review stated that 'Overall, Family Drug and Alcohol Courts had no effect on care re-entry or re-abuse. This is based on high-strength evidence from eight research studies with a total of 1,474 participants' (Foundations, 2023b: no page numbers). They pointed out that there was also no evidence of a harmful effect.

The model for such courts was developed in the USA and continues (County Health Rankings and Road Maps, 2025). Effects on the recurrence of child abuse and neglect and children's re-entry to the care system remain unclear. These courts allow parents to take more time to make the necessary changes than traditional courts, and parents tend to be more compliant with the court, perceiving the approach as fair. A large-scale review (Eggins et al., 2024) concluded that despite a large body of evaluation evidence, the quantity of missing data precluded analyses of the comparative effectiveness of multi-dimensional interventions for improving the outcomes for children with substance-misusing parents. But the authors concluded that these interventions can be effective when they holistically address multiple factors including parental well-being, mental health, parenting skills, substance misuse and wider factors associated with deprivation such as housing. It seems not unreasonable to suppose that any family approaching care proceedings is likely to benefit from such a joined-up inter-disciplinary approach that is authoritatively overseen, but data that might shed light on this does not appear to be available as these courts are only available to substance-misusing parents.

**Key Points from this Chapter**

- Parental vulnerability is ubiquitous in family court proceedings, occurring with significantly greater frequency than in the population at large.
- The FPR Part 3A places a duty on the court to consider whether the quality of evidence given by a party or witness is likely to be diminished by reason of vulnerability and, if so, whether it is necessary to make one or more participation directions.
- These include preventing a party or witness from seeing another party or witness; allowing the giving of evidence by live link; providing for the use of a device to help communication; providing for a party or witness to participate in proceedings with the assistance of an intermediary and providing for a party or witness to be questioned in court with the assistance of an intermediary.
- Vulnerable parents are not a homogeneous group. Some who present as robust may do so out of fear of the consequences of disclosure.
- Experts need to ensure that their approaches are adapted to take account of and make reasonable adjustments for a range of vulnerabilities including physical impairments, intellectual challenges, mental health conditions and drug and alcohol misuse.
- A great deal of care and a degree of scepticism are necessary in interpreting numerical data which can give the appearance of greater certainty than is warranted (e.g. IQ tests, hair strand analysis).
- Going to court is stressful and often harrowing for parents and in itself can contribute to and exacerbate existing vulnerabilities.
- Some conditions carry a risk for practitioners of being drawn into violation of professional boundaries. To assist recognition of the temptation to do so it is wise to have in place mechanisms (such as clinical supervision or team involvement where appropriate) that protect both the family members and the practitioner.

## Notes

1 Re C (A Child) [2014] EWCA Civ 128.
2 Lack of Multiagency Approach to Deaf Parents [2024] EWFC 364 (B).
3 Re D (A Child) (No 3) [2016] EWFC 1.
4 Re G and A (Care Order: Freeing Order: Parents with a Learning Disability) [2006] NIFam 8.
5 Re EF and GH (Children) (1980 Hague Child Abduction Convention) [2024] EWHC 3576 (Fam).
6 Re N (Children: Fact Finding – Perplexing Presentation/Fabricated or Induced Illness) [2024] EWFC 326.
7 Re D (Children: Interim Care Order: Hair Strand Testing) [2024] EWCA Civ 498.
8 H (A Child: Hair Strand Testing) [2017] EWFC 64.

Chapter 9

# Migration

According to the Annual Population Survey, in 2022 an estimated 10 million people born overseas were living in the UK. Of these, approximately 3.5 million said that they originally moved to the country mainly to join or accompany a British citizen or UK-settled resident (Migration Observatory, 2023). One in three children born in the UK in 2023 had at least one parent born overseas (Luthra, 2023). This is reflected in the school system, with around 20% of students speaking English as an additional language. It follows that, as in any family, a proportion of immigrant parents (where both parents are immigrants from the same country, both parents are immigrants from two different countries, and where one parent is UK-born and one parent is an immigrant) will experience separation from their partner and may appeal to the family court to resolve their differences. Like others, the children of immigrant parents may be assessed as suffering significant harm and be subject to public law proceedings. Some children arrive in the UK as unaccompanied minors. For professionals trying to assist such families, additional challenges arise through language barriers, diverse cultural perspectives and legal issues concerning asylum, migration and the right to remain.

People migrate to the UK for a variety of reasons: economic, seeking asylum, refugees fleeing war-torn countries, being trafficked and/or exploited. Not only may they be non-native English speakers (if they speak English at all) but language embodies cultural mores and expectations which reflect different ways of seeing or constructing experiential worlds, culture being defined as 'a shared mental model of the world' (Katan, 2004: 26). The discipline of psychology developed in the West and necessarily reflects its cultural context. When working with migrant families I cannot stand outside my own cultural history even though I may try to put myself in their shoes.

Constructions of behaviour are context-specific. In an account given by a Kosovan woman to a colleague of mine, during the civil war all the women in her village were rounded up by soldiers and the younger ones raped. A cousin of hers was shot for being unfaithful to her husband because by being the victim of rape she was considered 'soiled goods' and in some way complicit. The client's mother-in-law had witnessed the mother being raped but both had kept it secret from the woman's husband. To reveal such experiences in an assessment for the family court would

DOI: 10.4324/9781003453390-9

constitute an enormous risk, especially if an interpreter appointed for the proceedings belonged to the same community as the mother.

Forced migrants fleeing conflict and political persecution are in particularly perilous situations. Power differentials in the country of origin may adversely affect the relationship between clinician, interpreter and family member, particularly in the light of political and social conflict.

> Many asylum seekers and forced migrants report feeling that they were 'silenced' or their voices were taken away from them by political regimes which did not allow for multiple accounts or voices which stifled criticism prior to them seeking asylum. Thus, talking about psychological problems may have been and may remain difficult, issues of trust may have become compromised and secrecy may have been a functional and key survival strategy.
>
> (Tribe and Thompson, 2022: 614)

## Cultural and Language Barriers

The extract below is from a paper written by the 'bossy white woman' therein. To me it illustrates the difficulties in negotiating a path between family members, their cultural and linguistic history and the conventions of the family court.

> Today, your sister gave you a piece of paper that she got from the police. It was covered in strange symbols. You stared at them – lines, circles, and figures you recognised as numbers – but you couldn't work it out. You showed it to your cousin who can read a bit because she went to school until year 10, and she said 'you must be in big trouble because that paper says you have to go to court.' You have no idea what you've done wrong, but you're terrified… What will they do to you?
>
> …it's court day. Everyone sits out on the grass near the Council and waits. A white woman rushes over and asks you your name. You know a bit of white language, but she talks so fast you find it difficult to follow. She sits down beside you, but she's bossy and rude, asking you all kinds of personal questions and not giving you time to answer. You're hoping she will go away when she shows you a piece of paper with your signature on it, and tells you a story. Although it is filled with strange white words, you realise you know this story. It is your story. She is talking about an actual time your husband flogged you. How she knows about it, you have no idea. It happened a long time ago, and you'd both been drunk and jealous. You called the police, they took him away to dry out and took you to the Clinic, and the next day everything was fine. Why talk about it now?
>
> And then it dawns on you. Suddenly you know what's going on and you feel sick. This bossy white woman wants you to get up there in front of your family, your husband, and some white strangers and tell them how he flogged you. She wants you to send your husband to jail. Panic rises. How will you look after the children? How will you face your family? Your husband's mother? They will never understand. It will all be your fault.

This is what justice is like for many Indigenous Australians – a system alien not only in concept but in language. It is a problem found in most areas of rural Australia, and particularly in Queensland, Western Australia, South Australia and the Northern Territory.

(Heske, 2008: 5)

The contradiction between cultural and linguistic histories and the conventions of the family court are manifest in language whilst reflecting underlying contexts in which clashes and misconceptions present challenges to justice. Michael Cooke explains that even the question and answer style of the court is at odds with modes of communication of some Aboriginal cultures:

Police and lawyers in the Northern Territory and other parts of northern Australia admit to great difficulty in interviewing Aboriginal people, whether as clients, suspects or witnesses. Following standard practice, police and legal counsel usually attempt to elicit information by way of question and answer (Q&A) sequences. This is how lawyers interview their clients, how police interrogate suspects, and how counsel examine and cross examine witnesses. What we often forget is that the Q&A interview style is a learned discursive style; it is culturally specific. It is not a universal speech style. It is not found in the inventory of speech registers and speech genres of the Aboriginal people of northern Australia. For the Yolngu of North East Arnhemland children who ask curious questions, one after the other, are criticized or teased by grown-ups for behaving like white people.

(Cooke, 1996: 273)

Cooke (1996) gave an extended example of how a woman kept prisoner by her partner and seriously abused was charged with his murder because she did not understand the process of question and answer sequences employed by counsel. When allowed to give her own narrative account it became clear that the appropriate charge was manslaughter.

Differences between cultures, modes of expression and prejudice create many opportunities for misinterpretation. Reading of a court bundle may give an impression belied by subsequent full investigation. Particularly in private law disputes, the potential for professional bias may be exploited by warring parents when the issues may be complicated by the interconnection of social characteristics such as 'race' and gender. Three examples were cited by Williams et al. (2024) in which presumptions were made about South Asian and Middle Eastern, African and Arab fathers occupying traditional gender roles, exercising authority in the home and failing to adapt to the mainstream culture. One mother reported false stereotypes to professionals, saying 'Muslim men spit on their wives' which was subsequently repeated to other professionals involved in the proceedings. Williams et al. (2024) described key errors arising from cultural stereotypes which in each case resulted in harm to the children.

The language used in the family court is challenging for native English language speakers, let alone those for whom it is a subsidiary. Such clients are vulnerable because language and cultural issues act as a barrier to full participation. There are inherent difficulties in giving instructions, understanding advice and comprehending proceedings. When experts assess such clients, adjustments are needed to ensure fairness. Misjudgements about language proficiency can easily be made, often further compounded by parents' own misconceptions of their fluency in this context. People may over- or under-estimate their additional language skills. They may be reluctant to admit to weakness in these skills for personal and/or cultural reasons. If they say that they are struggling to understand legal professionals, the response tends to be direct repetition and a slower delivery which do not necessarily help and may hinder (Ogawa, 2007). In criminal cases, an expert forensic linguist may be recruited to assess a defendant's English language proficiency with a view to making a judgment about statements previously made to police (English, 2021). Alternatively:

> [t]he judgment of whether a person can "understand or speak the language used in the court" usually rests with the judge, who often makes the decision on the basis of considerable ignorance, both about details of the person's proficiency in the language of the court, and about broader applied linguistic issues… [D]efendant[s] may appear quite fluent and articulate in answering basic biographical questions (such as are usually asked by a judge before the decision about calling an interpreter is made), and yet lack the language proficiency to answer much more complex questions, such as can be expected in cross examination.
>
> (Eades, 2003: 116)

When families are referred for assessment by the family court, a judgment will have been made by their legal representative (if they have one) and/or by the judge about their language skill level. This may be conveyed to the expert but this assessment is unlikely to have been undertaken formally. The expert will need to decide whether family members would benefit from the appointment of an interpreter. The first step is to assess the needs and preferences of parents and children. It is possible to use surveys, questionnaires and/or informal conversations to find out what languages family members speak, how comfortable they are with English and what modes of communication they prefer, although this is more challenging the lower the level of fluency in English. My experience is that by the time families are referred to an expert, it has already been determined whether or not they would benefit from the appointment of an interpreter and where there is doubt, to err on the side of caution and appoint one in case. Although it may seem obvious, it is critical to ensure that the interpreter speaks the same language as the parent. This can be particularly important for languages where there is significant regional variation or multiple dialects. In the pre-hearing process of LB Croydon v D,[1] the mother was repeatedly provided with a Farsi interpreter when her language was Afghan Dari. The UK government website states that in the family court:

> You'll be given an interpreter if your case involves children, domestic violence or forced marriage. You might still be able to get an interpreter for other types of cases, but only if all of the following apply:
>
> • you cannot afford to pay for an interpreter yourself
> • you do not qualify for legal aid
> • you do not have a friend or family member who the judge says can act as your interpreter
>
> You'll always be given an interpreter if you're deaf or have difficulty hearing ('hard of hearing')
>
> You might be able to get an interpreter if you want to speak Welsh in a court in Wales.
>
> (UK Government, undated)

The government website states that the interpreter will normally be available only during the hearing although they may be able to take part in legal discussions before or after the hearing if the judge allows it.

Dubita (2025), an interpreter for the family court, argues that there is a lack of clear unified rules regarding the use of interpreters who can be appointed by the court or privately by members of the legal profession. This leads to ambiguity regarding roles and responsibilities as every county court and sometimes even individual judges have different opinions about how interpreters should be used:

> In some counties, court interpreters are booked only for witness evidence during fact-finding hearings, while solicitors hire private interpreters for all other stages. In others, only court-appointed interpreters are allowed in the courtroom, with privately booked interpreters limited to conferences outside it.
>
> Sometimes, judges ask privately hired interpreters to work in the courtroom while the court-appointed interpreters relax – or vice versa. Other times, interpreters arrive only to be told their services aren't needed, or multiple interpreters show up and are left to sort out roles among themselves.
>
> In the absence of a booked court interpreter, privately hired interpreters are often asked to interpret for the entire hearing, even though they were engaged for a specific task. This leaves interpreters facing a moral dilemma – decline the request and risk delaying proceedings for parents and children separated for months, or step in and shoulder the additional responsibility.
>
> (Dubita, 2025: no page numbers)

Dubita argued that clear unambiguous national standards are needed. In 2025 a report entitled 'Lost in Translation?' was published by the House of Lords Public Services Committee of an investigation carried out by select committee. They described the current process for appointment of interpreters by His Majesty's Courts and Tribunals Service (HMCTS). Interpreting for non-spoken languages such as British Sign Language is outsourced as part of the same tender. When this service becomes aware of the need for an interpreter they contact a provider contracted to the Ministry of Justice (thebigword, TBW). TBW makes the information available to interpreters via an app and they are able to book onto a job in this way. If TWB cannot secure an interpreter by 12 noon on the day before the hearing the MOJ can book an interpreter 'off contract', arranged by staff at individual courts. These bookings are made outside existing pay and quality assurance arrangements. Supply and demand vary by region and specific language. The government's outsourcing (a cost-saving exercise undertaken in 2012 which replaced direct booking by courts that had set fees, terms and conditions and vetting) was criticised in the select committee review by interpreters who regarded it as having resulted in lower qualification requirements, poorer working terms and conditions and poor administration of the service.

The select committee reported that the MoJ's published data masked problems in the service, that the quality control process for interpreters lacked transparency and may be absent altogether in closed court settings, with problems in recruitment and retention of highly qualified and experienced interpreters. Due to low pay rates many qualified interpreters have stopped working for TBW and will only undertake off-contract work where they are engaged directly by the court which allows them to set their own rates. This runs counter to the intentions of the Ministry of Justice. The select committee concluded that the current state of interpreting services in the courts is inefficient, ineffective and poses a risk to the administration of justice (Fouzder, 2025).

These arrangements only apply to the need for interpreters during the court hearing. When interpreters are required in earlier stages of the proceedings, they are appointed on an individual basis. For the purpose of developing trust and understanding it might be expected that one interpreter would be used throughout, although the impartiality required in the hearing might be compromised by a client's developing relationship with one of the parties.

## Use of Interpreters

Interpreters work with the spoken word and translators with the written word. The task of interpretation is complex and challenging, particularly in the field of mental health.

> [T]he myths of the interpreter's neutrality, impartiality and invisibility are frequently challenged in clinical practice. A number of roles emerged during the focus groups. The interpreter acts as an active translator, who is expected to detect hidden meanings and facilitate conversation, as a cultural informant/ broker, who mediates between two different cultural systems, as a co-therapist, who expresses his or her opinions about the service user or about the assessment, and occasionally even as an (almost) therapist, who personally and directly deals with patients in crisis.
>
> (Resera et al., 2015: 202)

Interpreters need to have knowledge and direct experience of the language, dialect and culture of the client's home milieu and of the location in which the litigation is taking place. This brings with it a danger that if both client and interpreter come from the same community, confidentiality may be breached or the client may be reluctant to reveal relevant information for fear of it becoming more widely known (Sawrikar, 2015). Specific dialects that carry social class markers may affect interview dynamics. Clients may not trust anyone from their own community within which they had very negative experiences. In selecting an interpreter, gender, age and faith considerations may be essential. Continuity is desirable in order to foster trust although agencies may try to provide a different interpreter for each session. As one interpreter in Resera et al.'s research put it:

> [T]rust is extremely, is probably crucial in the situation. The client needs to know that everything they're saying, you're passing on and they can say anything and that's why you can't show either shock, or disgust or any of your own emotions about what they're saying to you, because instantly they would stop being open.
>
> (Resera et al., 2015: 12)

It may not be possible for trust to be established with an interpreter present. Whilst people may be agreeable to disclosing unspeakable experiences to a professional tasked with providing assistance, they are less likely to risk making such disclosures to someone who might live on their street. In this case it may be possible to stumble through in English.

There is a question of whether machine translation could assist in overcoming this aspect of the interpretation process. It is being used for the translation of legal documents (White, 2023). There are issues with accuracy and security, particularly when inaccuracies in court documents can lead to delays in hearings or the undermining of evidence once discovered. White concluded that:

> Ultimately, legal firms and barristers should work with a translation provider that collaborates to understand the scenarios where machine translation would be a benefit, and where human input is required, depending on the type of text and language combination required.
>
> (White, 2023: no page numbers)

Friends or family members may be put forward as interpreters, but they are not neutral parties and are likely to have some sort of interest, be it personal, emotional or financial. They may even be a trafficker maintaining control of their victim. They may mistranslate in order to protect their relative and may omit, add, substitute or summarise, inject their own opinions or observations, advocate for or make their own judgements. They may be embarrassed to admit they do not understand. Their limited knowledge of ethical and professional responsibilities may interfere with the demands of confidentiality. Children may have acted as interpreters for their parents in other contexts, but this places too much responsibility upon them and involves a risk that they may learn about issues from which they need to be protected. Whilst translating can be a source of pride and empowerment, it may also be a burden that generates anxiety and may interfere negatively with the parent-child relationship dynamics (Crafter and Iqbal, 2020). Although these are risks associated with family members, it is my experience that professional interpreters may also fall into these traps.

## Positive Practice Guidelines

Rachel Tribe has written extensively about and offered guidelines for working with interpreters in mental health settings, also contributing to the British Psychological Guidelines (British Psychological Society, 2017; Tribe and Thompson, 2022). Her main points are summarised and adapted below:

- If you have not undertaken training in working with interpreters, undertake a training course. If you are working with an interpreter unexpectedly and training is not feasible, read these or other relevant guidelines and allocate time to consider the issues or discuss them with a more experienced colleague.
- Check that the interpreter is qualified and appropriate for the consultation/meeting and speaks the service user's first language.
- Allocate 10–15 minutes in advance of the session to brief the interpreter about the purpose of the meeting and to enable them to inform you about any cultural issues which may have bearing on the session.
- Be mindful of issues of confidentiality and trust when working with someone from a small language community as the service user may be anxious about being identifiable and mistrustful of an interpreter's professionalism. This has particular relevance when working with forced migrants.
- State clearly that you alone hold responsibility for the meeting.
- Commit to a collaborative working relationship based on trust and mutual respect.
- Match if appropriate for gender, age or religion, avoid using relatives and never use a child.
- Create an atmosphere where each member of the triad feels able to ask for clarification if anything is unclear and be respectful to your interpreter, they are an important member of the team who makes your work possible.
- Be aware of the well-being of your interpreter and mindful of the risk of vicarious traumatisation. Consider what support they will be offered, and if they are subcontracted from an external agency, be aware that there is often little support provided by their employer.
- At the end of the session always allocate 10–15 minutes to debrief the interpreter about the session and offer support and supervision as appropriate.

- Extreme caution should be exercised when considering the use of translated assessment measures as languages and concepts are not interchangeable and results may therefore not be valid or meaningful.
- All written translations used should have been back translated [where a translated document is translated back into the original language to verify the accuracy and consistency of the initial translation] to ensure they are fit for purpose.

(Tribe and Thompson, 2022: 613–614)

A colleague of mine advocates a longer meeting with the interpreter at the outset in order to discuss their prior experience and expectations and to clarify their role for the purposes of the family court. She explores whether the interpreter already knows the interviewee or whether they belong to different conflicted factions in the country of origin (such as Tamil and Sinhalese in Sri Lanka). The aim is to establish a collaborative relationship which supports the family member in telling their story. Prior discussion is particularly important when administering psychological tests. Interpreters benefit from understanding something of the purpose of the test and the instructions regarding the use of words and intonation that are specified in test manuals.

Confidentiality is of critical importance; nothing is 'off the record' and everything will be recorded but must be kept confidential to the court. She explains that she wants the interpretation to be in the first person i.e. a repeat of what the interviewee has said rather than a summary or reversion to the third person. She wants to know everything that the client has said. If the interpreter is of the opinion that she has asked an inappropriate question she wants them to tell her so that she can try and think of a different way to enquire into the issue. She explains that as well as helping the client to express themselves, it is also the interpreter's role to help her with getting what she is saying across to the family member without missing anything out. The client may be quiet or crying but it is important that the interpreter does not interject. If the interpreter has an urge to say something it is best that they hold onto it until the end of the session unless it is otherwise likely to be damaging to the relationship between her and the client.

She organises the seating in a triangle and addresses her questions directly to the interviewee in order to clarify that the enquiry is between her and the client with assistance from the interpreter. She discusses the inappropriateness of advocating or judging. When working with refugees and forced migrants traumatic events are often recounted. In describing these experiences clients may struggle to think straight and be triggered back to the sights and sounds of the time. Trying to get the right word can bring them into the here and now. Interpreters need to be aware that they may find this very distressing. Primarily qualitative studies have reported increased emotional stress in interpreters and difficulties in handling traumatic content from clients (Geiling et al., 2021). In such circumstances it may be necessary to work out how the interpreter will obtain their own support. In my experience they can easily and understandably be drawn into the expression of sympathy or offering of opinions and/or encouragement which can impact the purpose and continuity of the session.

It's not easy [to be emotionally detached], because it is in your mind. They're people, they're human beings like you. That person is suffering and you're listening to whatever she's suffering from and it's not easy to forget or to cancel it from your mind. It's natural because you know how they're coming and how they're suffering, so for me it is hard.

(Resera et al., 2015: 198)

Sessions involving interpretation inevitably take at least twice as long since each question and answer has to be repeated. The interpreter is likely to use non-verbal feedback from the client to ascertain whether a question has been understood, and if necessary rephrase it. For much terminology there is no literal translation. In instances where equivalent words or phrases are not available, it may take several attempts for interpreters adequately to interpret what has been said to the client. In consequence the interpreter may appear to be saying more than is desirable and the meaning of extended discussion may be ambiguous but can be clarified in discussion between expert and interpreter afterwards.

At the end of the session my colleague enquires as to how the interpreter thinks that it has gone. She asks how the interpreter is feeling especially when they have had to listen to accounts of distressing and traumatic experiences. On one occasion an interpreter explained that they felt angry with the client because they had experienced similar issues in their home country. He showed her how he had self-harmed and not had help. He was angry that the client was receiving assistance that had never been offered to him. He felt that she was not grateful for the help that she was being given.

In some circumstances, consideration may be given to the use of telephone or video-link interpreting. I have discussed issues arising from virtual interviews elsewhere (Scaife, 2024). At a very practical level some family members may not have access to a private space where confidentiality can be assured or the necessary technology to ensure a reliable connection. Guidance from the British Psychological Society (BPS) suggests that the nature of the work means that it is usually better conducted face-to-face so that nuances of non-verbal communication are not lost. Unless the interview is face-to-face the expert may not be aware of the presence of third parties which may considerably constrain conversations and in the worst case may mean that a trafficker orchestrates responses from a victim. The Association of Sign Language Interpreters (ASLI) in the UK stipulates that sign language interpreters should not participate in video-link interpretation for the purpose of police interviews, court hearings, psychiatric assessments or when meetings may be highly emotional (ASLI, 2015). The BPS offers helpful guidance for those working with interpreters online or via the telephone which became imperative during the Covid-19 pandemic (BPS, 2020).

Instructions in a range of languages on the use of the online platform Zoom can be found at www.burc.org/how-to-use-zoom-in-different-languages/.

The involvement of an interpreter has been reported, unsurprisingly, to influence the outcome of an interview and the data generated (Ingvarsdotter et al., 2010).

These authors argue that it is impossible to devise an all-embracing strategy for conducting interviews with an interpreter. Specific agreements need to be reached in preliminary meetings to suit the purposes of the session and accommodate the knowledge and skills of the parties, particularly when they involve open-ended interviews.

## Best Interests of the Child in Immigration and Asylum Law

The need to know about immigration and asylum law has arisen in my experience as an expert witness when migrants are contesting their right to remain in the UK on the basis of being the parent of a child who was born or has resided in the UK for an uninterrupted period of seven years. A separated parent with whom a child does not live may commence private law proceedings in conjunction with their immigration status application since they need to evidence their parental involvement with the child.

Although the United Nations Convention on the Rights of the Child 1989 (UNCRC) has not been incorporated into UK domestic law, it is applicable as international law with which public bodies are required to comply. Article 3(1) states that, 'In all actions concerning children, whether undertaken by public or private social welfare institutions, courts of law, administrative authorities or legislative bodies, the best interests of the child shall be a primary consideration.' Other legislation (Children Act, 1989; Section 55 of the Borders, Citizenship and Immigration Act, 2009) also makes explicit reference to the best interests of children. The UNCRC states that the child's best interests refer to their general well-being taking into consideration the need for a safe environment, family and close relationships, and development and identity needs (Coram Children's Legal Centre, 2017).

All agencies must comply with the duty to treat a child's best interests as a primary consideration irrespective of the child's immigration status and whether they are separated from or within a family. The duty applies to all of the agency's functions. Social workers, teachers and other professionals may become involved in the decision-making process and may be required to provide supporting evidence concerning what they believe to be in the child's best interests. In a landmark case of ZH v Secretary of State for Home Department[2] a mother was appealing a decision against her removal from the UK. The appeal court held that the best interests of the child should be the first consideration. The court also concluded that it is important to ascertain the child's own views; while a child's interests may be the same as their parents', this should not be taken for granted in every case; and although nationality is not a 'trump card' it is of 'particular importance' in assessing the best interests of a child (the children involved in this case were British citizens).

The Supreme Court has stated that the best interests of a child are a primary, although not always the only primary, but not a paramount consideration when making assessments under Article 8 of the European Convention on Human Rights (ECHR) which protects the right to respect for private and family life, home, and correspondence. The best interests assessment should be carried out in isolation from other factors and should be done at the beginning (Coram Children's Legal Centre, 2017: 4). The complexities of this area of law are discussed extensively in Wray (2023).

Under legislation contained in Section 3(1)(b) of the Immigration Act (1971) a parent may make an application to the Home Office for leave to remain in the UK, which may be for a fixed period or indefinitely. If it is considered to be in a child's best interests for a longer period of leave or indefinite leave to remain to be granted, the reasons need to be made clear in the parent's application. The Home Office may then reach a decision that takes into account the best interests of the child as a primary consideration.

There are a number of requirements that parents need to evidence in order to make an application to live in the UK to care for their child. The child must be under 18 years of age on the date of application or when leave was first granted. The child must live with the parent unless they are in full-time education (such as away at boarding school or university). The child must not be married or in a civil partnership. They must either be a British or Irish citizen, have indefinite leave to remain or proof of permanent residence, have pre-settled status prior to Brexit or have lived in the UK for seven years continuously and it would not be reasonable for them to leave (Gov.uk, undated c). The parent needs to have sole or shared PR for their child. If PR is shared, the child's other parent must not be their partner (they would then need to apply via a different route). The other parent must be a British or Irish citizen and have settled or pre-settled status in the UK. If the child lives with the other parent or carer the applicant must have access to the child in person, as agreed with the other parent or carer or by court order. The parent needs to provide evidence that they are taking an active role in the child's upbringing and has plans to continue to do so. The evidence needs to be dated within the previous four years, may come from the government, school, court or a medical profes- sional, and show that the parent is living with or caring for the child. If the parent is reliant on court evidence they need to obtain consent from the court to use court paperwork. Financial independence must also be evidenced unless the child is a cit- izen or has lived in the UK for seven years and it would be unreasonable for them to leave. On this visa, leave is given for two years and nine months after which an extension may be sought. I have learned that in contested private law where there are uncertainties regarding parental immigration status, it is wise to explore with parents the intersection of applications for leave to remain with applications for arrangements to spend time with children. Motivations may be mixed and can be difficult to disentangle.

In a separate issue, a high court judge highlighted the need to ensure that the immigration status of a child in public law proceedings is clarified at the earliest opportunity, and that any issues with respect to the child's immigration status are dealt with before final orders are made. This arose in Re Y[3] when a special guardi- anship order (SGO) was made to a child's aunt, it later being established that the child had no immigration status in the UK.

## Asylum Seekers and Refugees

The family court does not deal with immigration and asylum claims which are handled by specialist courts termed First-tier Tribunal (the Immigration and Asylum Chamber) and Upper Tribunal. Further levels of appeal are possible up to the level of the European Court of Justice. This does not mean that when working for the family court, asylum seekers and refugees will not feature. I have found that parents who have arrived in the UK fleeing oppressive regimes, ethnic cleansing and torture give some of the most distressing and moving accounts of their life histories. They nevertheless have often needed immense strength and resilience in fleeing their country of origin. In my experience, some pair up with vulnerable and needy partners which can lead them into contact with the local authority if they struggle to meet the needs of the children that they have conceived together or separately.

Refugees are typically impacted by economic hardship, social isolation and mental health difficulties. Wrestling with immigration claims contributes to stress and anxiety. The Mental Health Foundation (2025) cites evidence that exposure to violence and trauma increases refugees' risk of post-traumatic stress disorder (PTSD) (Steel et al., 2009). Depression and anxiety are widespread (Blackmore et al., 2020; Hameed et al., 2018; Tempany, 2009) and refugees are a high-risk group for suicidal ideation (Haase et al., 2022) although the frequency of suicide attempts in this study was reported to be similar to non-refugee populations. International data suggest that about 30% of refugees experience symptoms of PTSD and depression (Fazel et al., 2005). The Mental Health Foundation (2025) quotes asylum seekers describing issues with their status and fears of deportation:

> Everything is stressful. You can't sleep at night time, always thinking about the Home Office, maybe they want to send you back home, today or tomorrow, you never know.
>
> (Asylum seeker, MHF Perthyn programme)

> I was scared of people judging me [as an asylum seeker] so I always hid it. I didn't mention the word asylum seeker when I talked about myself until sixth form. For me, as a child, it was very overwhelming and burdensome because of the fear of being excluded.
>
> (Mental Health Foundation Young Leader)

> I've gone for the main interview five times – this is retraumatising. They think what I am telling them is a cover-up story, even though they can see the physical evidence [of what I have been through] and the government from my home country has sent through evidence to support my claim. They still think it's a hoax story. This is torturing me mentally.

The Mental Health Foundation describes a raft of disadvantages and hurdles faced by refugees and asylum seekers. Their already-tenuous situation is further impacted by barriers to resources, such as 'no recourse to public funds' which can lead to destitution, by public hostility and negative images in the press, loneliness, difficulties accessing public services, barriers to employment and fear of the authorities. Children of refugees, who have migrated with family members or arrive unaccompanied will also be subject to these disadvantages. A low level of reporting of ethnicities in research studies means that it is difficult to determine whether children from minoritised ethnicities are over-represented in the care system. But in 2024, unaccompanied asylum-seeking children (UASC) in England made up 8.8% of the population of children in care (Department for Education, 2024).

Migrant parents of different ethnicities have to meet the challenge of bringing together their individual expectations of children's behaviour and parental roles and responsibilities. I found this challenging enough myself when bringing up my children although my partner and I are ostensibly from similar backgrounds and speak the same language. Given the disadvantages that they face, it is unsurprising that migrants may struggle to meet the demands of parenthood. When carrying out assessments for the family court it is incumbent on practitioners to adopt a trauma-informed approach, recognising the obstacles faced by families in such circumstances.

Guidance is offered by the BPS to psychologists working in this domain (BPS, 2018b). It is advocated that children are never asked to interpret for their parents and that children are assessed separately as they may wish to avoid distressing their parents if seen together as a family. Turning 18 is a crucial event both in terms of applications for leave to remain and the support to which they are entitled if children stay. The BPS recommends a focus on strengths, not only needs; that families should be signposted to sound and reliable legal advice; and the avoidance of assumptions about the appropriate community to which these families belong.

This child's father was a refugee who had experienced torture by the regime in his home country and was not entitled to benefits when injured at work. But in the end, he was able to show that he could provide good quality care for his children and was supported by the local authority.

Dad's a lot stricter than mum so we don't get too much screen time 'cos Emily normally goes on her tablet a lot and starts shouting on it. So she didn't get so much screen time but neither did I. I don't really like a lot of screen time at dad's 'cos it's really fun at dad's. You can play out in the big street and he throws us on the bed and stuff and carries us upside down. Mum likes to be in bed and she has loads of tablets and she's always had a problem with her nerves and her blood pressure. If my dad was living with my mum I'd feel a lot better. At dad's I go to bed at 9 o'clock but at mum's I go to bed really late at about 12 o'clock but I can't fall asleep for worrying and sometimes I have a tantrum, screaming and shouting. Dad leaves me alone for a bit then gets me to join in a football game.

The Mental Health Foundation (undated) tells stories of hope shared by migrant children:

> When I arrived in Scotland as a 14 year old I didn't speak English, I had no friends and no connection with my new home. I needed to learn English to pursue my ambition to go to university. I knew reading would open up the world to me.... Where I come from it is unthinkable to have access to books unless you receive them as a present or have money to buy them. I remember when my teacher told me that I could borrow books from the library I couldn't believe it. I was so excited. So, the library in Glasgow and all the books were gifts of hope.

## International Family Law Issues

International family law concerns issues about children whose parents have residency or citizenship in different countries. Private law issues include situations where a child is taken or retained in a country different from their habitual residence without the consent of the other parent or guardian; determination of 'live with' and child arrangements when parents live in different countries, and disputes between parents when one of them wants to move abroad with the child.

In some public law proceedings, kinship carers who live overseas may be identified. Assessment of overseas carers may be facilitated by the International Child Abduction and Contact Unit (ICACU) provided that it involves either a Member State of the European Union (other than Denmark) or a State Party to the 1996 Hague Convention. The ICACU may have practical knowledge and experience of the processes and procedures in the other country which it can usefully share in response to an enquiry. The charity Children and Families Across Borders (CFAB) protects children who have become separated from their family across international borders. CFAB provides expertise and experience to local authorities, the courts and other public agencies to facilitate positive outcomes for children when different jurisdictions are involved.

---

### Key Points from this Chapter

- About 15% of the UK population was born overseas. Some of these families will be represented in referrals to expert witnesses in family proceedings.
- Experts need to become familiar with the law and issues related to culture, language, forced migration and asylum without making unwarranted assumptions.
- Experts need ongoing developing awareness of their own cultural contexts and histories in influencing their opinions.
- When working with interpreters, mutual expectations, methods of engagement and professional boundaries need to be clarified and the processes involved in working in partnership agreed.

- Sessions involving interpreters will necessarily take twice as long and this needs to be factored into arrangements for meeting with family members.
- Children, relatives or friends of the family are inappropriate interpreters in this context.
- Arrangements may need to be made for support of interpreters when sessions are harrowing or potentially traumatic.
- Migrants' applications for resident status in the UK may intersect with private law proceedings under the seven-year residence rule.
- The UNCRC Article 3(1) states that 'In all actions concerning children, whether undertaken by public or private social welfare institutions, courts of law, administrative authorities or legislative bodies, the best interests of the child shall be a primary consideration.' This approach is underpinned by additional domestic legislation.
- Asylum and migration claims are not handled by the family court but may arise there.

## Notes

1 LB Croydon v D (Critical Scrutiny of the Paediatric Overview) [2024] EWFC 438.
2 *ZH (Tanzania) v Secretary of State for the Home Department* [2011] UKSC 4.
3 *Y (Failure to Clarify Immigration Status), Re* [2024] EWFC 159.

Chapter 10

# Current Issues and Future Directions

## Introduction

This chapter focuses on recent preoccupations of the family court and issues under discussion at the time of writing. The most significant driver of these issues has been delay in family law courts. Proceedings have been taking months or years to resolve, during which time hostilities between separated parents have often continued to fester and grow. Reforms and initiatives, such as the introduction of the Pathfinder model in 2022 and relaunch of the Public Law Outline (PLO) in 2023, were designed to address this issue.

Whilst the intention in these initiatives has been to reduce the duration of proceedings and improve the lives of children and families, this was brought into question in a podcast hosted by Robertson (2025). Ayisha Robertson, Kate Hellin and Andrew Pack discussed systemic approaches to struggling families, with a focus on the support available to parents within the wider family and social system. They argued that the 26-week aspiration of the PLO is utterly inadequate as a timescale in which parents might be expected to change and overcome negative experiences and trauma dating from their early lives. By the time assessments have been completed and sources of assistance identified, the actual time parents have available in which to evidence change is only three to four months. The source for the 26-week deadline was identified as the Norgrave report (2011) which was written following the death of Peter Connolly. This took place during a period of austerity and cuts to welfare budgets. Pack argued that the conclusions of the Norgrave report were resource-driven with the intention of reducing demands on public funds, and that recent preoccupations of the family court have been process-oriented. When first working in the courts he never left a hearing without the judge having enquired into the child's state of well-being and more often than not, asking parents how their contact with the child was going. That is not to say that judges are no longer humane but that the current focus on process tends to have a dehumanising and distancing effect. When children are taken away from parents it is a failure of the state and in the longer term requires even greater public resources than are incurred through extended proceedings.

Nevertheless, the Norgrave report highlighted some issues that continue to gain attention. It referenced the need for the child's voice to be heard, pointed out

DOI: 10.4324/9781003453390-10

the benefits of Family Group Conferences, highlighted the focus on adversarial approaches that tend to fuel rather than help parents resolve conflict, argued for the development of mediation and other alternative dispute resolution (ADR) services, proposed the development of new means of protection for vulnerable witnesses, and recommended a reduction in commissioning of expert reports which was seen as contributing to delay. Transparency was raised as an issue but seen as a complex area requiring further consideration by the government. The report supported the Justice Select Committee's recommendation that the scheme to increase media access to the courts (contained in Part 2 of the Children, Schools and Families Act 2010) should not be implemented. The Transparency Project subsequently lobbied for greater transparency and progress was made on this issue.

## The Voice of the Child

We spoke to so many people involved in the family justice system – the guardian, family legal advisers, we wrote a letter to the judge, we had to speak to police at some points. You would think because we spoke to so many people we felt heard. Unfortunately, that was not the case. I was told in a meeting with my guardian I had no say. I thought she was supposed to be there as a voice for me in the court. I was a bit confused by that. I was told by people I was lying, being a drama queen. Even if I said what I wanted to say, it wouldn't go anywhere. I lost hope in the system and felt hopeless.

(Fouzder, 2024b: no page numbers)

The quote above was presented by CAFCASS chief executive Jacky Tiotto to an audience at the Family Justice Council Bridget Lindley lecture as an example highlighting the need to give greater priority and consideration to how a child's voice is heard. In Re D[1] Baroness Hale expressed the importance of listening to children in litigation which touches and concerns their lives:

There is a growing understanding of the importance of listening to the children involved in children's cases. It is the child, more than anyone else, who will have to live with what the court decides. Those who do listen to children understand that they often have a point of view which is quite distinct from that of the person looking after them. They are quite capable of being moral actors in their own right. Just as the adults may have to do what the court decides whether they like it or not, so may the child. But that is no more reason for failing to hear what the child has to say than it is for refusing to hear the parents' views.

In 2015 the Ministry of Justice gave a press release stating that children would have a greater say in family court cases (UK Government, 2015). Changes were made so that children aged ten years and above could communicate their views to the court via meetings, letters, pictures or by way of a third person in addition to their CAFCASS officer or social worker. The plans complemented reforms to guidance for judges seeing children which were set in train by the then President of the Family Division, Sir James Munby. The intention was to enable children to take an active role in decisions about them, referencing what they have to say and also what they do.

Sometimes there is a suggestion that a child be called to give evidence during proceedings. A presumption against such an arrangement was challenged in the case of Re W.[2] In consequence, the court decides whether a child should give evidence and be subject to cross-examination by striking a balance between Article 6 (requirement of fairness which includes the opportunity to challenge evidence) and Article 8 (respect for private and family life) of the Human Rights Act. In a 'Re W exercise', evidence is gathered about the merits and risks of a young person giving testimony and the impact that this may have on them. The court considers the assessment report and hears arguments for and against. If it is determined that the balance is in favour of the child giving evidence, the court considers whether any special arrangements need to be put in place to either safeguard the child or to minimise the emotional harm.

The principle that children have a right to be heard in legal matters affecting them is enshrined in the United Nations Convention on the Rights of the Child (CRC) and was first introduced in UK legislation in the Children Act (1989) with the Children and Families Act (2014) building on this foundation, introducing measures to ensure that children's voices are central to the family justice system. Working Together to Safeguard Children (2018) emphasised the importance of listening to children as a key element in safeguarding, further reinforced in Working Together (Department for Education, 2023b). Children's voices are crucial in giving them a sense of empowerment and respect, thereby increasing their self-esteem and confidence (Access Group, 2024). Children often have unique insights and perspectives. When they feel heard they are more likely to engage positively with services, with better outcomes in education, health and overall wellbeing. Children are typically aware when something is wrong which may mean earlier detection of difficulties.

The NSPCC (NSPCC Learning, 2024) analysed a sample of serious case reviews (SCRs) published between 2019 and 2023 where practice failures concerning the voice of the child pertained. These children were harmed, seriously injured or died of neglect, suspected FII and physical abuse, sexual abuse, serious self-harm, attempted suicide, unexplained death of an infant and death caused by a parent or carer.

Children in these cases were not seen frequently enough or asked about their views and feelings. This was particularly the case for children with disabilities or complex communication needs, sometimes due to a lack of professional confidence and knowledge. Children tended to be seen at the time of specific incidents rather than during more routine contacts so that changes in circumstances or developments were sometimes missed. Pre-verbal and non-verbal children's experiences were often sought through conversations with parents rather than observation of the child, the parents' interaction with the child, or through play. Teenagers were sometimes seen as uncooperative or hard to engage such that professionals sometimes stopped attempting to understand their experiences. Sometimes professionals were too ready to accept parental accounts, sometimes making assumptions about the child's wishes and feelings rather than seeking the child's views. The ways in which children's experiences could be explored were limited when they were not regularly in school. Sometimes children were not provided with opportunities to be seen on their own or this was resisted through parental objection which was not adequately challenged.

Home visits were not always used effectively as opportunities to communicate with children in their own environment. Questioning styles used by practitioners did not always open the door to the child's views, but rather gave the impression that they were more interested in parental needs. Inadequate steps were taken to understand and reflect upon what was being said by the child or the reasons that might account for the child's behaviour. Children's actual words were not always recorded; professional interpretations alone being documented. Frequent changes of worker and lengthy gaps between visits due to excessive workloads and staff turnover made it difficult for children to form enduring and trusting relationships with professionals. Other people's knowledge of the child and family was not always accessed. These people could have assisted with communication and helped with the engagement process. Information that could have been provided by siblings or extended family members was not sought. The NSPCC argued that greater emphasis needed to be placed on play, creative tools and observation.

Not only are there issues in children being heard in public law proceedings, but the Nuffield Family Justice Observatory (Hargreaves, 2024) reported that in around half of the children who were involved in private law cases starting in 2019 there was no indication that they participated. Only 5.2% of children in England and 7.2% of children in Wales had more than one marker indicating child participation. This showed little variation according to the age of the child although the older children were less likely to participate. The longer the case lasted, the more likely it was that the children had been consulted about their wishes and feelings. Welfare reports and those written by children's guardians are the primary methods for conveying children's views to the court but cannot be ordered prior to the first hearing (this may have changed subsequent to the introduction of Pathfinder courts). This means there is no universal mechanism giving children the opportunity to express their opinions in private law proceedings. When CAFCASS does become involved they have developed various resources to aid communication with children. Together with young people they have created a video to explain their role in hearing what young people have to say which can be accessed at https://www.cafcass.gov.uk/children-and-young-people.

HJ MacDonald, Deputy Head of International Justice for England and Wales, in an address to the Judicial Council in Dublin (Courts and Tribunals Judiciary, 2024c) emphasised the challenge of hearing the *authentic* voice of the child, particularly when this is impacted by developmental status, disability, minoritised ethnicity and cultural background. He argued that those seeking the authentic views of the child often do not have first-hand knowledge of the social, geographical, cultural, religious and linguistic traditions that underpin the child's identity and views. These need to be integrated into the whole effort to ascertain, understand and act on the child's views and experiences.

Not only do these factors impact obtaining the authentic views of the child, but the judgment of the Court of Appeal in Re C[3] dealt with the degree of influence that a parent may bring to bear on the expressed view of the child. It also raised issues about meetings between children and judges.

In Re C the parents were in conflict regarding arrangements for the care of the children. The appointed expert concluded:

> Whereas I acknowledge and agree that there is bound to be some degree of influence over a child by a parent, I also believe that in this situation, the degree of influence over A by his father is extreme and damaging. The papers that I have read describe the potential for the child to be 'parroting' a parent's beliefs/words, and to act as their mouthpiece. In my opinion, this situation is more insidious and far-reaching than that as A has absorbed a belief system of his father's…
>
> I would say that the majority of the areas under consideration outlined above lead to a view that A is not competent to instruct his own solicitor. The main arguments 'for' his doing so are his overall intelligence and his strength of feelings about this. However, I would say that his strength of feeling is at least in part based on false beliefs or premises. So although there is something of a balanced answer, I would say that the overall answer is that A is very probably not competent to instruct his own solicitor, on around a 90:10 balance.

The father in this case had published a book which contained significant personal information about the children, the case and professionals including foster carers. Injunctions were granted by the High Court and Amazon removed the book from sale.

When the case was returned to court by the parents, the judge agreed to meet with the eldest child. As a result, she concluded that A was very mature and insightful which was totally at odds with the evidence from two experts. Neither did she give a reason for rejecting their evidence despite previously having unhesitatingly accepted one of their assessments. The judge was regarded as having made her own assessment of A's ability to instruct that went well beyond the permissible use of such a meeting, the purpose of which is for the child to meet the judge, not for the judge to meet the child.

The use of such meetings is governed by guidelines produced by the Family Justice Council (Justice, 2010). The purpose can be to help children feel more involved and connected. They are not for the purpose of gathering evidence but rather to help children understand that it is the judge, after weighing up a lot of options, who makes decisions, and the outcomes are never the responsibility of the child. The guidelines lay out that the judge should explain to the child at an early stage that they cannot hold secrets. What is said by the child will, other than in exceptional circumstances, be communicated to their parents and other parties. Judges are advised to discuss with the child how their decisions will be communicated to the child. In 2025 the President of the Family Division published guidance on when, how and why judges should write to children to give an informative and accurate account of their decisions and the reasons underpinning them. A toolkit was produced to support judges in this task which is discussed in a podcast hosted by Opie (2025b). The podcast focuses on improving accessibility and compassion in court communication, highlighting how a well-crafted letter can empower children to understand decisions affecting their lives.

> Writing to children is one important way of ensuring that children have the opportunity to participate in family court proceedings. A child's right to participate in proceedings and to have the final decision communicated to them in a way they can understand is enshrined in international and domestic legislation and guidance – as a way of both informing welfare-based decisions and upholding children's rights and access to justice (Stalford & Hollingsworth, 2020).
>
> (President of the Family Division, 2025: 3)

There may be several health and social care professionals and their solicitors holding different opinions about what is in the best interests of the children. In my experience, there are times when it seems as if an expert has been instructed to resolve a difference of opinion between the local authority and a children's guardian. This is not stated explicitly but emerges out of an exploration of the issues. However impartial the expert attempts to be, whenever there are 'sides' in a dispute, the expert may be viewed as drawn into one or the other which tends to generate resistance from the other 'side'. The response to this may be the instruction of yet another expert although the rules of the family court are meant to protect against this by specifying the use of a single joint expert who acts on behalf of all of the involved parties (Practice Direction Part 25).

In my experience, direct questioning is not the most helpful way to try and establish the authentic views of children. They often have a wish to please (somebody) and are vulnerable to adult authority. Children have learned that there are 'right' and 'wrong' answers and they may try and make guesses about the adult's motivation in asking these questions. I have written extensively about methods for exploring a child's experience in Scaife (2024). Activities suited to the child's age and developmental level can be used to elicit experiences and opinions indirectly, with children sometimes recounting incidents that are quite shocking. They can be quite gleeful when posting cards with written statements into boxes representing family members since this distances them from expressing negative opinions directly. Audio recordings allow me to use the child's actual words in my report and in private law proceedings in particular, I hope that parents will take heed of what their children say.

I always talk to children's teachers who see them on a daily basis and are alert to changes in behaviour that may indicate issues at home. Alarm bells ring when a parent is opposed to a child being seen without their presence. But consent is invariably given since they recognise that this is likely to be seen unfavourably by the court. Sometimes a child is aware that it is their parent who is struggling and needs assistance. A child with a disability whom I saw in a CYPMHS service was quite clear that it was his mother who needed help and if I did not provide it he was going to kill me.

No matter how hard I have tried to engage children, there are times when I have found it impossible and I am then reliant on reports by others who play a part in their lives, and their reluctance to communicate is in itself information about the child in their context.

## Alternative Dispute Resolution

Traditional approaches to private law disputes between separated parents have been called into question since their adversarial approach tends to exacerbate animosity. Approaches have been introduced under the umbrella of ADR with a greater emphasis on investigation and the resolution of differences out of court. The Family Solutions Group (2022) has argued that the use of the term 'dispute' is not widely used outside legal circles and would benefit from being dropped and replaced with 'alternative' or 'non-court' resolution. Alternative approaches were summarised by Reed (2022).

Mediation is probably the most widely used of the alternatives to proceedings. Since 2014 it has been a requirement that parents attend a Mediation Information and Advice Meeting (MIAM) prior to lodging an application for child arrangements to the court. They may be attended by parents separately or together. There are limited exceptions to this requirement including when there is evidence of domestic abuse. Mediators are impartial and trained to assist parents in agreeing arrangements for the care of the children. But there are no formal rules for mediation which may contribute to difficulties in resolving disagreements. Agreements reached through mediation are not legally binding but can be made so through the terms being drawn up into a consent order. This is then sent to court to be approved by a judge when it is attributed the same status as a court order.

Mediation can be useful where parents recognise the need for some compromise. It is regarded as being much cheaper, less time-consuming and less stressful than going to court and some services may be free or funded by legal aid. People on low incomes can attend a MIAM and mediation without payment and the government has provided £500 vouchers to encourage parents to take this path.

In Collaborative Law each parent is represented by their own lawyer who gives advice but tries to work constructively with the other parent's lawyer to reach an agreement. If this attempt is unsuccessful and they subsequently make an application to court, parents need to appoint a different lawyer. Psychologists or counsellors can be invited to join the meetings to provide support to parents. Round Table

Discussion describes an approach in which each parent is represented by a solicitor and barrister. It is similar to collaborative law but solicitors may be retained if proceedings are subsequently instigated.

Arbitration is a process that takes place alongside legal advice. Parents agree that the decision of the arbitrator will be legally binding. It is a relatively new approach to disputes about the care of the children and demands considerable resources to pay legal costs, the costs of the arbitrator and of obtaining an order to approve their payment. It has the advantages of speed, choice and continuity of arbitrator, choice of issues and some flexibility and control. There is a range of other novel legal services available using divorce coaches rather than lawyers to help parents work through and resolve their disputes.

In an attempt to manage family court backlogs the government considered whether to make mediation mandatory in private law proceedings. Whilst this was not ultimately agreed, in 2024 the Family Procedure Rules were extended to strengthen the provisions on alternative forms of dispute resolution. Limits were placed on exemptions from attending a MIAM and additional forms were introduced requiring litigants to explain how they have meaningfully engaged in the process. These have to be completed prior to the first court hearing. There is provision for judges to encourage alternatives to the proceedings during court hearings and to postpone them to allow for this if it is considered desirable. Parents can be penalised for lack of engagement with non-court dispute resolution (NCDR) through costs orders.

Since 2009, parents could be recommended by CAFCASS or ordered by the courts to attend a Separated Parents Information Programme. Separated parents were not required to attend the same programme as each other. The programme entailed a day-long four-hour course in which the impact of parental separation on children was explored. This was revised collaboratively with parents in 2023 and is now called 'Planning Together for Children' in England and 'Working Together for Children' (WT4C) in Wales. It combines e-learning, group work and online support for parents.

Mediation has been emphasised by policymakers as a preferred form of dispute resolution. I have found it difficult to locate *convincing* evidence of improvements in outcomes achieved through mediation. Morris et al. (2018) claimed that there were only two randomised controlled trials comparing mediation and court litigation which were both conducted in the USA in 1987 and 1991. Those studies reported that mediation was cheaper, quicker, had higher rates of consumer satisfaction and lower rates of future court presentation, but there was no published research comparing parental adherence to court-determined as opposed to mediation-determined agreements.

The Family Mediation Council carried out a survey of mediators in 2019. Forty-nine per cent of cases were reported by mediators to have resulted in full agreement and were written up, 8% reached agreement on some issues and were written up and a further 16% agreed proposals but they were not written up. It is not clear whether these agreements involved arrangements for the care of the children or other issues such as financial settlements.

Only a small number of respondents knew what happened to cases after they had produced outcome documentation. Those did know (sic) commonly said 80% or over obtained a court order by consent for financial matters. Those respondents who mentioned children only cases said that they rarely resulted in an order, instead resulting in either an open letter or parenting plan.

(Family Mediation Council, 2019: 4)

The Family Mediation Council is not a disinterested party as the title of its 2025 conference suggests: 'FMC 10th Anniversary Conference: ensuring the growth of the profession'.

For parents in a study carried out by the Nuffield Family Justice Observatory (2022), mediation did not always meet parents' needs:

It was common for it to be frustrating and sometimes distressing, because the information was not clear or realistic, the mediator was not able to effectively identify and manage the power dynamics between parents, or because there were misplaced expectations. In some cases, there had not been effective screening for domestic abuse to assess whether mediation was appropriate. Counselling, on the other hand, was found to be valuable. Parents appreciated the emotional support they received, and the opportunity to express and process their feelings about the separation to someone who was impartial.

(Symonds et al., 2022, 2022: no page numbers)

The study also reported that contrary to the commonly-held view, if at all possible parents avoided court, being concerned about the repercussions for their relationship and excessive costs. The authors argued that policy development should move away from a binary model of either court or mediation and give a greater emphasis to advice, guidance and emotional support for parents and children. Even legal formalisation rarely marked the end of a parental relationship, because ongoing negotiation was invariably necessary, especially when circumstances changed.

## Child Sexual Abuse, Exploitation, and Online Abuse

"I couldn't talk about the sexual abuse. It was too difficult. I wanted them all to notice and to ask me what was going on." (Interview with child who was sexually abused). Yet when children did tell someone, as they did in nearly three-quarters of the reviews we looked at, they were often not listened to or were disbelieved, with subsequent retractions taken as proof that the abuse had not occurred, and leaving them at further risk of harm.

(Child Safeguarding Review Panel, 2024: 8)

This quote is from a study carried out between 2018 and 2023, during which time the independent Child Safeguarding Practice Review Panel received over 130 rapid reviews, related SCRs and local child safeguarding practice reviews (LCSPRs) which featured child sexual abuse in the family environment. They termed this 'intrafamilial child sexual abuse', perpetrated by a child's family member/s or other people close to and involved with the family. The panel decided that this volume of cases warranted further investigation. They noted that intrafamilial child sexual abuse often overlapped with child sexual abuse out-with the family because family members were not infrequently involved in the production and distribution of child sexual abuse material (such as images or videos), in child sexual exploitation, and in the organised abuse of children by multiple abusers. They concluded that practitioners should consider the risk of other forms of child sexual abuse occurring when assessing children for whom there are concerns of intra-familial child sexual abuse.

They reported that in over a third of the reviews, the people who sexually abused children (98% of whom were men) were already known to pose a risk of sexual harm, often over a period of years, but this knowledge was ignored, denied or deflected. They argued that 'the system' did not notice or comprehend this kind of risk. My own sense is that it takes practice for professionals to feel comfortable with talking about sexual matters and using the associated vocabulary. What might raising these issues say about them/us? Feelings of shame, fear and concern about betraying their families meant that children struggled to tell others what was happening. So, many factors conspired to allow children to continue to be sexually abused within their families for months and years with appalling long-term consequences for mental health.

Not long before the report by the Safeguarding Review Panel, the Independent Inquiry into Child Sexual Abuse was published (IICSA) (Jay et al., 2022). That inquiry set up the Truth Project which gave more than 6,000 victims and survivors of child sexual abuse an opportunity to share their experiences and make suggestions for change.

> The Inquiry held 325 days of public hearings. It processed over two million pages of evidence and heard from 725 witnesses. The Inquiry has also published 61 reports and publications. Over 7,300 victims and survivors engaged with the work of the Inquiry. More than 700 gave evidence at public hearings or provided statements. Over 6,200 came forward to share their experiences at the Truth Project and nearly 1,800 joined the Inquiry's Victims and Survivors' Forum.
>
> (Jay et al., 2022: 1)

For each of the people who shared their experiences, their lives had been fundamentally altered and negatively impacted by the abuse. The inquiry reported that the deviousness and cruelty of perpetrators was limitless, involving threats, beatings and humiliation of the children. Disabled and other vulnerable children were often selected as easy victims. They were groomed and their parents befriended in order to create a veneer of genuine affection which allowed the abuse to continue and also reduced the likelihood of subsequent reporting of disclosures. The children suffered harm to their mental, emotional and physical well-being with life-long consequences. For most, their education, familial relationships, sexual relationships and job prospects were affected. In many cases the abuse led to self-harm and for some, suicide.

Children often tried to tell or show adults what was happening. This was sometimes in 'acting out' behaviours or in ways that led them to be given a diagnosis themselves. Often adults either disbelieved them or failed to provide a trusted space in which they could make disclosures. Many gave up trying to report what had happened to them. They were powerless in the institutions such as churches, schools, foster placements or residential care homes where the abuse was taking place.

The inquiry found that institutions were guilty of protecting their reputations and those of their staff at the expense of children who had been abused. Many lacked appropriate policies and procedures for handling disclosures. Instead of being held to account, perpetrators were moved on or given support when this was not provided to victims. Records about the allegations of abuse were not kept.

> Several cross-cutting themes recurred throughout the investigation, including undue deference by police, prosecutors and political parties towards politicians and others in public life; differences in the treatment of wealthy and well-connected individuals, as opposed to those who were poorer, more deprived and without access to networks of influence; failures to put children and their welfare first; and the prioritisation of reputation over the needs and safety of children. Political parties showed themselves to be more concerned about political fallout than safeguarding and, in some cases in the past, the honours system prioritised reputation and discretion in making awards with little or no regard for victims of nominated persons.
>
> (Jay et al., 2022: 11)

The report highlighted how perpetrators were grooming children and manipulating them into engaging in sexual acts on screen, often for the purpose of sexual exploitation. The internet was being used to distribute indecent images of children and live-stream sexual abuse. A raft of recommendations was made to the UK and devolved governments.

In clinical practice and in my role as an expert witness it has always been my understanding that disclosures of any form of child abuse must be reported to the local authority or police. However, IICSA recommended that laws should be introduced mandating people who work with children ('mandated reporters') to report any disclosures, observations of sexual abuse, or signs that indicate a child has been or is being sexually abused. In some circumstances, failure to make such a report would be a crime. Mandated reporters are those who work in regulated activity with children in positions of trust (under the Safeguarding and Vulnerable Groups Act 2006, as amended) and police officers.

The report recommended that all child victims of sexual abuse should be offered specialist and accredited therapeutic support and that a code of practice should be introduced regarding keeping and accessing records of child sexual abuse which should be kept for 75 years with appropriate review periods. Jess Phillips (Under-Secretary of State in the Home Office) announced to parliament in April 2025 that in the Crime and Policing Bill the government, with the aim of creating a culture of openness and honesty, would be taking forward the new mandatory duty to report child sexual abuse for individuals in England undertaking activity with children. They would introduce a new criminal offence of obstructing an individual from making a report under that duty. She said that the government was instructing the Information Commissioner's Office to produce a code of practice on the retention of personal data relating to child sexual abuse. They planned to remove the three-year limitation period on victims and survivors bringing personal injury claims in the civil courts and shift the burden of proof from survivors to defendants, thereby protecting victims from having to relive their trauma to obtain compensation they are owed. They planned to bring forward proposals regarding the provision of therapeutic services for victims and survivors of child sexual abuse, although the details were reserved until after the next spending review. But in July 2025 the Human Rights Select Committee expressed concern that without stronger penalties for failing to act, the new duty to report child sexual abuse may fail to have an impact.

Expert witnesses in the family court are bound to encounter children who have been and/or are being sexually abused, and also adults who suffered such abuse in their childhoods. I have met adult clients who have disclosed their own historical abuse and their current fears or evidence that the abuser was continuing to target children. Sometimes these parents do not want to disclose their identity for fear of retribution. It is to be hoped that this kind of disclosure would also meet the requirements for mandatory reporting by the practitioner to whom it was revealed.

Individual reports to the inquiry by adults who had been sexually abused in childhood give pointers to practitioners about how professional responses could better have facilitated revelation of the abuse. 'Ruby' might have been able to make a disclosure if she had been seen alone and away from the family home where she always feared that she might be overheard. Another contributor found the Achieving Best Evidence (ABE) interviews 'horrendous'. She felt unsupported and did not know what to do. One interview lasted 4½ hours and the endless questioning made her feel as if she was on trial.

In my experience, when questioned by adults in authority, children sometimes cast around in order to find the 'correct' answer. In Re EF, GH and IJ,[4] the three brothers expressed feeling pressured into making a series of allegations in order for the police to believe them. At Paragraph 154 of his Judgment Mr Justice Keegan quoted one of the children as saying:

I was just searching for things to tell the police, it seemed to be what they wanted to hear. The police seemed to want more and more incidents; to me it felt like if I didn't say something, they wouldn't take me seriously.

Allegations of sexual abuse of a child arise in the context of both public and private law proceedings. It is not for the expert to determine the veracity of these and a clause in letters of instruction is usually included to remind experts of this:

> Unless you have been specifically asked to do so you should please avoid expressing a view with regard to the factual disputes as this is of course the province of the Judge at the final hearing. Where appropriate it would be of assistance if you are able to express your opinion on the basis of alternative findings regarding the factual disputes.

This means that questions in the letter of instruction tend to be expressed in terms of hypothetical risk: 'If the Court finds that the father has touched the child's bottom or vagina inappropriately, please comment upon this in terms of any risk the father may pose to the children and what work may be done to ameliorate any risk.'

Such questions mean that the allegations need to be explored with both parents and children. If the child has already been given an ABE interview by the police, there may be greater flexibility in how this is discussed with the child. If not, there is a need for caution about what may be interpreted as leading questions. In order best to represent what children have said in interview, I make an audio-recording which not only allows the court to hear the child's voice but can also provide evidence that the interview was not leading.

Children not infrequently make disclosures to adults or peers which they fail to repeat in ABE interviews. This does not mean that it did not happen, but the evidence available must be of sufficient substance to meet the balance of probabilities test in the family court. This was the case in KW v ST B.[5] The child's mother claimed that after contact with her father she said that her father had digitally penetrated her vagina and/or bottom. A forensic examiner found three injuries to the child's vagina which in her opinion were consistent with sexual assault by digital penetration. This was filmed and saved on a DVD. At a pre-ABE preparatory session the child repeated the claim to a police officer but during the ABE interview itself, the child disclosed nothing and the police decided to take no further action. A circuit judge found that the father had, on a single occasion, sexually abused the child by digital penetration of the vagina but on appeal by the father who had denied the incident, an independent paediatrician gave the following evidence

> Despite the lack of medical evidence, the fact remains that B disclosed on the 28/08/18 to her mother and subsequently in the presence of an intermediary and police officer during a pre-interview assessment (10/9/18) when talking to teddy, that "daddy hurts her bumby,…he puts his fingers down her bumby, … She indicated on a picture that she calls the genital area noony and the anal area bumby, and specified when it happened: "Grandma is in the toilet when daddy puts his fingers in my bumby." When asked directly where dad puts his finger, she replied: "…in the noony, in the little hole, …lots of times." However, in the archiving (sic, semble achieving) best evidence (ABE) interview, B would not

talk, was evasive, and repeatedly stated that she could not remember and finally said, "I can't remember what my dad did, like when he hurts me."

From my paediatric experience, I can think of several reasons why B didn't want to talk about her father during the video-interview. The strange new setting might have contributed, she might have felt that she had said it all already, felt pressured, had a conflict of interest and loyalty, realising that she had got her father into trouble, but also, she may have been uncomfortable because what she had previously said was not true. I also wonder if the child in the last 19 months expanded further on what she previously said. Children who have experienced maltreatment are often able to talk about what happened once they are in a secure setting and don't have further contact with their abuser.

The medical evidence, in my opinion, does not help to ascertain if the alleged sexual touching or any form of child sexual abuse to the genito-anal area has taken place. Despite the good quality of the recording, I cannot identify in the DVD of the genital examination two of the three lacerations described by Dr B. The third laceration is in my opinion likely to be the result of the examination technique, possibly facilitated by the previously noted nappy rash.

(Expert Court Reports, 2025)

The judge concluded that in the circumstances, the court would never find that it was more likely than not that the father had sexually abused his daughter in the manner alleged or at all. Thus, no findings were made of sexual impropriety by this father against his daughter. The judge opined that in such matters, the law treats as a certainty that the conduct alleged did not happen and the father was therefore entitled to be treated as exonerated.

In some cases, extensive fabricated allegations may be made in the intensity of the parental battle. In my experience children sometimes become pawns in this conflict and may be coached into making false allegations, and be subjected to intrusive medical investigations and circumstances in which they are required to repeat the false accounts. At times it is quite clear from a child's unusual responses that something is distinctly wrong about their disclosures. At other times, as in K W v ST B, experts are left with uncertainty and a range of possible explanations about what happened.

In Re: E[6] the parents made allegations of domestic abuse against each other. By later that year the mother was making allegations that the father had physically and sexually abused two of the children and, to a more limited degree, a third child, and that he enabled other men to sexually abuse them as part of a sex ring. The father alleged that the mother was fabricating these allegations in order to disrupt his relationship with the children. The allegations were investigated by the local authority and police who conducted ABE interviews as a result of which no further action was taken.

In 2024 at a subsequent fact-finding hearing, the judge said that there was 'considerable force in the argument that the allegations only emerged once it became clear to the mother that this was the only way to prevent the father from having contact with the children.' Her answers in evidence were rambling and avoidant; in marked contrast to her clear and determined approach outside the courtroom when trying to persuade professionals that the children had been sexually abused, and her anger when they did not accept her viewpoint. At Paragraph 184, the judge concluded that:

> The mother has convinced herself that the father sexually abused her children. Secure in her belief that the central allegation is true, she has pressed relentlessly for other professionals to accept her perspective and act accordingly. When they have not acted or not acted in the way that she has wanted, she has redoubled her efforts. She has, in my judgment, pressured her children to 'start talking'. She has convinced them that the father is a bad person and that he poses a danger to her and to them. The father's actions in attending the property and threatening the mother, once seen by the children or relayed to them, have reinforced that view.

At Paragraph 7 the judge concluded:

> The mother has behaved in an alienating way towards the children by expressing an ongoing pattern of negative attitudes and communications about the father which had the potential or intention to undermine or destroy the children's relationships with the father. I have not found the mother's allegations of rape or sexual abuse of the children against the father to be proved.

As discussed more extensively in Chapter 7, this is a complex area of work for the family court which demands significant experience of and precision in investigation and reporting. The expert's assessment is conducted in a context influenced by vested interests and pressure group perspectives made widely available through social media. But it is vitally important that the extent of child sexual abuse, its ramifications for the individuals upon whom it is perpetrated, and the lengths to which individuals and institutions can be drawn into covering it up are publicised and attempts made to change past attitudes and behaviours so that children can grow up being protected from such experiences. Expert witnesses can be of critical importance in providing independent carefully constructed opinions that assist the family court in reaching best decisions for children in these families.

## Deprivation of Liberty

Article 5 of the ECHR addresses the issue of 'deprivation of liberty' (DoL). This article of the convention protects everyone's right to liberty by setting out the circumstances in which deprivation may be imposed and the strict safeguards which must be applied for those who are thus deprived. Any deprivation of liberty must be determined by a 'procedure prescribed by law' with those confined having the right to a review of the lawfulness of the decision by a court. Arrangements for the care of children will give rise to a deprivation of liberty if (i) there is confinement in a particular restricted place for a not negligible period of time, (ii) there is a lack of valid consent and (iii) the state is responsible for the confinement. This test (comprising what are termed these three Storck components) differs for young people aged 16 and 17 and children under the age of 16. This was determined in a judgment Re D[7] when Lady Black argued that 'as a matter of common law, parental responsibility for a child of 16 or 17 years of age does not extend to authorising the confinement of a child in circumstances which would otherwise amount to a deprivation of liberty'.

For children under 16, parents' proper exercise of parental responsibilities may include the need to place restrictions on their child that might amount to 'continuous supervision and control'. Neither are under-16s free to choose where or with whom they live. This means that if children under the age of 16 are assessed as not being Gillick competent (having the maturity and capacity on their own to make relevant decisions and to understand the implications of them) to make decisions related to their confinement, those with parental responsibility may consent to confinement on their behalf, providing that this decision is a proper exercise of their parental responsibility. This is not then categorised as deprivation of liberty which means that the legal safeguards afforded by a DoL order do not apply. The door is thus opened to PR being exercised in a manner that is not in the child's best interests. This was not addressed in Re: D. The court's approach is to make such decisions on an individual basis. There is guidance available on this matter in the Mental Health Act 1983 Code of Practice (the MHA code) (Department of Health, 2015).

In order to secure their welfare, when children have a history of absconding as a result of which they are likely to suffer significant harm, or if kept in any accommodation other than a secure placement are likely to injure themselves or others, local authorities may seek a secure accommodation order under Section 25 of the Children Act (1989) or Section 119 of the Social Services and Well-being Act (Wales) (2014). Section 25 only applies to children who are accommodated (for at least 24 hours) under Section 20 of the Children Act (with some exclusions) or who are the subject of a care order. In 2024, there were 261 applications for secure accommodation orders to place children in a regulated secure children's home.

However, there is a great shortage of placements available in registered secure placements. And such placements are unable to meet the needs of some children who present with severe self-harming or aggressive behaviour arising from historical and current trauma and/or insecure or disorganised attachment difficulties. These difficulties can be so severe as to require specialist intensive therapeutic input, often in restrictive single occupancy placements, of which there are very few.

If a registered placement is not available, the local authority can use the inherent jurisdiction of the high court (a broad power allowing it to intervene to protect children when statutory intervention has been inadequate or inappropriate) to obtain a DoL order. This allows the child to be placed in residential units that are unregulated and often unregistered, with the intention of moving the child when a suitable registered alternative is found. But some children remain in what are often deemed 'emergency placements' for many months. These placements are often made in haste because the child's current placement has given notice that they are unable to accommodate the child. Because they are scarce, secure placements (both registered and unregistered) are often a significant distance from the child's home, generating problems in maintaining family relationships. Neither are the placements typically short-term since the majority of children are on DoL orders for longer than six months (Roe, 2023).

Regulations in England prohibit local authorities from using unregulated placements for under-16s (Care Planning, Placement and Case Review (England), Regulations 2021) but on account of the placement shortages, they continue to be made. Guidance provided by the government aims to ensure that when a child is placed in an unregistered home, application is made for registration so that it then falls into statutory monitoring and inspection regimes, but some placement providers decline to do so (Birmingham City Council v R and others[8]). In this case, Ofsted threatened to prosecute the placement if the child remained there. As a result, the placement served notice to terminate the placement, though they were prepared to continue to care for the child until an alternative had been found. In the absence of an alternative, the court authorised the placement's continuation whilst the local authority carried on its search for a registered placement.

In 2024, 1,280 children were subject to applications to deprive them of their liberty in England and Wales (Nuffield Family Justice Observatory, 2025b) compared with 261 applications for secure accommodation orders.

> This reflects a growing trend where applications for DoL orders – which authorise the deprivation of a child's liberty in an unregulated secure placement – vastly outnumber applications to place children in registered secure accommodation. There is severe shortage of places in secure children's homes, with around 50 children waiting for a place on any given day.
>
> (Nuffield Family Justice Observatory, 2025b: no page numbers)

For a number of reasons there are concerns about children in secure accommodation and whose liberty has been withdrawn. The Family Justice Observatory (Roe et al., 2022) reported that children subject to DoL orders were typically under constant supervision, were kept in locked environments with no access to a mobile phone or the internet and were frequently the subjects of restraint interventions. A lot of children spent time in suboptimal placements without access to the therapeutic support that they needed, with very few opportunities to engage with other children and often many miles away from home. Whilst some cases returned to court, in most it was unknown what happened after the order was made.

This runs counter to the guidelines of the Committee of Ministers of the Council of Europe (2010) which state that any form of deprivation of liberty of children should be a measure of last resort and be for the shortest appropriate period of time. Children should have the right to:

a  maintain regular and meaningful contact with parents, family and friends through visits and correspondence, except when restrictions are required in the interests of justice and the interests of the child. Restrictions on this right should never be used as a punishment.
b  receive appropriate education, vocational guidance and training, medical care, and enjoy freedom of thought, conscience and religion and access to leisure, including physical education and sport.
c  access programmes that prepare children in advance for their return to their communities, with full attention given to them in respect of their emotional and physical needs, their family relationships, housing, schooling and employment possibilities and socio-economic status.

(Guidelines of the Committee of Ministers
of the Council of Europe, 2010: 14)

Expert witnesses may be asked to carry out assessments of capacity for children who are regarded as needing confinement for their own or others' safety. This involves assessment of the child's cognitive functioning, emotional maturity, communication skills, mental health, the extent to which they are being influenced by others and whether their decisions are authentically their own. Whilst the Gillick competence standard ostensibly guides this process, Daly (2020) claimed that what children's capacity actually entails is little understood, proving notoriously difficult to define (Hein et al., 2015). Daly suggested reconceptualising approaches to assessing children's capacity in a rights-based way via the UN Convention on the CRC, taking into consideration articles of the CRC as follows

- Autonomy (Article 12): Children have autonomy rights, and to deny them their wishes should be considered a matter of seriousness.
- Evidence (Article 2): Decision-makers should have basic knowledge about childhood including psychology and other relevant theories.
- Support (Article 5): Capacity can be increased through appropriate support, guidance and information.
- Protection (Article 3): Children are a group who are in a unique position of relative vulnerability and adults are obliged to offer them protection from harm.

Guidance is provided in the case of CS v SBH[9] in respect of the child's capacity to pursue an appeal to a decision regarding a child arrangements order. The judge concluded that in determining whether the child has sufficient understanding to give instructions to pursue an appeal and to conduct the appeal, a range of factors needs to be considered including:

   i  The level of intelligence of the child.

  ii  The emotional maturity of the child.

 iii  Factors which might undermine their understanding such as issues arising from their emotional, psychological, psychiatric or emotional (sic) state.

 iv  Their reasons for wishing to instruct a solicitor directly or to act without a guardian and the strength of feeling accompanying the wish to play a direct role.

  v  Their understanding of the issues in the case and their desired outcome [in]any matter which sheds light on the extent to which those are authentically their own or are mere parroting of one parent's position.

 vi  Their understanding of the process of litigation including the function of their lawyer, the role of the judge, the role they might play and the law that is applied and some of the consequences of involvement in litigation.

vii  The court's assessment of the risk of harm to the child of direct participation for (sic) the risk of harm arising from excluding the child from direct participation and the child's appreciation of the risks of harm.

(Mental Health Law Online, 2019)

Experts may also be requested to assess such children in order to identify the package of support and features of a placement that will meet their holistic needs and keep them safe. Letters of instruction typically request a full psychological assessment of the child and an analysis of future needs in terms of the nature of care, education, and therapeutic support required. An opinion may be sought on the placement options open to the child and the extent to which each of these may meet their needs. A comparison of foster placements, specialist residential placements and secure accommodation may be requested, identifying the implications, advantages and disadvantages of each option for the child. Local authorities need to justify their requests to deprive a child of liberty, and in the case of children under the age of 13 years, approval for the placement can only be given by the Secretary of State to whom such evidence must be provided.

Many judges have raised concerns about the lack of appropriate placements for children and young people who have experienced the most adverse of childhoods with resulting complex needs. Nuffield Family Justice Observatory research and briefings conclude that there is a need for a wider discussion on these gaps in provision for children and young people whose complex needs require specialist input, and on how they might be addressed.

## Use of AI

In 2024 I attended a Family Law Week conference addressed to Public and Private Children Law. The final speaker focused on the use of AI in the family court and to give an illustration, told the delegates that he had asked ChatGPT to write his speech. He felt that it had not done a bad job except that he would normally use more humour. He asked ChatGPT to rewrite the address including some jokes. He considered these to be rather weak but otherwise the speech was passable. Following his example, I asked ChatGPT to write me a 200-word summary of the Advantages and Disadvantages of AI for Expert Witnesses in Family Court. This is what it produced:

### Advantages

AI technology can significantly enhance the efficiency and accuracy of expert witness analysis in family court. Its ability to process vast amounts of data quickly allows for more comprehensive evaluations of financial records, communication histories, and behavioral patterns. AI-driven tools can assist in identifying inconsistencies, patterns of abuse, or financial discrepancies that may impact custody or divorce settlements. Additionally, AI can reduce human biases by providing objective, data-driven insights, which can contribute to fairer outcomes.

### Disadvantages

However, reliance on AI also brings concerns. One major issue is the potential lack of transparency in how AI algorithms reach conclusions, which may be challenging for judges and attorneys to interpret and question effectively. This "black box" problem can undermine trust in AI-generated reports. Furthermore, AI systems can inadvertently reflect biases present in the data they are trained on, potentially perpetuating systemic inequalities. The lack of emotional and contextual understanding in AI analysis is another drawback, as family court cases often require sensitive interpretation of emotional dynamics that AI cannot fully comprehend.

In summary, while AI has the potential to enhance objectivity and efficiency in family court proceedings, concerns around transparency, bias, and emotional interpretation must be carefully managed.

I then refined my query and asked ChatGPT the same question, but specifying that the expert was a clinical psychologist. This was the result:

### Advantages

AI technologies offer significant benefits for clinical psychologist expert witnesses in family court settings. They can streamline the analysis of large datasets, such as medical records, psychological assessments, and case histories, allowing for quicker and more efficient evaluations. AI-driven tools can enhance the accuracy of diagnostic conclusions by cross-referencing symptoms and behaviors with vast psychological databases. Additionally, AI can assist in reducing biases by providing objective data analysis, supporting expert testimonies with quantifiable evidence.

AI's predictive analytics can also help assess risk factors, such as the potential for domestic violence or child neglect, which aids in making informed recommendations for child custody and parental fitness. Moreover, digital tools can enhance transparency and standardization in psychological assessments, contributing to fairer decision-making processes.

### Disadvantages

However, the integration of AI in expert witness roles is not without challenges. There are concerns about the dehumanization of sensitive family matters, where emotional and contextual understanding is crucial. Over-reliance on AI might also overlook nuanced, case-specific factors that require human judgment. Ethical concerns about privacy and data security are significant, particularly when handling sensitive psychological information. Furthermore, biases can still emerge if AI systems are trained on datasets that reflect existing disparities.

Lastly, the use of AI could potentially undermine the expert's perceived credibility if legal professionals or judges are skeptical of technology-driven assessments. Balancing technological advancements with human expertise is crucial for effective and ethical use in family courts.

The concerns about the use of AI in the family court summarised above by AI itself are recognised in advice provided in a range of relevant contexts. Guidance and discussion have been published by the Courts and Tribunals Judiciary (2025b); the Bar Council (2024); the Alan Turing Institute (Leslie, 2019); the European Parliament (2023) which has introduced an Artificial Intelligence Act placing controls on high risk systems used in education, healthcare and law enforcement; the Solicitor's Regulation Authority (2023); and the British Psychological Society (MacRae, 2024). The judiciary has introduced an AI tool (Microsoft's 'Copilot Chat') which is available on judicial office holders' devices through eJudiciary to which their guidance applies. This is summarised below:

### Understand AI, Its Applications, Capabilities and Limitations

AI tools work by generating new text using an algorithm based on the data upon which they have been trained. The user is not able to determine whether this is the most appropriate data or the accuracy of the resulting response. Any new information which is produced may be difficult to verify so should not be seen as fact. The underlying datasets may include misinformation and be inaccurate, incomplete, misleading or biased.

### Uphold Confidentiality and Privacy

The judiciary recommends that information not already in the public domain should not be entered into a public AI programme as it is effectively then available to anyone with the technology all over the world. Everything that is entered becomes public and may be used to respond to queries from other users. If possible, chat history should be disabled which prevents the user's data from being available for further training and after 30 days will be deleted. This is available in ChatGPT and Google Bard.

Some AI platforms, particularly if used as an App on a smartphone, may request various permissions which give access to other information on the device. All such permissions should be refused.

### Ensure Accountability and Accuracy

Information obtained from an AI tool must be checked before it is used since it is capable of generating fictitious cases, citations or quotes and referencing texts that do not exist. The presence of 'legal hallucinations', responses that are inconsistent with legal facts, was reported by Dahl et al. (2024). In their study, legal hallucinations were alarmingly prevalent, occurring between 69% of the time with ChatGPT 3.5 and 88% with Llama 2, when these models were asked specific, verifiable questions about random federal court cases. They often failed to correct a user's incorrect legal assumptions in a contra-factual question set-up and they could not always predict or recognise when they were producing legal hallucinations.

### Be Aware of Bias

Information generated by AI will inevitably reflect errors and biases in its training data. Because machine learning algorithms use data generated by humans, they are likely to reproduce or exacerbate existing biases. The COMPAS system predicted a higher risk of reoffending for black defendants and Google Ads showed fewer adverts for high-paying jobs to women (cited in Ntoutsi et al., 2020) although the research on which this was based was published in 2015 and 2016, since when AI programmes are reported to have become more adept.

### Maintain Security

To follow best practices for maintaining personal and court/tribunals' security, professionals are advised to use work devices and email addresses. Programmes involving paid subscriptions are regarded as more secure than those available for free.

### Take Responsibility

Judicial office holders are personally responsible for material which is produced in their name. If assistants or other colleagues are producing material on behalf of the office holder, they need to be able to confirm that they have independently verified the accuracy of any research or case citations that have been generated with the assistance of an AI tool. AI tools are capable of producing fake material either maliciously or without intent.

## Approaches to Identifying Material Produced by AI

The Iowa Office of Teaching, Learning, and Technology (2024) published the following strategies to identify work that may have been produced by AI:

- Examine your output for common-sense answers. AI-generated content can include odd or highly improbable scenarios, characters, or events.
- Look for responses that seem out of context or like part of a different conversation than the one you're conducting.
- Watch for internal consistency. Depending on the size of the AI's memory, previous prompts will be forgotten as a conversation is held.
- Be especially cautious of specific facts like names, dates, and locations. These should be fact-checked against authoritative sources.
- Consult with experts. While AI may be convenient, consulting with a real human expert can help you identify inaccuracies or inconsistencies typical of AI hallucinations.

Although they are easily anthropomorphised, computers cannot empathise, think or reason. Whilst pressure of work may lead practitioners to take short-cuts using AI, some of which are legitimate and helpful, for the critical decisions that reverberate through children and parents' entire lives, only careful, critical, empathic consideration will do.

## Keeping Up-to-Date

In this chapter I have explored some of the current and future issues in the family court. My experience of the law is that it is constantly in flux, developing all the time in response to new issues and precedents established in relation to individual cases. Experts need to keep abreast of these developments, which can be accomplished with regular reference to various publications.

Even within the months during which I was writing this text the law changed, although fundamentals remain as pillars to the process. In constantly updating my knowledge I have found the following invaluable:

The Nuffield Family Justice Observatory carries out research to fill gaps in understanding in the family court with a view to supporting better outcomes for children and families. Local Government Lawyer runs articles of interest. In 2024 the President of the Family Division commenced publication of an annual report.

Approximately once a year (on 14 August 2023, 31 July 2024 and 16 April 2025) the Courts and Tribunals Judiciary publishes *A View from the President's Chambers* which documents news and updates to family law.

I have found essential the publications of *Family Law Week* which provides summary articles on topical issues, important judgments, hosts updating CPD events such as conferences and podcasts, and astute summaries of cases impacting the law. It can be accessed at: https://www.familylawweek.co.uk/.

*The Transparency Project* website posts articles clarifying and commenting on media reports of family law, explains and comments on family court judgments, and conducts projects aimed at making the family justice system more transparent and accessible. This can be accessed at: https://transparencyproject.org.uk/.

*Today's Family Lawyer* provides daily news, industry insight, best practice and opinion on the stories that affect practitioners day-to-day through a newsletter, podcasts and CPD training events. It can be accessed at: https://todaysfamilylawyer.co.uk/.

The *Law Society Gazette* publishes articles online addressing contemporary issues in the family court which can be accessed at: https://www.lawgazette.co.uk/family-and-children/67.subject.

The CAFCASS website provides resources for professionals at: https://www.cafcass.gov.uk/professionals/our-resources-professionals.

*Bond Solon* offers support and training events for experts at: https://www.bondsolon.com/, as does the *Expert Witness Institute*: https://www.ewi.org.uk/About.

I have been provided with valuable support and formal learning opportunities by *Carter Brown Associates* at: https://www.carterbrownexperts.co.uk/. I would highly recommend that beginning experts engage with a company that will provide referrals, ongoing training, quality assurance and support. No doubt there are other sources of relevant information. Wherever it is located, my advice is to keep abreast of the changes to family law, vocabulary and approaches in order best to serve the children and families who find themselves there.

## Key Points from this Chapter

- There is a growing understanding that the voice of the child is central in legal matters affecting them. Experts need ways of ascertaining a child's independent perspective adapted to their age and developmental status.
- In private law disputes the family court is moving away from an adversarial towards an investigative approach with encouragement for families to engage in alternative forms of dispute resolution such as mediation. Although this is not mandated, it is encouraged through the requirement to attend a MIAM and the provision of financial incentives.
- Parents can be recommended by CAFCASS or ordered by the courts to attend a Planning Together for Children programme exploring the impact of separation on children.
- Two major inquiries into child sexual abuse and exploitation report the harrowing and tragic long-term adverse consequences. In response, the government has introduced mandatory reporting by those who work with children in positions of trust and in some circumstances, failure to do so is a criminal offence.

- The Information Commissioner's Office has been instructed to produce a code of practice on the retention of personal data relating to child sexual abuse with a proposed timescale of 75 years.
- It is not for expert witnesses to determine the veracity of disclosures of sexual abuse as this is the remit of the judge. But the issues do need to be explored with parents and children, requiring comfort with the use of sexual vocabulary and open exploration of the disclosure taking care not to lead. Recordings can assist with giving voice to the child and evidencing a non-leading approach.
- The numbers of children experiencing deprivation of liberty have increased, many of them being cared for in unregistered facilities. Expert witnesses may be asked to carry out assessments of capacity or to identify the package of support and features of a placement that are capable of meeting their needs.
- AI is increasingly being used across different occupations for time-saving and digital assistance. Microsoft's Copilot Chat has been made available to judicial office holders. AI tools work by generating new text using an algorithm based on data on which they have been trained. The programme cannot empathise, think or reason. Caution needs to be exercised in terms of its limitations and dangers related to issues of confidentiality, accuracy, accountability, bias, security and vulnerability to fake material. Anything obtained via an AI tool needs to be checked against reliable sources.
- Aspects of the law relating to the family court can change rapidly. Experts need ways of keeping up-to-date with these changes in order to maintain credibility and provide critical opinions that benefit children and their families appearing in the family court.

## Notes

1 Re D (a child) [2006] UKHL 51.
2 Re W (a child) [2016] EWCA Civ 1140.
3 Re C (Child: ability to instruct solicitor) [2023] EWCA Civ 889.
4 *EF, GH, IJ (care proceedings) [2019] EWFC.*
5 *KW v ST B (by her Guardian)* [2020] EWFC 34, 2020 WL 02069863.
6 Re E (Children: Costs) [2025] EWCA Civ 183.
7 Re *D (A Child)* [2019] UKSC 42 (Supreme Court (Hale, Carnwath, Black, Lloyd-Jones and Arden SCJJ)).
8 Birmingham City Council v R & Ors [2021] EWHC 2556 (Fam).
9 CS v SBH [2019] EWHC 634 (Fam).

# References

Access Group (2024). *Voice of the child legislation in the UK: what it is and why it matters.* Retrieved 3 May 2025 from: https://www.theaccessgroup.com/en-gb/blog/hsc-voice-of-the-child-legislation-uk-what-it-is-and-why-it-matters/

Advocates Gateway (2024). *Responding to communication needs in the justice system.* Retrieved 11 February 2025 from: https://www.theadvocatesgateway.org/

Allen, R., Olsen, J., Soorenian, A. and Verlot, M. (2021). *UK disability survey research report, June 2021.* Retrieved 12 February 2025 from: https://www.gov.uk/government/publications/uk-disability-survey-research-report-june-2021/uk-disability-survey-research-report-june-2021

Altieri, N.A., Pisoni, D.B. and Townsend, J.T. (2011). Some normative data on lip-reading skills (L). *The Journal of the Acoustical Society of America, 130*(1), 1–4. Doi: 10.1121/1.3593376

Association of Sign Language Interpreters (2015). *ASLI's position paper on the use of video interpreting services for public services.* Retrieved 2 May 2025 from: https://test80.toucantech.com/news/best-practice-guidance/42/42-ASLIs-Position-paper-on-the-use-of-video-interpreting-services-for-public-services-

Austen, S. and Holmes, B. (2021). *An introductory guide for professionals working with deaf and hard of hearing clients in clinical, legal, educational and social care settings.* Independently published. ISBN-13 979-8520594826.

Austin, W.G., Kline Pruett, M., Kirkpatrick, H.D., Flens, J.R. and Gould, J.W. (2013). Parental gatekeeping and child custody/child access evaluation: part 1: conceptual framework, research and application. *Family Court Review, 51*(3), 485–501.

BAILII (2018). *England and Wales family court decisions (other judges).* Retrieved 3 May 2024 from: https://www.bailii.org/ew/cases/EWFC/OJ/2018/B9.html

BAILII (2000). *England and Wales court of appeal (civil division) decisions.* Retrieved 29 November 2024 from: https://www.bailii.org/cgi-bin/format.cgi?doc=/ew/cases/EWCA/Civ/2000/194.html&query=(%22civ+194%22)

BAILII (2022). *England and Wales court of appeal (civil division) decisions.* Retrieved 4 May 2024 from: https://www.bailii.org/ew/cases/EWCA/Civ/2022/468.html

BAILII (2023). *England and Wales family court decisions (other judges).* Retrieved 8 November 2025 from: https://www.bailii.org/cgi-bin/format.cgi?doc=/ew/cases/EWFC/OJ/2023/69.html&query=(alleged)+AND+(FII)

BAILII (2024). *England and Wales court of appeal (civil division) decisions.* Retrieved 21 October 2024 from: https://www.bailii.org/cgi-bin/format.cgi?doc=/ew/cases/

EWCA/Civ/2024/241.html&query=(Re)+AND+(T)+AND+((Children:)+AND+(Non-Disclosure))+AND+(.2024.)+AND+(EWCA)+AND+(Civ)+AND+(241)

Baker, A.J.L. (2005). The long-term effects of parental alienation on adult children: a qualitative research study. *American Journal of Family Therapy 33*, 289–302. Doi: 10.1080/01926180 590962129

Bar Council (2024). *Considerations when using ChatGPT and generative AI software based on large language models.* https://www.barcouncilethics.co.uk/wp-content/uploads/2024/01/Considerations-when-using-ChatGPT-and-Generative-AI-Software-based-on-large-language-models-January-2024.pdf

Barnes, H. (2024, March 31). Why the Tavistock gender identity clinic was forced to shut … and what happens next. *The Guardian.* Retrieved 9 September 2024 from: https://www.theguardian.com/society/2024/mar/31/why-the-tavistock-gender-identity-clinic-was-forced-to-shut-and-what-happens-next

Barnett, A. (2020). *Domestic abuse and private law children's cases. Ministry of Justice. Crown Copyright.* Retrieved 18 July 2025 from: https://assets.publishing.service.gov.uk/media/5ef3dd32d3bf7f7142efc034/domestic-abuse-private-law-children-cases-literature-review.pdf

Basicmedical Key (2020). *Diagnosis and classification of substance use disorders.* Retrieved 5 May 2023 from: https://tinyurl.com/ydbzx394

Baum, S. (2014). *Parents with intellectual disabilities.* Retrieved 9 February 2025 from: https://www.intellectualdisability.info/family/articles/parents-with-intellectual-disabilities

BBC (2009, November 16). *Have you lost your father?* Radio 5 live phone-in.

Bentley, C. and Matthewson, M. (2020). The not-forgotten child: alienated adult children's experience of parental alienation. *The American Journal of Family Therapy, 48*(5), 509–529. Doi: 10.1080/01926187.2020.1775531

Birth Companions (2024). *Taking a strand.* Retrieved 30 March 2025 from: https://www.birthcompanions.org.uk/pages/taking-a-strand

Blackmore, R., Boyle, J.A., Fazel, M., Ranasinha, S., Gray, K.M., Fitzgerald, G., Misso, M. and Gibson-Helm, M. (2020). The prevalence of mental illness in refugees and asylum seekers: a systematic review and meta-analysis. *PLoS Medicine, 17*(9). Doi: 10.1371/JOURNAL.PMED.1003337

Blatt, M. (2024). *Case law update re: appointment of an intermediary.* Retrieved 11 February 2025 from: https://becket-chambers.co.uk/articles/case-law-update-re-appointment-of-an-intermediary/

Booth, T. (2003). Parents with learning difficulties, child protection and the courts. *Representing Children, 13*(3), 175–188.

Booth, T., Booth, W. and McConnell, D. (2005). The prevalence and outcomes of care proceedings involving parents with learning difficulties in the family courts. *Journal of Applied Research in Intellectual Disabilities, 18*, 7–17.

Branson, S. and Hunter, P. (2023). Recent scientific developments in hair strand testing and racial bias in current practices of hair strand testing. *Family Law, 669*, June 2023. Retrieved 2 July 2025 from: https://www.coramchambers.co.uk/news-events/how-we-believe-hair-strand-testing-evidence-could-be-instructed-in-the-family-justice-system-proposals-for-reform/

Bravata, D.M., Watts, S.A., Keefer, A.L., Madhusudhan, D.K., Taylor, K.T., Clark, D.M., Nelson, R.S., Cokley, K.O. and Hagg, H.K. (2020). Prevalence, predictors, and treatment of impostor syndrome: a systematic review. *Journal of General Internal Medicine, 35*(4), 1252–1275. Doi: 10.1007/s11606-019-05364-1

British Psychological Society (2011). *Good practice guidance for clinical psychologists when assessing parents with learning disabilities.* Retrieved 14 February 2025 from: https://explore.bps.org.uk/content/report-guideline/bpsrep.2011.rep171

British Psychological Society (2017). *Working with interpreters: guidelines for psychologists.* Retrieved 2 May 2025 from: https://repository.uel.ac.uk/download/9bf5056282 1d7a150325d5756f5c1460ddb9df96f28377a9a71f1e72cae3df9a/207644/INF288%20 WEB.pdf

British Psychological Society (2018a). *Communicating test results: guidance for test users.* Retrieved 10 September 2024 from: https://www.bps.org.uk/guideline/communicating-test-results-guidance-test-users

British Psychological Society (2018b). *Guidance for psychologists working with refugees and asylum seekers in the UK: extended version.* Retrieved 3 May 2025 from: https://explore.bps.org.uk/content/report-guideline/bpsrep.2018.inf300b

British Psychological Society (2019a). *Constraints on disclosure and sharing of raw data from psychometric and structured professional judgements.* Retrieved 23 October 2024 from: https://www.bps.org.uk/guideline/constraints-disclosure-and-sharing-raw-data-psychometric-and-structured-professional

British Psychological Society (2019b). *Completing an assessment of capacity.* Retrieved 26 May 2025 from: https://explore.bps.org.uk/content/report-guideline/bpsrep.2019.rep127 Doi: 10.53841/bpsrep.2019.rep127.4

British Psychological Society (2020). *Working with interpreters online or via the telephone.* Retrieved 2 May 2025 from: https://www.bps.org.uk/guideline/working-interpreters-online-or-telephone

British Psychological Society (2021). *What is an expert witness?* Retrieved 20 November 2023 from: https://explore.bps.org.uk/content/report-guideline/bpsrep.2021.rep157/chapter/bpsrep.2021.rep157.3

British Psychological Society (2023). *How psychologists work.* Retrieved 29 February 2024 from: https://explore.bps.org.uk/content/report-guideline/bpsrep.2017.inf115/chapter/bpsrep.2017.inf115.3

British Psychological Society and Family Justice Council (2023). *Psychologists as expert witnesses in the family courts in England and Wales: standards, competencies and expectations* (2nd edition). Retrieved 14 September 2024 from: https://www.bps.org.uk/guideline/psychologists-expert-witnesses-family-courts-england-wales

British Psychological Society (BPS) (2025). We want to use the archive to constructively address this harmful part of UK psychology's history. *The Psychologist,* 38, March edition 2–3.

Burch, K., Simpson, A., Taylor, V., Bala, A. and Morgado De Queiroz, S. (2024). *Babies in care proceedings: what do we know about parents with learning disabilities or difficulties?* Nuffield Family Justice Observatory. Retrieved 9 February 2025 from: https://www.nuffieldfjo.org.uk/resource/babies-in-care-proceedings-what-do-we-know-about-parents-with-learning-disabilities-or-difficulties

Burnham, J. (2013). Developments in Social GGRRAAACCEEESSS: visible-invisible, voiced-unvoiced. In I. Krause (Ed.) *Cultural reflexivity.* London: Karnac.

Bütz, M.R., English, J.V., Meyers, J.E. and Cohen, L.J. (2023). Threats to the integrity of psychological assessment: the misuse of test raw data and manuals. *Applied Neuropsychology: Adult, 1–20.* Retrieved 23 October 2024 from: Doi: 10.1080/23279095.2023.2241094

CAFCASS (2024). *Domestic abuse practice policy.* Retrieved 3 May 2025 from: https://www.battens.co.uk/assets/uploads/documents/Domestic-Abuse-Practice-Policy.pdf

CAFCASS (2025a). *Annual data summaries*. Retrieved 22 November 2024 from: https://www.cafcass.gov.uk/about-us/our-data/annual-data-summaries

CAFCASS (2025b). *Domestic abuse practice policy.* Retrieved 4 May 2025 from: https://www.cafcass.gov.uk/sites/default/files/2024-10/Domestic%20Abuse%20Practice%20Policy.pdf

Callaghan, J.E.M. and Alexander, J.H. (2015). *Understanding agency and resistance strategies (UNARS): children's experiences of domestic violence.* Northampton: University of Northampton.

Cass, H. (2024). *The Cass review: independent review of gender identity services for children and young people: final report.* Retrieved 9 September 2024 from: https://cass.independent-review.uk/home/publications/final-report/

Chaloner, M. (2024, December 2). New domestic abuse measures come into force. *Family Law Week*. Retrieved 2 December 2024 from: https://www.familylawweek.co.uk/new-domestic-abuse-measures-come-into-force/

Child Protection Resource (2021). *What does 'section 20' mean? And when should it be used?* Retrieved 21 February 2024 from: https://childprotectionresource.online/what-does-section-20-mean/

Child Protection Resource (n.d.). *Why does everyone hate the family court? Part four.* Retrieved 1 December 2024 from: https://childprotectionresource.online/tag/family-court/

Child Rights International Network (2018). *J v. B. (ultra-orthodox Judaism: transgender).* Retrieved 17 November 2023 from: https://archive.crin.org/en/library/legal-database/j-v-b-ultra-orthodox-judaism-transgender.html

Child Safeguarding Practice Review Panel (2024). *I wanted them all to notice.* Retrieved 5 May 2025 from: https://assets.publishing.service.gov.uk/media/67446a8a81f809b32c8568d3/CSPRP_-_I_wanted_them_all_to_notice.pdf

Clance, P.R. and Imes, S.A. (1978). The imposter syndrome in high achieving women: dynamics and therapeutic intervention. *Psychotherapy: Theory, Research and Practice, 15*(3), 241–247. Doi: 10.1037/h0086006

Committee of Ministers of the Council of Europe (2010). *Guidelines of the Committee of Ministers of the Council of Europe on child-friendly justice.* Retrieved 9 May 2025 from: https://search.coe.int/cm?i=09000016804b2cf3

Community Care (2013, June 7). *Family courts calling fewer expert witnesses, finds Cafcass study.* Community Care. Retrieved 18 July 2025 from: https://www.communitycare.co.uk/2013/06/07/family-courts-calling-fewer-expert-witnesses-finds-cafcass-study/

Conn, F. (2014). *Re C (A Child) [2014] EWCA Civ 128.* Retrieved 11 February 2025 from: https://www.familylawweek.co.uk/judgments/re-c-a-child-2014-ewca-civ-128/

Cooke, M. (1996). A different story: narrative versus 'question and answer' in Aboriginal evidence. *The International Journal of Speech, Language and the Law, 3*(2), 273–288.

Coram Children's Legal Centre (2017). *Best interests of the child in immigration and asylum law.* Retrieved 2 May 2025 from: https://childrenslegalcentre.com/wp-content/uploads/2016/10/Best.interests-May-2017.final_.pdf

County Health Rankings and Road Maps (2025). *What works for health: family treatment drug courts.* Retrieved 1 July 2025 from: https://www.countyhealthrankings.org/strategies-and-solutions/what-works-for-health/strategies/family-treatment-drug-courts

Courts and Tribunals Judiciary (2022). *A View from the president's chambers: November 2022.* Retrieved 24 November 2024 from: https://www.judiciary.uk/guidance-and-resources/a-view-from-the-presidents-chambers-november-2022/

Courts and Tribunals Judiciary (2023). *Speech by the president of the family division: parents with intellectual impairment in public law proceedings – the need to be alert.* Retrieved 4 August 2025 from: https://www.judiciary.uk/speech-by-the-president-of-the-family-division-parents-with-intellectual-impairment-in-public-law-proceedings-the-need-to-be-alert/

Courts and Tribunals Judiciary (2024a). *Wholesale reform to adoption process is needed, says public law working group.* Retrieved 20 June 2025 from: https://www.judiciary.uk/guidance-and-resources/wholesale-reform-to-adoption-process-is-needed-says-public-law-working-group/

Courts and Tribunals Judiciary (2024b). *Local practice note: ensuring adherence to the public law outline in London.* Retrieved 1 July 2025 from: https://www.judiciary.uk/guidance-and-resources/local-practice-note-ensuring-adherence-to-the-public-law-outline-in-london/

Courts and Tribunals Judiciary (2024c). *The challenges in hearing the authentic voice of the child in public and private family law proceedings.* Retrieved 3 May 2025 from: https://www.judiciary.uk/wp-content/uploads/2024/11/The-Judicial-Council-Dublin-9-November-2024-The-Challenges-of-Hearing-the-Authentic-Voice-of-the-Child-MacDona.pdf

Courts and Tribunals Judiciary (2025a). *Practice guidance by the PFD: the use of intermediaries, lay advocates and cognitive assessments in the family court.* Retrieved 11 February 2025 from: https://www.judiciary.uk/guidance-and-resources/practice-guidance-by-the-pfd-the-use-of-intermediaries-lay-advocates-and-cognitive-assessments-in-the-family-court/

Courts and Tribunals Judiciary (2025b). *Artificial Intelligence (AI) guidance for judicial office holders.* Retrieved 9 May 2025 from: https://www.judiciary.uk/guidance-and-resources/artificial-intelligence-ai-judicial-guidance-2/

Cox, J. (2020). *The Children and Families Act 2014 – changes to.* Retrieved 25 February 2024 from: https://creighton.co.uk/news/2014/05/28/the-children-and-families-act-2014-changes-to-public-law-care-proceedings/

Crafter, S. and Iqbal, H. (2020). *Child interpreters: source of pride or cultural burden?* Retrieved 16 November 2022 from: https://tinyurl.com/43thv4p5

Criminal Injuries Helpline (2023). *The reality for male victims of domestic abuse.* Retrieved 5 December 20234 from: https://criminalinjurieshelpline.co.uk/blog/the-reality-for-male-victims-of-domestic-violence/

Cubas (2023). *What is Cubas?* Retrieved 15 March 2023 from: https://cubas.co.uk/

Cusworth, L., Bedston, S., Alrouh, B., Broadhurst, K., Johnson, R.D., Akbari, A. and Griffiths, L.J. (2021). *Uncovering private family law: who's coming to court in England?* London: Nuffield Family Justice Observatory. Retrieved 2 December 2024 from: https://www.nuffieldfjo.org.uk/wp-content/uploads/2021/05/nfjo_whos_coming_to_court_England_full_report_FINAL-1-.pdf

Cusworth, L., Bedston, S., Trinder, L., Broadhurst, K., Pattinson, B., Harwin, J. et al. (2020). *Who's coming to court? Private family law applications in Wales.* London: Nuffield Family Justice Observatory.

Dabhi, K., Anand, T. and Tu, T. (2022). *Survey of separated parents.* DWP Ad Hoc Research Report No 1015. Department for Work and Pensions.

Dahl, M., Magesh, V., Suzgun, M. and Ho, D.E. (2024). Large legal fictions: profiling legal hallucinations in large language models. *Journal of Legal Analysis, 16*(1), 64–93. Retrieved 10 November 2025 from: https://doi.org/10.1093/jla/laae003

Dalgarno, E., Ayeb-Karlsson, S., Bramwell, D., Barnett, A. and Verma, A. (2024). Health-related experiences of family court and domestic abuse in England: a looming public health crisis. *Journal of Family Trauma, Child Custody & Child Development, 21*(3), 277–305. Doi: 10.1080/26904586.2024.2307609

Daly, A. (2020). Assessing children's capacity: reconceptualising our understanding through the UN Convention on the Rights of the Child. *International Journal of Children's Rights, 28*(3), 471–499. Doi: 10.1163/15718182-02803011

Davis, M. (2021). *Experts in the family court: the basics.* Retrieved 27 November 2023 from: https://www.judiciary.uk/wp-content/uploads/2021/05/Maud-Davis-the-basics.pdf

Department for Education (2016). *Analysis of serious case reviews: 2011 to 2014.* Retrieved 28 March 2025 from: https://www.gov.uk/government/publications/analysis-of-serious-case-reviews-2011-to-2014

Department for Education (2018). *Applying corporate parenting principles to looked-after children and care leavers: statutory guidance for local authorities.* Retrieved 20 February 2024 from: https://www.gov.uk/government/publications/applying-corporate-parenting-principles-to-looked-after-children-and-care-leavers

Department for Education (2020). *Characteristics of children in need 2019 to 2020.* Retrieved 28 March 2025 from: https://www.gov.uk/government/statistics/characteristics-of-children-in-need-2019-to-2020

Department for Education (2023a). *Gender questioning children: non-statutory guidance for schools and colleges in England.* Retrieved 9 September 2024 from: https://consult.education.gov.uk/equalities-political-impartiality-anti-bullying-team/gender-questioning-children-proposed-guidance/supporting_documents/Gender%20Questioning%20Children%20%20nonstatutory%20guidance.pdf

Department for Education (2023b). *Working together to safeguard children 2023: statutory guidance.* Retrieved 7 November 2025 from: https://www.gov.uk/government/publications/working-together-to-safeguard-children--2

Department for Education (2024). *Children looked after in England including adoptions.* Retrieved 3 May 2025 from: https://explore-education-statistics.service.gov.uk/find-statistics/children-looked-after-in-england-including-adoptions/2024

Department of Health (2015). *Mental Health Act 1983: code of practice.* Retrieved 8 May 2025 from: https://assets.publishing.service.gov.uk/media/5a80a774e5274a2e87dbb0f0/MHA_Code_of_Practice.PDF

Department of Health and Social Care (2024a). *Puberty blockers temporary ban extended.* Retrieved 9 September 2024 from: https://www.gov.uk/government/news/puberty-blockers-temporary-ban-extended

Department of Health and Social Care (2024b). *Care and support statutory guidance.* Retrieved 14 February 2025 from: https://www.gov.uk/government/publications/care-act-statutory-guidance/care-and-support-statutory-guidance

Department for Science, Innovation and Technology (2025). *Independent review of data, statistics and research on sex and gender.* Retrieved 21 June 2025 from: https://www.gov.uk/government/publications/independent-review-of-data-statistics-and-research-on-sex-and-gender

Department for Work and Pensions (2021). *Reducing parental conflict: the impact on children.* Retrieved 21 January 2025 from: https://www.gov.uk/guidance/reducing-parental-conflict-the-impact-on-children

Department for Work and Pensions (2024a). *Separated families statistics: April 2014 to March 2023.* Retrieved 23 November 2024 from: https://www.gov.uk/government/

statistics/separated-families-statistics-april-2014-to-march-2023/separated-families-statistics-april-2014-to-march-2023

Department for Work and Pensions (2024b). *Family resources survey: financial year 2022–2023.* Retrieved 10 February 2025 from: https://www.gov.uk/government/statistics/family-resources-survey-financial-year-2023-to-2024/family-resources-survey-financial-year-2023-to-2024

Dolan, B. (2018). *Poppi Worthington's abuser fails to remove an account of his acts from the record of inquest.* Retrieved 26 May 2025 from: https://www.ukinquestlawblog.co.uk/poppi-worthington-abuser-fails-to-remove-account-of-his-acts-from-roi/

Domestic Abuse Commissioner (2023). *The family court and domestic abuse: achieving cultural change.* Retrieved 29 November 2024 from: https://domesticabuse commissioner.uk/

Dubita, E. (2025). *Clarity needed for court interpreters in family proceedings: it's time for action.* Retrieved 1 May 2025 from: https://www.linkedin.com/posts/elenadubita_interpreters-familycourt-legalsupport-activity-7263121079500509184-66UM

Eades, D. (2003). Participation of second language and second dialect speakers in the legal system. *Annual Review of Applied Linguistics, 23*, 113–133.

Edwards, O. (2021). *Race and culture in family law.* Retrieved 10 May 2024 from: https://www.18sjs.com/wp-content/uploads/2021/09/Race_and_culture_in_family_law_-_2021_Fam_.pdf

Eggins, E., Wilson, D.B., Betts, J., Roetman, S., Chandler-Mather, N., Theroux, B. and Dawe, S. (2024). Psychosocial, pharmacological, and legal interventions for improving the psychosocial outcomes of children with substance misusing parents: a systematic review. *Campbell Systematic Reviews, 20*(3), e1413. Doi: 10.1002/cl2.1413

Emerson, E.B., Davies, I., Spencer, K. and Malam, S. (2005, Jun 1). *Adults with learning difficulties in England 2003/4.* Leeds: Health & Social Care Information Centre.

English, F. (2021). Assessing non-native speaking detainees' English language proficiency. In M. Coulthard, A. May and R. Sousa-Silva (Ed.) *The Routledge Handbook of Forensic Linguistics.* Abingdon, Oxon: Routledge.

Equality and Human Rights Commission (2018). *The Human Rights Act.* Retrieved 26 February 2024 from: https://www.equalityhumanrights.com/human-rights/human-rights-act

Erikson, S.K., Lilienfeld, S.O. and Vitacco, M.J. (2007). Failing the burden of proof: the science and ethics of projective tests in custody evaluations. *Family Court Review, 45*(2), 185–192.

European Court of Human Rights (2022). *Guide on article 6 of the European Convention on Human Rights: right to a fair trial.* Retrieved 23 November 2023 from: www.echr.coe.int/Documents/Guide_Art_6_ENG.pdf

European Parliament (2023, December 19). *EU AI Act: first regulation on artificial intelligence.* Retrieved 19 July 2025 from: https://www.europarl.europa.eu/topics/en/article/20230601STO93804/eu-ai-act-first-regulation-on-artificial

Expert Court Reports (2025). *Proving accusations of abuse in children law cases.* Retrieved 6 September 2025 from: https://www.expertcourtreports.co.uk/blog/proving-accusations-of-abuse/

Family Justice Council (2022). *Interim guidance in relation to expert witnesses in cases where there are allegations of alienating behaviours – conflicts of interest.* Retrieved 5 May 2024 from: https://www.judiciary.uk/related-offices-and-bodies/advisory-bodies/family-justice-council/resources-and-guidance/parental-alienation/

Family Justice Council (2024). *Family Justice Council guidance on responding to a child's unexplained reluctance, resistance or refusal to spend time with a parent and allegations of alienating behaviour.* Retrieved 11 December 2024 from: https://www.judiciary.uk/related-offices-and-bodies/advisory-bodies/family-justice-council/resources-and-guidance/parental-alienation/

Family Law Week (2011). *Doncaster MBC v Haigh, Tune and X [2011] EWHC B16 (Fam).* Retrieved 1 December 2024 from: https://www.familylawweek.co.uk/judgments/doncaster-mbc-v-haigh-tune-and-x-2011-ewhc-b16-fam/

Family Mediation Council (2019). *Family mediation survey autumn 2019 results.* Retrieved 5 May 2025 from: https://www.familymediationcouncil.org.uk/wp-content/uploads/2020/01/Family-Mediation-Survey-Autumn-2019-Results.pdf

Family Rights Group (undated). *Child assessment order.* Retrieved 20 February 2024 from: https://frg.org.uk/get-help-and-advice/a-z-of-terms/child-assessment-order/

Family Solutions Group (2022). *Language matters: a review of language for separating families.* Retrieved 11 May 2025 from: https://www.familysolutionsgroup.co.uk/language-matters/

Fazel, M., Wheeler, J. and Danesh, J. (2005). Prevalence of serious mental disorder in 7000 refugees resettled in western countries: a systematic review. *Lancet* (London, England), *365*(9467), 1309–1314. Doi: 10.1016/S0140-6736(05)61027-6

FDAC (2025). *What is FDAC?* Retrieved 11 May 2025 from: https://fdac.org.uk/what-is-fdac/

Fleming, P.J., Blair, P.S.P., Bacon, C. and Berry, P.J. (2000). *Sudden unexpected death in infancy. The CESDI SUDI studies 1993–1996.* Bristol Medical School, Centre for Academic Primary Care. London: The Stationery Office.

Ford, D.Y. (2005). *Intelligence testing and cultural diversity: pitfalls and promises.* University of Connecticut, National Research Center on the Gifted and Talented (1990–2013). Retrieved 23 November 2022 from: https://nrcgt.uconn.edu/newsletters/winter052/

Foster, D. (2024). *An overview of child protection legislation in England.* Retrieved 20 February 2024 from: https://commonslibrary.parliament.uk/research-briefings/sn06787/

Foster, D. and Danechi, S (2023). *Government proposals for children's social care reform.* Retrieved 25 February 2024 from: https://commonslibrary.parliament.uk/research-briefings/cbp-9818/

Foundations (2023a). *Over 827,000 children estimated to have experienced domestic abuse this year.* Retrieved 30 November 2024 from: https://foundations.org.uk/press-release/over-827000-children-estimated-to-have-experienced-domestic-abuse-this-year-with-concerns-of-increase-at-christmas-underscoring-urgent-need-for-stronger-support/

Foundations (2023b). *Evaluation of family drug and alcohol court.* Retrieved 11 May 2025 from: www.foundations.org.uk/our-work/publications/evaluation-of-family-drug-and-alcohol-courts/

Fouzder, M. (2024a). *Renewed bid to tackle 'unacceptable' family court backlog.* The Law Society Gazette. Retrieved 24 November 2024 from: https://www.lawgazette.co.uk/news/renewed-bid-to-tackle-unacceptable-family-court-backlog/5120682.article

Fouzder, M. (2024b). *'We weren't being heard': siblings share family justice experience.* The Law Society Gazette. Retrieved 3 July 2025 from: https://www.lawgazette.co.uk/news/we-werent-being-heard-siblings-share-family-justice-experience/5118962.article

Fouzder, M. (2025). *Court interpreting system 'poses significant risk to justice'.* The Law Society Gazette. Retrieved 29 April 2025 from: https://www.lawgazette.co.uk/news/court-interpreting-system-poses-significant-risk-to-justice/5122769.article

Geiling, A., Knaevelsrud, C., Böttche, M. and Stammel, N. (2021). Mental health and work experience of interpreters in the mental health care of refugees: a systematic review. *Frontiers in Psychiatry, 12,* 710789.

George, R. and Marsh, R. (2024). Do we need physical family courts? *Journal of Social Welfare and Family Law, 46*(1), 59–81. Doi: 10.1080/09649069.2024.2305028

Gordon, C. (2023). *Instructing an expert in children proceedings.* Retrieved 3 December 2023 from: https://www.farrer.co.uk/news-and-insights/instructing-an-expert-in-children-proceedings/

Gould, J.R., Prentice, N.M. and Ainslie, R.C. (1996). The splitting index: construction of a scale measuring the defense mechanism of splitting. *Journal of Personality Assessment, 66,* 414–430.

Gov.uk (2025). *Consultation on the standards required for expert witnesses: proposed practice direction changes.* Retrieved 6 September 2025 from: https://www.gov.uk/government/consultations/family-procedure-rules-new-draft-255a-changes-to-252-and-practice-directions-25b-and-25c/consultation-on-the-standards-required-for-expert-witnesses-proposed-practice-direction-changes

Gov.uk (undated a). *Parental rights and responsibilities.* Retrieved 15 July 2025 from: https://www.gov.uk/parental-rights-responsibilities/print

Gov.uk (undated b). *Surrogacy: legal rights of parents and surrogates.* Retrieved 15 July 2025 from: https://www.gov.uk/legal-rights-when-using-surrogates-and-donors.

Gov.uk (undated c). *Family visas: apply, extend or switch.* Retrieved 10 November 2025 from: https://www.gov.uk/uk-family-visa/parent

Gowen, A. (2025). *The crucial role of intermediaries in family court proceedings.* Retrieved 11 February 2025 from: https://hanne.co.uk/the-crucial-role-of-intermediaries-in-family-court-proceedings/

Haase, E., Schönfelder, A., Nesterko, Y. and Glaesmer, H. (2022). Prevalence of suicidal ideation and suicide attempts among refugees: a meta-analysis. *BMC Public Health, 22*(1), 1–12. Retrieved 3 May 2025 from: https://pubmed.ncbi.nlm.nih.gov/35365108/

Hackett, P. (2025, March 11). How hair strand testing should be instructed for family court proceedings. *Local Government Lawyer.* Retrieved 11 May 2025 from: https://www.localgovernmentlawyer.co.uk/child-protection/543-sponsored-editorial/60234-how-hair-strand-testing-should-be-instructed-for-family-court-proceedings

Hackett, R.A., Steptoe, A., Lang, R.P., et al. (2020). Disability discrimination and well-being in the United Kingdom: a prospective cohort study. *BMJ Open,* 10, e035714. Doi: 10.1136/bmjopen-2019-035714

Hale, B. (1998). Private lives and public duties: what is family law for? *Journal of Social Welfare and Family Law, 20*(2), 125. Doi: 10.1080/09649069808410239

Hameed, S., Sadiq, A. and Din, A.U. (2018). The increased vulnerability of refugee population to mental health disorders. *Journal of Medicine, 11*(1), 20–23. Doi: 10.17161/kjm.v11i1.8680

Hardcastle, G.W. (2005). Adversarialism and the family court: a family court judge's perspective. *UC Davis Journal of Juvenile Law and Policy, 9*(1), 57–125. Retrieved 25 November 2023 from: https://sjlr.law.ucdavis.edu/archives/vol-9-no-1/02_Hardcastle.pdf

Hargreaves, C. (2024). *Uncovering private family law: how often do we hear the voice of the child?* Nuffield Family Justice Observatory. Retrieved 3 May 2025 from: https://www.nuffieldfjo.org.uk/resource/uncovering-private-family-law-how-often-do-we-hear-the-voice-of-the-chid

Hein, I.M., Troost, P.W., Broersma, A., de Vries, M.C., Daams, J.G. and Lindauer, R.J. (2015). Why is it hard to make progress in assessing children's decision-making competence? *BMC Medical Ethics, 16*(1). Doi: 10.1186/1472-6939-16-1

Herbert, A. (2025). *The pathfinder scheme and practice direction 36Z: a new approach to private law proceedings.* Retrieved 10 June 2025 from: https://www.familylawweek.co.uk/articles/the-pathfinder-scheme-and-practice-direction-36z-a-new-approach-to-private-law-proceedings/

Heske, C. (2008). Interpreting Aboriginal justice in the Territory. *Alternative Law Journal, 33*(1), 5–9.

Hine, B. and Bates, E. (2023). There is no part of my life that hasn't been destroyed: the impact of parental alienation and intimate partner violence on fathers. *Partner Abuse, 15*(1). Retrieved 28 February 2025 from: https://insight.cumbria.ac.uk/7049/1/Hine%20and%20Bates%202023%20accepted.pdf

Hine, B., Harman, J., Leder-Elder, S. and Bates, E. (2024). *Alienation behaviours in separated mothers and fathers in the UK.* Retrieved 22 December 2024 from: https://www.uwl.ac.uk/sites/uwl/files/2024-04/Alienating%20behaviours_v3.pdf

HM Courts and Tribunals Service (2013, updated 2025). *Sharing information outside of court in family proceedings.* Retrieved 14 September 2024 from: https://www.gov.uk/guidance/sharing-information-outside-of-court-in-family-proceedings

HM Courts and Tribunals Service (2025). *Jurisdictional guidance to support media access to courts and tribunals: family courts guide (accessible version).* Retrieved 22 July 2025 from: https://www.gov.uk/government/publications/guidance-to-staff-on-supporting-media-access-to-courts-and-tribunals/jurisdictional-guidance-to-support-media-access-to-courts-and-tribunals-family-courts-guide-accessible-version

HM Government (2003). *Every child matters: change for children.* London: Crown Copyright. Retrieved 21 February 2024 from: https://www.gov.uk/government/publications/every-child-matters

HM Government (2023). *Working together to safeguard children 2023: a guide to multi-agency working to help, protect and promote the welfare of children.* London: The Stationery Office. Retrieved 16 December 2023 from: https://www.gov.uk/government/publications/working-together-to-safeguard-children--2

HM Government (undated). *Data protection.* Retrieved 21 October 2024 from: https://www.gov.uk/data-protection

Holt, K. (2019). *Child protection.* London: Bloomsbury Publishing PLC.

Home Office (2023). *Supporting male victims.* Retrieved 5 December 2024 from: https://www.gov.uk/government/publications/supporting-male-victims/supporting-male-victims-accessible

Home Office (2024). *Domestic Abuse Act, 2021: overarching fact sheet.* Retrieved 21 October 2024 from: https://www.gov.uk/government/publications/domestic-abuse-bill-2020-factsheets/domestic-abuse-bill-2020-overarching-factsheet

Honeyman, G. (2024). *Re N (Children: Fact Finding – Perplexing Presentation/Fabricated or Induced Illness) [2024] EWFC 326.* Retrieved 10 December 2024 from: https://www.

familylawweek.co.uk/judgments/re-n-children-fact-finding-perplexing-presentation-fabricated-or-induced-illness-2024-ewfc-326/

Hood, R., Goldacre, A., Davies, A., Jones, E., Webb, C. and Bywaters, P. (2021). *The social gradient in children's social care.* Retrieved 7 May 2024 from: https://www.nuffield foundation.org/wp-content/uploads/2019/11/The-social-gradient-in-CSC_ Executive-Summary_Final_June-2021.pdf

Howe, D., Wiley, F., Ciborowska, C. and Japp, K. (2024, March 8). Alienation and domestic abuse-what on earth is going on? *Family Law Week.* Retrieved 7 December 2024 from: https:// www.familylawweek.co.uk/articles/alienation-and-domestic-abuse-what-on-earth-is-going-on/

Hunter, G., Thomas, M. and Campbell, N. (2024). *Experiences of public law care proceedings: a briefing on interviews with parents and special guardians.* Retrieved 12 February 2025 from: https://revolving-doors.org.uk/wp-content/uploads/2024/03/RD-Experiences-of-Public-Law-Care-Proceedings-single-page.pdf

Hunter, R., Burton, M. and Trinder, L. (2020). *Assessing risk of harm to children and parents in private law children cases: final report.* London: Ministry of Justice (KAR id:81894). Retrieved 25 November 2023 from: https://assets.publishing.service.gov.uk/ media/5ef3dcade90e075c4e144bfd/assessing-risk-harm-children-parents-pl-childrens-cases-report_.pdf

ICO (2023). *Understanding and assessing risk in personal data breaches.* Retrieved 22 October 2024 from: https://ico.org.uk/for-organisations/advice-for-small-organisations/ understanding-and-assessing-risk-in-personal-data-breaches/

ICO (2025). *How to deal with a request for information: a step-by-step guide.* Retrieved 21 July 2025 from: https://ico.org.uk/for-organisations/advice-for-small-organisations/subject-access-requests-sar/how-to-deal-with-a-request-for-information-a-step-by-step-guide/

Ingvarsdotter, K., Johnsdotter, S. and Östman, M. (2010). Lost in interpretation: the use of interpreters in research on mental ill health. *International Journal of Social Psychiatry,* *58*(1), 34–40. Doi: 10.1177/0020764010382693

Iowa Office of Teaching, Learning, and Technology (2024). *When AI gets lost in its own reality: an introduction to AI hallucinations.* Retrieved 10 May 2025 from: https://teach. its.uiowa.edu/news/2024/04/when-ai-gets-lost-its-own-reality

Ireland, G., Wijlaars, L., Jay, M.A., Grant, C., Pearson, R., Downs, J. and Gilbert, R. (2024). Social and health characteristics of mothers involved in family court care proceedings in England. Retrieved 16 February 2025 from: https://www.nuffieldfoundation.org/ wp-content/uploads/2019/11/Nuffield_Social_Health_Mothers-in-care-proceedings_ final20240829.pdf

Jay, A., Evans, Sir M., Frank, I. and Sharpling, D. (2022). *The report of the independent inquiry into child sexual abuse.* Retrieved 6 May 2025 from: https://www.gov.uk/ government/publications/iicsa-report-of-the-independent-inquiry-into-child-sexual-abuse

Johnson, D. (2023). *The victim-or-perpetrator dichotomy harms both those who commit crime and those who suffer it.* Children and Young People's Centre for Justice. Retrieved 4 May 2024 from: https://www.cycj.org.uk/perpetrators-are-often-victims-dan-johnson/

Johnston, J.R. and Sullivan, M.J. (2020). Parental alienation: in search of common ground for a more differentiated theory. *Family Court Review,* *58*(2), 270–292.

Judiciary (2013). *View from the president's chambers (3) the process of reform: expert evidence.* Retrieved 11 September 2024 from: https://www.judiciary.uk https://www.

judiciary.uk/wp-content/uploads/JCO/Documents/FJC/Publications/VIEW+President+Expert(3).pdf

Judiciary (2014). *Guidance for the instruction of experts in civil claims.* Retrieved 21 October 2024 from: https://www.judiciary.uk/wp-content/uploads/2014/08/experts-guidance-cjc-aug-2014-amended-dec-8.pdf

Judiciary (2021a). *Confidence and confidentiality transparency in the family court.* Retrieved 14 September 2024 from: https://www.judiciary.uk/wp-content/uploads/2021/10/Confidence-and-Confidentiality-Transparency-in-the-Family-Courts-final.pdf

Judiciary (2021b). *Re: H-N and others (children) judgment.* Retrieved 28 November 2024 from: https://www.judiciary.uk/wp-content/uploads/2022/07/H-N-and-Others-children-judgment-1.pdf

Judiciary NI (2024). *Evaluating the expert witness in the modern legal landscape.* Retrieved 23 November 2024 from: https://www.judiciaryni.uk/files/judiciaryni/2024-05/Macfadyen%20Lecture%202024%20-%20Edinburgh%20-%20LCJ%20-%2018%20Apr%2024%20-%20SPEECH%20FINAL%20-%20290424.pdf

Justice (2010). *Guidelines for judges meeting children who are subject to family proceedings.* Retrieved 18 February 2024 from: https://www.judiciary.uk/wp-content/uploads/JCO/Documents/FJC/voc/Guidelines_+Judges_seeing_+Children.pdf

Justice (2017). *Practice direction 25B – the duties of an expert, the expert's report and arrangements for an expert to attend court.* Retrieved 27 November 2023 from: https://www.justice.gov.uk/courts/procedure-rules/family/practice_directions/practice-direction-25b-the-duties-of-an-expert,-the-experts-report-and-arrangements-for-an-expert-to-attend-court

Justice (2020). *Part 1 – overriding objective.* Retrieved 25 March 2024 from: https://www.justice.gov.uk/courts/procedure-rules/family/parts/part_01

Justice (2022). *Practice direction part 25: experts and assessors.* Retrieved 27 November 2023 from: https://www.justice.gov.uk/courts/procedure-rules/family/parts/part_25

Justice (2023a). *Practice direction 12B – child arrangements programme.* Retrieved 8 February 2024 from: https://www.justice.gov.uk/courts/procedure-rules/family/practice_directions/pd_part_12b

Justice (2023b). *Practice direction 3AA – Vulnerable persons: participation in proceedings and giving evidence.* Retrieved 11 February 2025 from: https://www.justice.gov.uk/courts/procedure-rules/family/practice_directions/practice-direction-3aa-vulnerable-persons-participation-in-proceedings-and-giving-evidence

Justice (2024). *Practice Direction 12J – Child arrangements and contact orders: domestic abuse and harm.* Retrieved 5 December 2024 from: https://www.justice.gov.uk/courts/procedure-rules/family/practice_directions/pd_part_12j

Justice (2025). *Family procedure rules: what's new?* Retrieved 4 July 2025 from: https://www.justice.gov.uk/courts/procedure-rules/family

Katan, D. (2004). *Translating cultures.* Abingdon, Oxon: Routledge.

Kelly, J. and Johnston, J. (2001). The alienated child: a reformulation of parental alienation. *Family Court Review, 39,* 249–266.

Learning Disability Allies (undated). *Human Rights Act.* Retrieved 10 February 2025 from: https://www.hft.org.uk/resources-and-guidance/disability-rights-and-legal/human-rights-act/

Legal Aid Agency (2025). *Guidance on the remuneration of expert witnesses in family cases.* Retrieved 3 July 2025 from: https://assets.publishing.service.gov.uk/media/

67ecea97632d0f88e8248b83/Guidance_on_Remuneration_of_Expert_Witnesses_v11_
April_2025_.pdf

Lekas, H-M, Pahl, K. and Lewis, C.F. (2020). Rethinking cultural competence: shifting to cultural humility. *Health Service Insights, 13*. Doi: 10.1177/1178632920970580. Retrieved 30 May 2025 from: https://journals.sagepub.com/doi/10.1177/1178632920970580

Leslie, D. (2019). *Understanding artificial intelligence ethics and safety: a guide for the responsible design and implementation of AI systems in the public sector.* The Alan Turing Institute. Doi: 10.5281/zenodo.3240529

Long, R. (2024). *Provisions to support gender-questioning children in schools.* Department for Education. Retrieved 9 September 2024 from: https://commonslibrary.parliament.uk/research-briefings/cbp-9078/

Luthra, R. (2023). *Separating immigrant families: negotiating care for children.* Retrieved 30 March 2025 from: https://www.iser.essex.ac.uk/blog/2023/08/09/separating-immigrant-families-negotiating-care-for-children

MacAlister, J. (2022). *The independent review of children's social care.* Retrieved 10 November 2025 from: https://www.gov.uk/government/publications/independent-review-of-childrens-social-care-final-report

MacRae, I. (2024). *AI and the work of psychologists: practical applications and ethical considerations.* Retrieved 10 May 2025 from: https://www.bps.org.uk/blog/ai-and-work-psychologists-practical-applications-and-ethical-considerations

Major Family Law (2022). *How to give evidence in the family court.* Retrieved 21 November 2024 from: https://www.majorfamilylaw.co.uk/how-to-give-evidence-in-the-family-court/

McGaw, S., Beckley, K., Connolly, N. and Ball, K. (1998). *Parent assessment manual.* Truro: Pill Creek Publishing.

McGaw, S. and Sturmey, P. (1993). Identifying the needs of parents with learning disabilities: a review. *Child Abuse Review, 2,* 101–117.

McLean, M. and George, R. (2021). *Family practice during COVID and access to justice.* Retrieved 22 November 2024 from: https://discovery.ucl.ac.uk/10115589/3/George_Family%20Practice%20During%20Covid%20and%20Access%20to%20Justice.pdf

Mental Health Foundation (2025). *The mental health of asylum seekers and refugees in the UK: 2025 edition.* Retrieved 3 May 2025 from: https://www.mentalhealth.org.uk/sites/default/files/2025-04/MHF%20Mental%20health%20of%20asylum%20seekers%20and%20refugees%20-%202025%20report.pdf

Mental Health Foundation (undated). *Short stories from refugees and asylum seekers: this is what hope looks like.* Retrieved 3 May 2025 from: https://www.mentalhealth.org.uk/our-work/programmes/refugees/resources/hope-posters

Mental Health Law Online (2019). *CS v SBH [2019] EWHC 634 (Fam).* Retrieved 22 July 2025 from: https://www.mentalhealthlaw.co.uk/CS_v_SBH_(2019)_EWHC_634_(Fam)

Migration Observatory (2023). *Family migration to the UK.* Retrieved 2 May 2025 from: https://migrationobservatory.ox.ac.uk/resources/briefings/family-migration-to-the-uk/

Ministry of Housing, Communities and Local Government (2019). *The English indices of deprivation 2019 (IoD2019).* Retrieved 7 May 2024 from: https://www.gov.uk/government/publications/english-indices-of-deprivation-2019-research-report

Ministry of Justice (2020). *Assessing risk of harm to children and parents in private law children cases: final report.* Retrieved 29 November 2024 from: https://assets.publishing.service.gov.uk/media/5ef3dcade90e075c4e144bfd/assessing-risk-harm-children-parents-pl-childrens-cases-report_.pdf

Ministry of Justice (2023). *Achieving best evidence in criminal proceedings*. Retrieved 20 February 2024 from: https://www.gov.uk/government/publications/achieving-best-evidence-in-criminal-proceedings

Ministry of Justice (2024). *Family court statistics quarterly: April to June 2024*. Retrieved 2 December 2024 from: https://www.gov.uk/government/statistics/family-court-statistics-quarterly-april-to-june-2024/family-court-statistics-quarterly-april-to-june-2024

Ministry of Justice (2025a). *Family court statistics quarterly: October to December 2023*. Retrieved 3 July 2025 from: https://www.gov.uk/government/statistics/family-court-statistics-quarterly-october-to-december-2024/family-court-statistics-quarterly-october-to-december-2024

Ministry of Justice (2025b). *Private law pathfinder project: an update on the implementation of the government's pathfinder programme for private law reform*. Retrieved 28 April 2025 from: https://assets.publishing.service.gov.uk/media/67e277f770323a45fe6a7067/pathfinder-programme-update.pdf

Ministry of Justice (2025c) *Government action to protect children from abusive parents*. Retrieved 7 November 2025 from: https://www.gov.uk/government/news/government-action-to-protect-children-from-abusive-parents

Ministry of Justice, Department for Education and the Welsh Government (2011). *Family justice review: final report*. Retrieved 26 November 2023 from: https://assets.publishing.service.gov.uk/media/5a7c4b3ae5274a1b00422c9e/family-justice-review-final-report.pdf

Morris, M., Halford, W.K. and Petch, J. (2018). A randomized controlled trial comparing family mediation with and without motivational interviewing. *Journal of Family Psychology, 32*(2), 269–275. Doi: 10.1037/fam0000367 PMID: 29658764

Munby, J. (2014). *21st century family law*. The 2014 Michael Farmer Memorial Lecture delivered by Sir James Munby President of the Family Division at the 2014 Legal Wales Conference at Bangor University on 10 October 2014. Retrieved 26 November 2023 from: https://www.judiciary.gov.uk/wp-content/uploads/2014/10/munby-speech-bangor-10102014.pdf

National Archives (2023). *Children Act 1989*. Retrieved 15 December 2023 from: https://www.legislation.gov.uk/ukpga/1989/41/contents

National Archives (2024a). *Children Act 1989*. Retrieved 10 February 2024 from: https://www.legislation.gov.uk/ukpga/1989/41/schedule/3

National Archives (2024b) *GB (Parental Alienation: factual findings), Re [2024] EWFC 75 (B)*. Retrieved 7 December 2024 from: https://caselaw.nationalarchives.gov.uk/ewfc/b/2024/75

National Archives (undated a). *Domestic Violence and Matrimonial Proceedings Act 1976 (repealed 1.10.1997)*. Retrieved 28 November 2024 from: https://www.legislation.gov.uk/ukpga/1976/50

National Archives (undated b). *Adoption and Children Act 2002*. Retrieved 20 June 2025 from: https://www.legislation.gov.uk/ukpga/2002/38/notes/division/2

NHS England (2023). *Mental health of children and young people in England, 2023 - wave 4 follow up to the 2017 survey*. Retrieved 30 November 2024 from: https://digital.nhs.uk/data-and-information/publications/statistical/mental-health-of-children-and-young-people-in-england/2023-wave-4-follow-up#data-sets

Nicole, L. (2023). *Children of parents with a learning disability 54 times more likely to be taken into care*. Retrieved 9 February 2025 from: https://www.learningdisabilitytoday.co.uk/education/children-of-parents-with-a-learning-disability-54-times-more-likely-to-be-taken-into-care/

Norgrave, D. (2011). *Family justice review: final report*. Retrieved 5 May 2025 from: https://assets.publishing.service.gov.uk/media/5a7c4b3ae5274a1b00422c9e/family-justice-review-final-report.pdf

NSPCC (2023). *Looked after children*. Retrieved 12 February 2024 from: https://learning.nspcc.org.uk/children-and-families-at-risk/looked-after-children/

NSPCC Learning (2024). *NSPCC voice of the child, learning from case reviews*. Retrieved 3 May 2025 from: https://learning.nspcc.org.uk/research-resources/learning-from-case-reviews/voice-child

Ntoutsi, E., Fafalios, P., Gadiraju, U., Iosifidis, V., Nejdl, W., Vidal, M.-E., Ruggieri, S., Turini, F., Papadopoulos, S., Krasanakis, E., Kompatsiaris, I., Kinder-Kurlanda, K., Wagner, C., Karimi, F., Fernandez, M., Alani, H., Berendt, B., Kruegel, T., Heinze, C., Broelemann, K., Kasneci, G., Tiropanis, T. and Staab, S. (2020). *Bias in data-driven artificial intelligence systems – an introductory survey*. Wiley Interdisciplinary Reviews: Data Mining and Knowledge Discovery. Retrieved 10 May 2025 from: https://wires.onlinelibrary.wiley.com/doi/10.1002/widm.1356

Nuffield Family Justice Observatory (2025a). *What are the experiences of parents with learning disabilities or difficulties in care proceedings?* Retrieved 13 February 2025 from: https://www.nuffieldfjo.org.uk/resource/what-are-the-experiences-of-parents-with-learning-disabilities-or-difficulties-in-care-proceedings

Nuffield Family Justice Observatory (2025b). *Data released by the Ministry of Justice shows 1,280 children subject to DoL applications in 2024*. Retrieved 8 May 2025 from: https://www.nuffieldfjo.org.uk/news/data-released-by-the-ministry-of-justice-shows-1280-children-subject-to-dol-applications-in-2024

Office for Health Improvement and Disparities (2025). *Learning disability - applying all our health*. Retrieved 9 February 2025 from: https://www.gov.uk/government/publications/learning-disability-applying-all-our-health/learning-disabilities-applying-all-our-health

Office for National Statistics (2008). *Non-residential parental contact: 2007–2008 Results*. London: HMSO. No 38.

Office for National Statistics (2024). *Domestic abuse in England and Wales overview: November 2024*. Retrieved 2 December 2024 from: https://www.ons.gov.uk/peoplepopulationandcommunity/crimeandjustice/bulletins/domesticabuseinenglandandwalesoverview/november2024

Ogawa, M. (2007). A second language speaker in court: linguistic phenomena threatening justice. *Alternative Law Journal 8, 32*(1). Retrieved 6 August 2025 from: https://www.austlii.edu.au/cgi-bin/viewdoc/au/journals/AltLawJl/2007/8.html

Olsen, R. and Clarke, H. (2003). *Parenting and disability: disabled parents' experience of raising children*. Bristol: The Policy Press.

Opie, D. (Host) (2025a, April 10). *Today's family lawyer podcast: splitting hairs: cut off levels and consistency in hair strand testing*. Retrieved 2 July 2025 from: https://todaysfamilylawyer.co.uk/splitting-hairs-cut-off-levels-and-consistency-in-hair-strand-testing/

Opie, D. (Host) (2025b, July 3). *Today's family lawyer podcast: the 'writing to children' toolkit in practice*. Retrieved 24 July from: https://todaysfamilylawyer.co.uk/the-writing-to-children-toolkit-in-practice/

Organ, J. and Sigafoos, J. (2018). *The impact of LASPO on routes to justice*. Equality and Human Rights Commission: research report 118. Retrieved 3 January 2023 from: https://www.equalityhumanrights.com/sites/default/files/the-impact-of-laspo-on-routes-to-justice-september-2018.pdf

Ososami, K. (2021). *Striking the balance between Articles 8 and 10 when family and criminal law proceedings collide*. Youth Justice Legal Centre. Retrieved 26 February

2024 from: https://yjlc.uk/resources/legal-updates/striking-balance-between-articles-8-and-10-when-family-and-criminal-law

Powell, A. and Francis-Devine, B. (2022). *UK labour market statistics*. House of Commons Library. Retrieved 28 November 2022 from: https://tinyurl.com/mr273zyz

President of the Family Division (2025). *Writing to children – a toolkit for judges*. Retrieved 23 July 2025 from: https://www.judiciary.uk/guidance-and-resources/president-of-the-family-division-publishes-guidance-on-writing-to-children-developed-with-the-family-justice-young-peoples-board/

Preston, R. (2021, July 6). *Children's services focus ever more on poorer households the more they intervene in family life, research finds*. Community Care. Retrieved 7 May 2024 from: https://www.communitycare.co.uk/2021/07/06/childrens-services-focus-ever-poorer-households-intervene-family-life-research-finds/

Process Unity (2020). *7 security controls you need for General Data Protection Regulation (GDPR)*. Retrieved 22 October 2024 from: https://www.processunity.com/6-security-controls-need-general-data-protection-regulation-gdpr/

Prochaska, J.O., Norcross, J.C. and DiClemente, C.C. (2013). Applying the stages of change. *Psychotherapy in Australia, 19*(2), 10–15.

Professional Indemnity Insurance Brokers (2018). *GDPR and professional indemnity insurance – what you need to know*. Retrieved 23 October 2024 from: https://www.professionalindemnity.co.uk/news/gdpr-and-professional-indemnity-insurance/

Proudman, C. (2021, July 21). The discredited legal tactic that's putting abused UK children in danger. *The Guardian*. Retrieved 8 December 2024 from: https://www.theguardian.com/commentisfree/2021/jul/21/abused-uk-children-family-courts-parental-alienation

Public Health England (2021). *Parents with alcohol and drug problems: adult treatment and children and family services*. Retrieved 28 March 2025 from: https://www.gov.uk/government/publications/parents-with-alcohol-and-drug-problems-support-resources/parents-with-alcohol-and-drug-problems-guidance-for-adult-treatment-and-children-and-family-services#:~:text=2.%20Prevalence.%20According%20to%20the%20Children%27s%20Commissioner,2020%2C%20a%20rate%20of%2040%20per%201%2C000

Pyper, D. and Uwazuruike, A. (2025). *A short introduction to equality law and policy*. House of Commons Library. Retrieved 10 February 2025 from: https://commonslibrary.parliament.uk/research-briefings/cbp-9448/

Rassool, G.H. (2009). *Alcohol and drug misuse: a handbook for students and health professionals*. Abingdon, Oxon: Routledge.

Reed, L. (2022). *The family court without a lawyer: a handbook for litigants in person*. Bath: Bath Publishing Ltd.

Reiss Edwards (2024). *UK parent visa application guide*. Retrieved 28 February 2024 from: https://immigrationlawyers-london.com/blog/uk-parent-visa-application-guidance.php

Resera, E., Tribe, R. and Lane, P. (2015). Interpreting in mental health, roles and dynamics in practice. *International Journal of Culture and Mental Health, 8*(2), 192–206.

Richardson, M. (2016). Judgments: Re D (A Child) (No 3) [2016] EWFC 1. *Family Law Week*. Retrieved 9 November 2025 from: https://www.familylawweek.co.uk/judgments/re-d-a-child-no-3-2016-ewfc-1/

Robertson, A. (Host) (2025, April 17). *Family law week podcast season 9 episode 3* [Audio podcast episode] Retrieved 19 July 2025 from: https://www.familylawweek.co.uk/resources/family-law-week-weekly-podcast-season-9-episode-3/

Roe, A. (2023). *Children subject to deprivation of liberty orders: briefing.* Nuffield Family Justice Observatory. Retrieved 9 May 2025 from: https://www.nuffieldfjo.org.uk/resource/children-subject-to-deprivation-of-liberty-orders

Roe, A., Ryan, M. and Powell, A. (2022). *Deprivation of liberty: a review of published judgments.* Retrieved 8 May 2025 from: https://www.nuffieldfjo.org.uk/resource/deprivation-of-liberty-a-review-of-published-judgments

Rollins, D.E., Wilkins, D.G., Krueger, G.G., Augsburger, M.P., Mizuno, A., O'Neal, C., Borges, C.R. and Slawson, M.H. (2003). The effect of hair color on the incorporation of codeine into human hair. *Journal of Analytical Toxicology, 27*(8), 545–551. Doi: 10.1093/jat/27.8.545

Ross, L. (2018). From the fundamental attribution error to the truly fundamental attribution error and beyond: my research journey. *Perspectives on Psychological Science, 13*(6). Doi: 10.1177/1745691618769855

Rudkin, A. (2024). *Family law week weekly podcast season 8 episode 9.* Retrieved 22 December 2024 from: https://www.familylawweek.co.uk/resources/family-law-week-weekly-podcast-season-8-episode-9/

Ryan, M., Harker, L. and Rothera, S. (2020). *Remote hearings in the family justice system: reflections and experiences.* London: Nuffield Family Justice Observatory.

Samuel, M. (2024, January 14). Child in need cases opened up to non-social work staff despite risk concerns. *Community Care.* Retrieved 10 February 2024 from: https://www.communitycare.co.uk/2024/01/14/child-in-need-cases-opened-up-to-non-social-work-staff-despite-risk-concerns/

Samuel, M. (2025). Spending review: children's services cash boost means Labour delivering on care review – MacAlister. *Community Care,* June 2025. Retrieved 22 June 2025 from: https://www.communitycare.co.uk/2025/06/12/spending-review-childrens-services-cash-boost-means-labour-delivering-on-care-review-macalister/

SASC (2021 updated 2023). *Updated list of tests available for use in the assessment of specific learning difficulties via remote online assessment.* Retrieved 10 September 2024 from: https://www.sasc.org.uk/media/5pzinxgo/eon-and-remote-assessment-test-list-sasc-may-2021_-links-updated.pdf

Sawrikar, P. (2015). How effective do families of non-English-speaking background (NESB) and child protection caseworkers in Australia see the use of interpreters? A qualitative study to help inform good practice principles. *Child and Family Social Work, 20,* 396–406. Doi: 10.1111/cfs.12088

Scaife, J. (2019). *Supervision in clinical practice: a practitioner's guide* (3rd edition). London: Routledge.

Scaife, J. (2024). *Deciding children's futures: an expert guide to assessments for safeguarding and promoting children's welfare in the family court* (2nd edition). Abingdon, Oxfordshire: Routledge.

Scott-Storey, K., O'Donnell, S., Ford-Gilboe, M., Varcoe, C., Wathen, N., Malcolm, J., and Vincent, C. (2022). What about the men? A critical review of men's experiences of intimate partner violence. *Trauma, Violence and Abuse, 24*(2), 858–872. Doi: 10.1177/15248380211043827.

Sellbom, M., Flens, J., Gould, J., Ramnath, R., Tringone, R. and Grossman, S. (2022). The Millon Clinical Multaxial Inventory-IV (MCMI-IV) and Millon Adolescent Clinical Inventory-II (MACI-II) in legal settings. *Journal of Personality Assessment, 104*(2), 203–220. Doi: 10.1080/00223891.2021.2013248

Shared Lives Plus (2025). *Abby's story: what's it like as a parent in shared lives?* Retrieved 14 February 2025 from: https://sharedlivesplus.org.uk/our-work-and-campaigns/our-shared-lives-programmes/supporting-parents-in-shared-lives/abbys-story-whats-it-like-as-a-parent-in-shared-lives/

Shek, M. (2015, October 10). Conflict of interest – or just a different perspective. *The Expert Witness Journal.* Retrieved 5 May 2024 from: https://cowan-architects.co.uk/wp-content/uploads/2018/05/Conflict-of-Interest-Expert-Witness-Mag-Autumn-15.pdf

Sigurjónsdóttir, H.B. and Rice, J.G. (2018). 'Evidence' of neglect as a form of structural violence: parents with intellectual disabilities and custody deprivation. *Social Inclusion, 6*(2), 66–73. Doi: 10.17645/si.v6i2.1344. Retrieved 11 February 2025 from: https://www.cogitatiopress.com/socialinclusion/article/view/1344/774

Social Care Institute for Excellence (2017). *Mental Capacity Act (MCA): care planning, involvement and person-centred care.* Retrieved 14 February 2025 from: https://www.scie.org.uk/mca/practice/care-planning/person-centred-care/

Society for Emotion and Attachment Studies (SEAS) (2021). *Explanations of attachment theoretical concepts.* Retrieved 4 July 2025 from: https://seasinternational.org/explanations-of-attachment-theoretical-concepts/

Steel, Z., Chey, T., Silove, D., Marnane, C., Bryant, R.A. and Van Ommeren, M. (2009). Association of torture and other potentially traumatic events with mental health outcomes among populations exposed to mass conflict and displacement: a systematic review and meta-analysis. *JAMA, 302*(5), 537–549. Doi: 10.1001/JAMA.2009.1132

Summers, H. (2024). *Children taken away from parents due to misreporting of drug tests, say experts.* Retrieved 30 March 2025 from: https://www.theguardian.com/law/2024/nov/09/uk-children-taken-away-from-parents-due-to-misreporting-of-drug-tests-say-experts

Symonds, J., Dermott, E., Hitchings, E. and Staples, E. (2022). *Separating families: experiences of separation and support.* Nuffield Family Justice Observatory. Retrieved 5 May 2025 from: https://www.nuffieldfjo.org.uk/news/new-qualitative-study-on-family-separation-shows-experiences-are-shaped-by-access-to-support-and-families-often-try-to-avoid-using-court

Tempany, M. (2009). What research tells us about the mental health and psychosocial wellbeing of Sudanese refugees: a literature review. *Transcultural Psychiatry, 46*(2), 300–315. Doi: 10.1177/1363461509105820

Templer, K., Matthewson, M., Haines, J. and Cox, G. (2017). Recommendations for best practice in response to parental alienation: findings from a systematic review. *Journal of Family Therapy, 39*, 103–122. Doi: 10.1111/1467-6427.12137

Theodore, K., Foulds, D., Wilshaw, P., Colborne, A., Lee, J.N.Y., Mallaghan, L., Cooper, M. and Skelton, J. (2018). 'We want to be parents like everybody else': stories of parents with learning disabilities. *International Journal of Developmental Disability, 8,* 64(3): 184–194. Doi: 10.1080/20473869.2018.1448233. PMID: 34141305; PMCID: PMC 8115499. Retrieved 14 February 2025 from: https://pmc.ncbi.nlm.nih.gov/articles/PMC8115499/

Tilbury, N. and Tarleton, B. (2023). *'Substituted parenting': what does this mean for parents with learning disabilities in the family court context?* University of Bristol/Nuffield Foundation. Retrieved 13 February 2025 from: www.nuffieldfoundation.org/wp-content/uploads/2021/10/Substituted-parenting-What-does-this-mean-for-parents-with-learning-disabilities-in-the-family-court-context.pdf

Transparency Project (2024). *Contempt of court by publication of information relating to family (children) proceedings – a simple question without a simple answer.* Retrieved 24 October 2024 from: https://transparencyproject.org.uk/contempt-of-court-by-publication-of-information-relating-to-family-children-proceedings-a-simple-question-without-a-simple-answer/

Tribe, R. and Thompson, K. (2022). Working with interpreters in mental health. *International Review of Psychiatry, 34*(6), 613–621.

Trinder, E., Hunt, J., Macleod, A., Pearce, J. and Woodward, H. (2013). *Enforcing contact orders: problem-solving or punishment?* Exeter: Exeter Law School. Retrieved 25 November 2024 from: https://ore.exeter.ac.uk/repository/handle/10871/16765

Trinder, L., Beek, M. and Connolly, J. (2005). *Making contact: how parents and children negotiate and experience contact after divorce.* York: Joseph Rowntree Foundation. Retrieved 14 January 2023 from: https://www.jrf.org.uk/sites/default/files/jrf/migrated/files/1842630938.pdf

Trinder, L., Hunter, R., Hitchings, E., Miles, J., Moorhead, R., Smith, L., Sefton, M., Hinchly, V., Bader, K. and Pearce, J. (2014). *Litigants in person in private family law cases.* Ministry of Justice. Retrieved 8 May 2024 from: https://www.gov.uk/government/uploads/system/uploads/attachment_data/file/380479/litigants-in-person-in-private-family-law-cases.pdf

Tulshyan, R. and Burey, J-A. (2021, February 11). Stop telling women they have imposter syndrome. *Harvard Business Review.* Retrieved 18 July 2025 from: https://hbr.org/2021/02/stop-telling-women-they-have-imposter-syndrome?kuid=31ba29f1-4186-437f-9ab0-df56eaf7fd8b-1748131200&kref=zBsLcbpPQCZa

UK Government (2015). *Voice of the child: children to be more clearly heard in decisions about their future.* Retrieved 3 May 2025 from: https://www.gov.uk/government/news/voice-of-the-child-children-to-be-more-clearly-heard-in-decisions-about-their-future

UK Government (undated). *Get an interpreter at a court or tribunal.* Retrieved 29 April 2025 from: https://www.gov.uk/get-interpreter-at-court-or-tribunal

United Nations (2022). *Disability-inclusive language guidelines.* Retrieved 19 July from: https://www.ungeneva.org/sites/default/files/2021-01/Disability-Inclusive-Language-Guidelines.pdf

van Eldik, W.M., de Haan, A.D., Parry, L.Q., Davies, P.T., Luijk, M.M., Arends, L.R. and Prinzie, P. (2020). The interparental relationship. *Psychological Bulletin, 146*(7), 553–594. Doi: 10.1037/bul0000233

Verhaar, S., Matthewson, M.L. and Bentley, C. (2022). The impact of parental alienating behaviours on the mental health of adults alienated in childhood. *Children (Basel), 9*(4), 575, 1–16. Doi: 10.3390/children9040475

Victim Support (2022). *Domestic abuse.* Retrieved 23 November 2022 from: https://www.victimsupport.org.uk/crime-info/types-crime/domestic-abuse/

Walsh, K. (2023). The gap between facts and norms: contact, harm and futility. *Child and Family Law Quarterly, 35*(1), 27–48. https://lexisweb.co.uk/sources/child-and-family-law-quarterly

Welbourne, P. (2014). Adversarial courts, therapeutic justice and protecting children in the family justice system. *Child and Family Law Quarterly, 28*(3), 205–222.

Whelan, A. (2024). *'Secret' disclosure within family law proceedings.* Retrieved 21 October 2024 from: https://www.tlt.com/insights-and-events/insight/secret-disclosure-within-family-law-proceedings/

White, A. (2023). The role of machine translation in the legal sector. *The Barrister, January 11, 2023.* Retrieved 1 July 2025 from: https://barristermagazine.com/the-role-of-machine-translation-in-the-legal-sector/

Whitman, B. and Accardo, P.J. (1990). *When a parent is mentally retarded.* Baltimore, MD: Paul H. Brookes.

Williams, M.T., Faber, S., Zare, M., Barker, T. and Abdulrehman, R.Y. (2024). Intersectional racial and gender bias in the family court. *Discover Psychology, 4*, 178. Doi: 10.1007/s44202-024-00282-8

Wired (2024). *What is GDPR? The summary guide to GDPR compliance in the UK.* Retrieved 21 October 2024 from: https://www.wired.com/story/what-is-gdpr-uk-eu-legislation-compliance-summary-fines-2018/

Women's Aid (2024a). *Women's Aid respond to new protective measures for survivors of domestic abuse being launched by the Ministry of Justice and Home Office.* Retrieved 2 December 2024 from: https://www.womensaid.org.uk/womens-aid-respond-to-new-protective-measures-for-survivors-of-domestic-abuse-being-launched-by-the-ministry-of-justice-and-home-office/

Women's Aid (2024b). *Domestic abuse, the facts.* Retrieved 2 December 2024 from: https://www.womensaid.org.uk/what-we-do/research/domestic-abuse-the-facts/

Working Together with Parents Network (2021). *Good practice guidance on working with parents with a learning disability.* Retrieved 14 February 2025 from: https://www.bristol.ac.uk/sps/wtpn/resources/

World Health Organization (1994). *Lexicon of alcohol and drug terms.* Retrieved 24 November 2022 from: http://www.who.int/substance_abuse/terminology/who_lexicon/en/index.html

World Health Organization (2022). *ICD–11 2022 release.* Retrieved 3 June 2025 from: https://www.who.int/news/item/11-02-2022-icd-11-2022-release

World Health Organization (2024). *Violence against women.* Retrieved 7 December 2024 from: https://www.who.int/news-room/fact-sheets/detail/violence-against-women

Wray, H. (2023). *Article 8 ECHR, family reunification and the UK's supreme court: family matters?* Oxford: Hart. ISBN:9781509902583

Zack, P. (2014). *Medico-legal – patients who record their consultations.* Retrieved 6 November 2024 from: www.gponline.com/medico-legal-patients-record-consultations/article/1227228

Zhang, S., Huang, H., Wu, Q., Li, Y. and Liu, M. (2019). The impacts of family treatment drug court on child welfare core outcomes: a meta-analysis. *Child Abuse & Neglect, 88,* 1–14. Doi: 10.1016/j.chiabu.2018.10.01

# Index

For Product Safety Concerns and Information please contact our EU
representative  GPSR@taylorandfrancis.com
Taylor & Francis Verlag GmbH, Kaufingerstraße 24, 80331 München, Germany

www.ingramcontent.com/pod-product-compliance
Lightning Source LLC
Chambersburg PA
CBHW070324270326
41926CB00017B/3749